DATA STRUCTURES AND ALGORITHMS USING C#

C# programmers: no more translating data structures from C++ or Java to use in your programs! Mike McMillan provides a tutorial on how to use data structures and algorithms plus the first comprehensive reference for C# implementation of data structures and algorithms found in the .NET Framework library, as well as those developed by the programmer.

The approach is very practical, using timing tests rather than Big O notation to analyze the efficiency of an approach. Coverage includes array and ArrayLists, linked lists, hash tables, dictionaries, trees, graphs, and sorting and searching algorithms, as well as more advanced algorithms such as probabilistic algorithms and dynamic programming. This is the perfect resource for C# professionals and students alike.

Michael McMillan is Instructor of Computer Information Systems at Pulaski Technical College, as well as an adjunct instructor at the University of Arkansas at Little Rock and the University of Central Arkansas. Mike's previous books include *Object-Oriented Programming with Visual Basic.NET*, *Data Structures and Algorithms Using Visual Basic.NET*, and *Perl from the Ground Up*. He is a co-author of *Programming and Problem-Solving with Visual Basic.NET*. Mike has written more than twenty-five trade journal articles on programming and has more than twenty years of experience programming for industry and education.

DATA STRUCTURES AND ALGORITHMS USING C#

MICHAEL MCMILLAN
Pulaski Technical College

CAMBRIDGE
UNIVERSITY PRESS

CAMBRIDGE UNIVERSITY PRESS
Cambridge, New York, Melbourne, Madrid, Cape Town, Singapore, São Paulo, Delhi

Cambridge University Press
32 Avenue of the Americas, New York, NY 10013-2473, USA

www.cambridge.org
Information on this title: www.cambridge.org/9780521670159

First published 2007
Reprinted 2008 (twice)

Printed in the United States of America

A catalog record for this publication is available from the British Library.

Library of Congress Cataloging in Publication Data

McMillan, Michael, 1957–
Data structures and algorithms using C# / Michael McMillan.
   p.   cm.
Includes bibliographical references and index.
ISBN-13: 978-0-521-67015-9 (pbk.)
ISBN-10: 0-521-67015-2 (pbk.)
1. C# (Computer program language) I. Title. II. Series.
QA76.73.C154M43   2006
005.13'3–dc22   2006024382

ISBN   978-0-521-87691-9 hardback
ISBN   978-0-521-67015-9 paperback

Contents

Preface

The study of data structures and algorithms is critical to the development of the professional programmer. There are many, many books written on data structures and algorithms, but these books are usually written as college textbooks and are written using the programming languages typically taught in college—Java or C++. C# is becoming a very popular language and this book provides the C# programmer with the opportunity to study fundamental data structures and algorithms.

C# exists in a very rich development environment called the .NET Framework. Included in the .NET Framework library is a set of data structure classes (also called collection classes), which range from the Array, ArrayList, and Collection classes to the Stack and Queue classes and to the HashTable and the SortedList classes. The data structures and algorithms student can now see how to use a data structure before learning how to implement it. Previously, an instructor had to discuss the concept of, say, a stack, abstractly until the complete data structure was constructed. Instructors can now show students how to use a stack to perform some computation, such as number base conversions, demonstrating the utility of the data structure immediately. With this background, the student can then go back and learn the fundamentals of the data structure (or algorithm) and even build their own implementation.

This book is written primarily as a practical overview of the data structures and algorithms all serious computer programmers need to know and understand. Given this, there is no formal analysis of the data structures and algorithms covered in the book. Hence, there is not a single mathematical formula and not one mention of Big Oh analysis (if you don't know what this means, look at any of the books mentioned in the bibliography). Instead, the various data structures and algorithms are presented as problem-solving tools.

Simple timing tests are used to compare the performance of the data structures and algorithms discussed in the book.

PREREQUISITES

The only prerequisite for this book is that the reader have some familiarity with the C# language in general, and object-oriented programming in C# in particular.

CHAPTER-BY-CHAPTER ORGANIZATION

Chapter 1 introduces the reader to the concept of the data structure as a collection of data. The concepts of linear and nonlinear collections are introduced. The Collection class is demonstrated. This chapter also introduces the concept of generic programming, which allows the programmer to write one class, or one method, and have it work for a multitude of data types. Generic programming is an important new addition to C# (available in C# 2.0 and beyond), so much so that there is a special library of generic data structures found in the System.Collections.Generic namespace. When a data structure has a generic implementation found in this library, its use is discussed. The chapter ends with an introduction to methods of measuring the performance of the data structures and algorithms discussed in the book.

Chapter 2 provides a review of how arrays are constructed, along with demonstrating the features of the Array class. The Array class encapsulates many of the functions associated with arrays (UBound, LBound, and so on) into a single package. ArrayLists are special types of arrays that provide dynamic resizing capabilities.

Chapter 3 is an introduction to the basic sorting algorithms, such as the bubble sort and the insertion sort, and Chapter 4 examines the most fundamental algorithms for searching memory, the sequential and binary searches.

Two classic data structures are examined in Chapter 5: the stack and the queue. The emphasis in this chapter is on the practical use of these data structures in solving everyday problems in data processing. Chapter 6 covers the BitArray class, which can be used to efficiently represent a large number of integer values, such as test scores.

Strings are not usually covered in a data structures book, but Chapter 7 covers strings, the String class, and the StringBuilder class. Because so much data processing in C# is performed on strings, the reader should be exposed to the special techniques found in the two classes. Chapter 8 examines the use of regular expressions for text processing and pattern matching. Regular expressions often provide more power and efficiency than can be had with more traditional string functions and methods.

Chapter 9 introduces the reader to the use of dictionaries as data structures. Dictionaries, and the different data structures based on them, store data as key/value pairs. This chapter shows the reader how to create his or her own classes based on the DictionaryBase class, which is an abstract class. Chapter 10 covers hash tables and the HashTable class, which is a special type of dictionary that uses a hashing algorithm for storing data internally.

Another classic data structure, the linked list, is covered in Chapter 11. Linked lists are not as important a data structure in C# as they are in a pointer-based language such as C++, but they still have a role in C# programming. Chapter 12 introduces the reader to yet another classic data structure—the binary tree. A specialized type of binary tree, the binary search tree, is the primary topic of the chapter. Other types of binary trees are covered in Chapter 15.

Chapter 13 shows the reader how to store data in sets, which can be useful in situations in which only unique data values can be stored in the data structure. Chapter 14 covers more advanced sorting algorithms, including the popular and efficient QuickSort, which is the basis for most of the sorting procedures implemented in the .NET Framework library. Chapter 15 looks at three data structures that prove useful for searching when a binary search tree is not called for: the AVL tree, the red-black tree, and the skip list.

Chapter 16 discusses graphs and graph algorithms. Graphs are useful for representing many different types of data, especially networks. Finally, Chapter 17 introduces the reader to what algorithm design techniques really are: dynamic algorithms and greedy algorithms.

ACKNOWLEDGEMENTS

There are several different groups of people who must be thanked for helping me finish this book. First, thanks to a certain group of students who first sat through my lectures on developing data structures and algorithms. These students include (not in any particular order): Matt Hoffman, Ken Chen, Ken Cates, Jeff Richmond, and Gordon Caffey. Also, one of my fellow instructors at Pulaski Technical College, Clayton Ruff, sat through many of the lectures and provided excellent comments and criticism. I also have to thank my department dean, David Durr, and my department chair, Bernica Tackett, for supporting my writing endeavors. I also need to thank my family for putting up with me while I was preoccupied with research and writing. Finally, many thanks to my editors at Cambridge, Lauren Cowles and Heather Bergman, for putting up with my many questions, topic changes, and habitual lateness.

CHAPTER 1

An Introduction to Collections, Generics, and the Timing Class

This book discusses the development and implementation of data structures and algorithms using C#. The data structures we use in this book are found in the .NET Framework class library System.Collections. In this chapter, we develop the concept of a collection by first discussing the implementation of our own Collection class (using the array as the basis of our implementation) and then by covering the Collection classes in the .NET Framework.

An important addition to C# 2.0 is generics. Generics allow the C# programmer to write one version of a function, either independently or within a class, without having to overload the function many times to allow for different data types. C# 2.0 provides a special library, System.Collections.Generic, that implements generics for several of the System.Collections data structures. This chapter will introduce the reader to generic programming.

Finally, this chapter introduces a custom-built class, the Timing class, which we will use in several chapters to measure the performance of a data structure and/or algorithm. This class will take the place of Big O analysis, not because Big O analysis isn't important, but because this book takes a more practical approach to the study of data structures and algorithms.

COLLECTIONS DEFINED

A collection is a structured data type that stores data and provides operations for adding data to the collection, removing data from the collection, updating data in the collection, as well as operations for setting and returning the values of different attributes of the collection.

Collections can be broken down into two types: linear and nonlinear. A linear collection is a list of elements where one element follows the previous element. Elements in a linear collection are normally ordered by position (first, second, third, etc.). In the real world, a grocery list is a good example of a linear collection; in the computer world (which is also real), an array is designed as a linear collection.

Nonlinear collections hold elements that do not have positional order within the collection. An organizational chart is an example of a nonlinear collection, as is a rack of billiard balls. In the computer world, trees, heaps, graphs, and sets are nonlinear collections.

Collections, be they linear or nonlinear, have a defined set of properties that describe them and operations that can be performed on them. An example of a collection property is the collections Count, which holds the number of items in the collection. Collection operations, called methods, include Add (for adding a new element to a collection), Insert (for adding a new element to a collection at a specified index), Remove (for removing a specified element from a collection), Clear (for removing all the elements from a collection), Contains (for determining if a specified element is a member of a collection), and IndexOf (for determining the index of a specified element in a collection).

COLLECTIONS DESCRIBED

Within the two major categories of collections are several subcategories. Linear collections can be either direct access collections or sequential access collections, whereas nonlinear collections can be either hierarchical or grouped. This section describes each of these collection types.

Direct Access Collections

The most common example of a direct access collection is the array. We define an array as a collection of elements with the same data type that are directly accessed via an integer index, as illustrated in Figure 1.1.

FIGURE 1.1. Array.

Arrays can be static so that the number of elements specified when the array is declared is fixed for the length of the program, or they can be dynamic, where the number of elements can be increased via the ReDim or ReDim Preserve statements.

In C#, arrays are not only a built-in data type, they are also a class. Later in this chapter, when we examine the use of arrays in more detail, we will discuss how arrays are used as class objects.

We can use an array to store a linear collection. Adding new elements to an array is easy since we simply place the new element in the first free position at the rear of the array. Inserting an element into an array is not as easy (or efficient), since we will have to move elements of the array down in order to make room for the inserted element. Deleting an element from the end of an array is also efficient, since we can simply remove the value from the last element. Deleting an element in any other position is less efficient because, just as with inserting, we will probably have to adjust many array elements up one position to keep the elements in the array contiguous. We will discuss these issues later in the chapter. The .NET Framework provides a specialized array class, ArrayList, for making linear collection programming easier. We will examine this class in Chapter 3.

Another type of direct access collection is the string. A string is a collection of characters that can be accessed based on their index, in the same manner we access the elements of an array. Strings are also implemented as class objects in C#. The class includes a large set of methods for performing standard operations on strings, such as concatenation, returning substrings, inserting characters, removing characters, and so forth. We examine the String class in Chapter 8.

C# strings are immutable, meaning once a string is initialized it cannot be changed. When you modify a string, a copy of the string is created instead of changing the original string. This behavior can lead to performance degradation in some cases, so the .NET Framework provides a StringBuilder class that enables you to work with mutable strings. We'll examine the StringBuilder in Chapter 8 as well.

The final direct access collection type is the struct (also called structures and records in other languages). A struct is a composite data type that holds data that may consist of many different data types. For example, an employee record consists of employee' name (a string), salary (an integer), identification number (a string, or an integer), as well as other attributes. Since storing each of these data values in separate variables could become confusing very easily, the language provides the struct for storing data of this type.

A powerful addition to the C# struct is the ability to define methods for performing operations stored on the data in a struct. This makes a struct somewhat like a class, though you can't inherit or derive a new type from a structure. The following code demonstrates a simple use of a structure in C#:

```
using System;

public struct Name {

private string fname, mname, lname;

public Name(string first, string middle, string last) {
   fname = first;
   mname = middle;
   lname = last;
}

public string firstName {
   get {
     return fname;
   }

   set {
     fname = firstName;
   }
}
public string middleName {
   get {
     return mname;
   }

   set {
     mname = middleName;
   }
}

public string lastName {
   get {
```

```
      return lname;
   }
   set {
      lname = lastName;
   }
}

public override string ToString() {
   return (String.Format("{0} {1} {2}", fname, mname,
         lname));
}

public string Initials() {
   return (String.Format("{0}{1}{2}", fname.Substring(0,1),
         mname.Substring(0,1), lname.Substring(0,1)));
}
}
public class NameTest {
   static void Main() {
      Name myName = new Name("Michael", "Mason", "McMillan");
      string fullName, inits;
      fullName = myName.ToString();
      inits = myName.Initials();
      Console.WriteLine("My name is {0}.", fullName);
      Console.WriteLine("My initials are {0}.", inits);
   }
}
```

Although many of the elements in the .NET environment are implemented as classes (such as arrays and strings), several primary elements of the language are implemented as structures, such as the numeric data types. The Integer data type, for example, is implemented as the Int32 structure. One of the methods you can use with Int32 is the Parse method for converting the string representation of a number into an integer. Here's an example:

```
using System;

public class IntStruct {
   static void Main() {
```

```
        int num;
        string snum;
        Console.Write("Enter a number: ");
        snum = Console.ReadLine();
        num = Int32.Parse(snum);
        Console.WriteLine(num);
    }
}
```

Sequential Access Collections

A sequential access collection is a list that stores its elements in sequential order. We call this type of collection a linear list. Linear lists are not limited by size when they are created, meaning they are able to expand and contract dynamically. Items in a linear list are not accessed directly; they are referenced by their position, as shown in Figure 1.2. The first element of a linear list is at the front of the list and the last element is at the rear of the list.

Because there is no direct access to the elements of a linear list, to access an element you have to traverse through the list until you arrive at the position of the element you are looking for. Linear list implementations usually allow two methods for traversing a list—in one direction from front to rear, and from both front to rear and rear to front.

A simple example of a linear list is a grocery list. The list is created by writing down one item after another until the list is complete. The items are removed from the list while shopping as each item is found.

Linear lists can be either ordered or unordered. An ordered list has values in order in respect to each other, as in:

Beata Bernica David Frank Jennifer Mike Raymond Terrill

An unordered list consists of elements in any order. The order of a list makes a big difference when performing searches on the data on the list, as you'll see in Chapter 2 when we explore the binary search algorithm versus a simple linear search.

Front   Rear

FIGURE 1.2. Linear List.

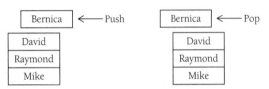

FIGURE 1.3. Stack Operations.

Some types of linear lists restrict access to their data elements. Examples of these types of lists are stacks and queues. A stack is a list where access is restricted to the beginning (or top) of the list. Items are placed on the list at the top and can only be removed from the top. For this reason, stacks are known as Last-in, First-out structures. When we add an item to a stack, we call the operation a push. When we remove an item from a stack, we call that operation a pop. These two stack operations are shown in Figure 1.3.

The stack is a very common data structure, especially in computer systems programming. Stacks are used for arithmetic expression evaluation and for balancing symbols, among its many applications.

A queue is a list where items are added at the rear of the list and removed from the front of the list. This type of list is known as a First-in, First-out structure. Adding an item to a queue is called an EnQueue, and removing an item from a queue is called a Dequeue. Queue operations are shown in Figure 1.4.

Queues are used in both systems programming, for scheduling operating system tasks, and for simulation studies. Queues make excellent structures for simulating waiting lines in every conceivable retail situation. A special type of queue, called a priority queue, allows the item in a queue with the highest priority to be removed from the queue first. Priority queues can be used to study the operations of a hospital emergency room, where patients with heart trouble need to be attended to before a patient with a broken arm, for example.

The last category of linear collections we'll examine are called generalized indexed collections. The first of these, called a hash table, stores a set of data

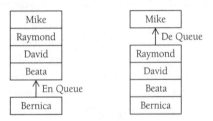

FIGURE 1.4. Queue Operations.

"Paul E. Spencer"
37500
5
"Information Systems"

FIGURE 1.5. A Record To Be Hashed.

values associated with a key. In a hash table, a special function, called a hash function, takes one data value and transforms the value (called the key) into an integer index that is used to retrieve the data. The index is then used to access the data record associated with the key. For example, an employee record may consist of a person's name, his or her salary, the number of years the employee has been with the company, and the department he or she works in. This structure is shown in Figure 1.5. The key to this data record is the employee's name. C# has a class, called HashTable, for storing data in a hash table. We explore this structure in Chapter 10.

Another generalized indexed collection is the dictionary. A dictionary is made up of a series of key–value pairs, called associations. This structure is analogous to a word dictionary, where a word is the key and the word's definition is the value associated with the key. The key is an index into the value associated with the key. Dictionaries are often called associative arrays because of this indexing scheme, though the index does not have to be an integer. We will examine several Dictionary classes that are part of the .NET Framework in Chapter 11.

Hierarchical Collections

Nonlinear collections are broken down into two major groups: hierarchical collections and group collections. A hierarchical collection is a group of items divided into levels. An item at one level can have successor items located at the next lower level.

One common hierarchical collection is the tree. A tree collection looks like an upside-down tree, with one data element as the root and the other data values hanging below the root as leaves. The elements of a tree are called nodes, and the elements that are below a particular node are called the node's children. A sample tree is shown in Figure 1.6.

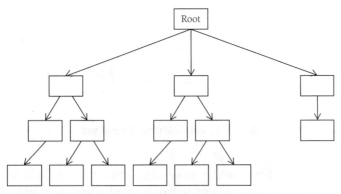

FIGURE 1.6. A Tree Collection.

Trees have applications in several different areas. The file systems of most modern operating systems are designed as a tree collection, with one directory as the root and other subdirectories as children of the root.

A binary tree is a special type of tree collection where each node has no more than two children. A binary tree can become a binary search tree, making searches for large amounts of data much more efficient. This is accomplished by placing nodes in such a way that the path from the root to a node where the data is stored is along the shortest path possible.

Yet another tree type, the heap, is organized so that the smallest data value is always placed in the root node. The root node is removed during a deletion, and insertions into and deletions from a heap always cause the heap to reorganize so that the smallest value is placed in the root. Heaps are often used for sorts, called a heap sort. Data elements stored in a heap can be kept sorted by repeatedly deleting the root node and reorganizing the heap.

Several different varieties of trees are discussed in Chapter 12.

Group Collections

A nonlinear collection of items that are unordered is called a group. The three major categories of group collections are sets, graphs, and networks.

A set is a collection of unordered data values where each value is unique. The list of students in a class is an example of a set, as is, of course, the integers. Operations that can be performed on sets include union and intersection. An example of set operations is shown in Figure 1.7.

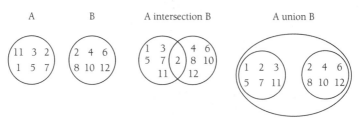

FIGURE **1.7. Set Collection Operations.**

A graph is a set of nodes and a set of edges that connect the nodes. Graphs are used to model situations where each of the nodes in a graph must be visited, sometimes in a particular order, and the goal is to find the most efficient way to "traverse" the graph. Graphs are used in logistics and job scheduling and are well studied by computer scientists and mathematicians. You may have heard of the "Traveling Salesman" problem. This is a particular type of graph problem that involves determining which cities on a salesman's route should be traveled in order to most efficiently complete the route within the budget allowed for travel. A sample graph of this problem is shown in Figure 1.8.

This problem is part of a family of problems known as NP-complete problems. This means that for large problems of this type, an exact solution is not known. For example, to find the solution to the problem in Figure 1.8, 10 factorial tours, which equals 3,628,800 tours. If we expand the problem to 100 cities, we have to examine 100 factorial tours, which we currently cannot do with current methods. An approximate solution must be found instead.

A network is a special type of graph where each of the edges is assigned a weight. The weight is associated with a cost for using that edge to move from one node to another. Figure 1.9 depicts a network of cities where the weights are the miles between the cities (nodes).

We've now finished our tour of the different types of collections we are going to discuss in this book. Now we're ready to actually look at how collections

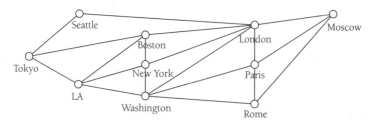

FIGURE **1.8. The Traveling Salesman Problem.**

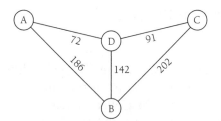

FIGURE **1.9. A Network Collection.**

are implemented in C#. We start by looking at how to build a Collection class using an abstract class from the .NET Framework, the CollectionBase class.

THE COLLECTIONBASE CLASS

The .NET Framework library does not include a generic Collection class for storing data, but there is an abstract class you can use to build your own Collection class—CollectionBase. The CollectionBase class provides the programmer with the ability to implement a custom Collection class. The class implicitly implements two interfaces necessary for building a Collection class, ICollection and IEnumerable, leaving the programmer with having to implement just those methods that are typically part of a Collection class.

A Collection Class Implementation Using ArrayLists

In this section, we'll demonstrate how to use C# to implement our own Collection class. This will serve several purposes. First, if you're not quite up to speed on object-oriented programming (OOP), this implementation will show you some simple OOP techniques in C#. We can also use this section to discuss some performance issues that are going to come up as we discuss the different C# data structures. Finally, we think you'll enjoy this section, as well as the other implementation sections in this book, because it's really a lot of fun to reimplement the existing data structures using just the native elements of the language. As Don Knuth (one of the pioneers of computer science) says, to paraphrase, you haven't really learned something well until you've taught it to a computer. So, by teaching C# how to implement the different data structures, we'll learn much more about those structures than if we just choose to use the classes from the library in our day-to-day programming.

Defining a Collection Class

The easiest way to define a Collection class in C# is to base the class on an abstract class already found in the System.Collections library—the Collection-Base class. This class provides a set of abstract methods you can implement to build your own collection. The CollectionBase class provides an underlying data structure, InnerList (an ArrayList), which you can use as a base for your class. In this section, we look at how to use CollectionBase to build a Collection class.

Implementing the Collection Class

The methods that will make up the Collection class all involve some type of interaction with the underlying data structure of the class—InnerList. The methods we will implement in this first section are the Add, Remove, Count, and Clear methods. These methods are absolutely essential to the class, though other methods definitely make the class more useful.

Let's start with the Add method. This method has one parameter – an Object variable that holds the item to be added to the collection. Here is the code:

```
public void Add(Object item) {
   InnerList.Add(item);
}
```

ArrayLists store data as objects (the Object data type), which is why we have declared item as Object. You will learn much more about ArrayLists in Chapter 2.

The Remove method works similarly:

```
public void Remove(Object item) {
   InnerList.Remove(item);
}
```

The next method is Count. Count is most often implemented as a property, but we prefer to make it a method. Also, Count is implemented in the underlying class, CollectionBase, so we have to use the new keyword to hide the definition of Count found in CollectionBase:

```
public new int Count() {
   return InnerList.Count;
}
```

The Clear method removes all the items from InnerList. We also have to use the new keyword in the definition of the method:

```
public new void Clear() {
   InnerList.Clear();
}
```

This is enough to get us started. Let's look at a program that uses the Collection class, along with the complete class definition:

```
using System;
using System.Collections;
public class Collection : CollectionBase<T> {
   public void Add(Object item) {
      InnerList.Add(item);
   }
   public void Remove(Object item) {
      InnerList.Remove(item);
   }
   public new void Clear() {
      InnerList.Clear();
   }
   public new int Count() {
      return InnerList.Count;
   }
}
   class chapter1 {
```

```
static void Main() {
  Collection names = new Collection();
  names.Add("David");
  names.Add("Bernica");
  names.Add("Raymond");
  names.Add("Clayton");
  foreach (Object name in names)
    Console.WriteLine(name);
  Console.WriteLine("Number of names: " + names.
                    Count());
  names.Remove("Raymond");
  Console.WriteLine("Number of names: " + names.
                    Count());
  names.Clear();
  Console.WriteLine("Number of names: " + names.
                    Count());
  }
}
```

There are several other methods you can implement in order to create a more useful Collection class. You will get a chance to implement some of these methods in the exercises.

Generic Programming

One of the problems with OOP is a feature called "code bloat." One type of code bloat occurs when you have to override a method, or a set of methods, to take into account all of the possible data types of the method's parameters. One solution to code bloat is the ability of one value to take on multiple data types, while only providing one definition of that value. This technique is called generic programming.

A generic program provides a data type "placeholder" that is filled in by a specific data type at compile-time. This placeholder is represented by a pair of angle brackets (< >), with an identifier placed between the brackets. Let's look at an example.

A canonical first example for generic programming is the Swap function. Here is the definition of a generic Swap function in C#:

```
static void Swap<T>(ref T val1, ref T val2) {
  T temp;
  temp = val1;
  val1 = val2;
  val2 = temp;
}
```

The placeholder for the data type is placed immediately after the function name. The identifier placed inside the angle brackets is now used whenever a generic data type is needed. Each of the parameters is assigned a generic data type, as is the temp variable used to make the swap. Here's a program that tests this code:

```
using System;

class chapter1 {
  static void Main() {
    int num1 = 100;
    int num2 = 200;
    Console.WriteLine("num1: " + num1);
    Console.WriteLine("num2: " + num2);
    Swap<int>(ref num1, ref num2);
    Console.WriteLine("num1: " + num1);
    Console.WriteLine("num2: " + num2);
    string str1 = "Sam";
    string str2 = "Tom";
    Console.WriteLine("String 1: " + str1);
    Console.WriteLine("String 2: " + str2);
    Swap<string>(ref str1, ref str2);
    Console.WriteLine("String 1: " + str1);
    Console.WriteLine("String 2: " + str2);
  }

  static void Swap<T>(ref T val1, ref T val2) {
    T temp;
    temp = val1;
    val1 = val2;
    val2 = temp;
  }
}
```

The output from this program is:

```
C:\WINDOWS\system32\cmd.exe                                _ □ x

C:\WINDOWS\Microsoft.NET\Framework\v2.0.50727>ch1
num1: 100
num2: 200
num1: 200
num2: 100
String 1: Sam
String 2: Tom
String 1: Tom
String 2: Sam

C:\WINDOWS\Microsoft.NET\Framework\v2.0.50727>_
```

Generics are not limited to function definitions; you can also create generic classes. A generic class definition will contain a generic type placeholder after the class name. Anytime the class name is referenced in the definition, the type placeholder must be provided. The following class definition demonstrates how to create a generic class:

```
public class Node<T> {

  T data;
  Node<T> link;
  public Node(T data, Node<T> link) {
    this.data = data;
    this.link = link;
  }
}
```

This class can be used as follows:

```
Node<string> node1 = new Node<string>("Mike", null);
Node<string> node2 = new Node<string>("Raymond", node1);
```

We will be using the Node class in several of the data structures we examine in this book.

While this use of generic programming can be quite useful, C# provides a library of generic data structures already ready to use. These data structures are found in the System.Collection.Generics namespace and when we discuss a data structure that is part of this namespace, we will examine its use. Generally, though, these classes have the same functionality as the nongeneric data structure classes, so we will usually limit the discussion of the generic class to how to instantiate an object of that class, since the other methods and their use are no different.

Timing Tests

Because this book takes a practical approach to the analysis of the data structures and algorithms examined, we eschew the use of Big O analysis, preferring instead to run simple benchmark tests that will tell us how long in seconds (or whatever time unit) it takes for a code segment to run.

Our benchmarks will be timing tests that measure the amount of time it takes an algorithm to run to completion. Benchmarking is as much of an art as a science and you have to be careful how you time a code segment in order to get an accurate analysis. Let's examine this in more detail.

An Oversimplified Timing Test

First, we need some code to time. For simplicity's sake, we will time a subroutine that writes the contents of an array to the console. Here's the code:

```
static void DisplayNums(int[] arr) {
  for(int i = 0; i <= arr.GetUpperBound(0); i++)
    Console.Write(arr[i] + " ");
}
```

The array is initialized in another part of the program, which we'll examine later.

To time this subroutine, we need to create a variable that is assigned the system time just as the subroutine is called, and we need a variable to store the time when the subroutine returns. Here's how we wrote this code:

```
DateTime startTime;
TimeSpan endTime;
startTime = DateTime.Now;
endTime = DateTime.Now.Subtract(startTime);
```

Running this code on my laptop (running at 1.4 mHz on Windows XP Professional), the subroutine ran in about 5 seconds (4.9917). Although this code segment seems reasonable for performing a timing test, it is completely inadequate for timing code running in the .NET environment. Why?

First, the code measures the elapsed time from when the subroutine was called until the subroutine returns to the main program. The time used by other processes running at the same time as the C# program adds to the time being measured by the test.

Second, the timing code doesn't take into account garbage collection performed in the .NET environment. In a runtime environment such as .NET, the system can pause at any time to perform garbage collection. The sample timing code does nothing to acknowledge garbage collection and the resulting time can be affected quite easily by garbage collection. So what do we do about this?

Timing Tests for the .NET Environment

In the .NET environment, we need to take into account the thread our program is running in and the fact that garbage collection can occur at any time. We need to design our timing code to take these facts into consideration.

Let's start by looking at how to handle garbage collection. First, let's discuss what garbage collection is used for. In C#, reference types (such as strings, arrays, and class instance objects) are allocated memory on something called the *heap*. The heap is an area of memory reserved for data items (the types mentioned previously). Value types, such as normal variables, are stored on the *stack*. References to reference data are also stored on the stack, but the actual data stored in a reference type is stored on the heap.

Variables that are stored on the stack are freed when the subprogram in which the variables are declared completes its execution. Variables stored on the heap, on the other hand, are held on the heap until the garbage collection process is called. Heap data is only removed via garbage collection when there is not an active reference to that data.

Garbage collection can, and will, occur at arbitrary times during the execution of a program. However, we want to be as sure as we can that the garbage collector is not run while the code we are timing is executing. We can head off arbitrary garbage collection by calling the garbage collector explicitly. The .NET environment provides a special object for making garbage collection calls, GC. To tell the system to perform garbage collection, we simply write:

```
GC.Collect();
```

That's not all we have to do, though. Every object stored on the heap has a special method called a finalizer. The finalizer method is executed as the last step before deleting the object. The problem with finalizer methods is that they are not run in a systematic way. In fact, you can't even be sure an object's finalizer method will run at all, but we know that before we can be sure an object is deleted, it's finalizer method must execute. To ensure this, we add a line of code that tells the program to wait until all the finalizer methods of the objects on the heap have run before continuing. The line of code is:

```
GC.WaitForPendingFinalizers();
```

We have one hurdle cleared and just one left to go – using the proper thread. In the .NET environment, a program is run inside a process, also called an *application domain*. This allows the operating system to separate each different program running on it at the same time. Within a process, a program or a part of a program is run inside a *thread*. Execution time for a program is allocated by the operating system via threads. When we are timing the code for a program, we want to make sure that we're timing just the code inside the process allocated for our program and not other tasks being performed by the operating system.

We can do this by using the Process class in the .NET Framework. The Process class has methods for allowing us to pick the current process (the process our program is running in), the thread the program is running in, and a timer to store the time the thread starts executing. Each of these methods can be combined into one call, which assigns its return value to a variable to store the starting time (a TimeSpan object). Here's the line of code (okay, two lines of code):

```
TimeSpan startingTime;
startingTime = Process.GetCurrentProcess.Threads(0).
          UserProcessorTime;
```

All we have left to do is capture the time when the code segment we're timing stops. Here's how it's done:

```
duration =
Process.GetCurrentProcess.Threads(0).UserProcessorTime.
Subtract(startingTime);
```

Now let's combine all this into one program that times the same code we tested earlier:

```
using System;
using System.Diagnostics;
class chapter1 {
  static void Main() {
    int[] nums = new int[100000];
    BuildArray(nums);
    TimeSpan startTime;
    TimeSpan duration;
    startTime =
      Process.GetCurrentProcess().Threads[0].
        UserProcessorTime;
    DisplayNums(nums);
    duration =
      Process.GetCurrentProcess().Threads[0].
        UserProcessorTime.
      Subtract(startTime);
    Console.WriteLine("Time: " + duration.TotalSeconds);
  }

  static void BuildArray(int[] arr) {
    for(int i = 0; i <= 99999; i++)
      arr[i] = i;
  }

  static void DisplayNums(int[] arr) {
    for(int i = 0; i <= arr.GetUpperBound(0); i++)
      Console.Write(arr[i] + " ");
  }
}
```

Using the new and improved timing code, the program returns 0.2526. This compares with the approximately 5 seconds returned using the first timing code. Clearly, there is a major discrepancy between these two timing techniques and you should use the .NET techniques when timing code in the .NET environment.

A Timing Test Class

Although we don't need a class to run our timing code, it makes sense to rewrite the code as a class, primarily because we'll keep our code clear if we can reduce the number of lines in the code we test.

A Timing class needs the following data members:

- startingTime—to store the starting time of the code we are testing
- duration—the ending time of the code we are testing

The starting time and the duration members store times and we chose to use the TimeSpan data type for these data members. We'll use just one constructor method, a default constructor that sets both the data members to 0.

We'll need methods for telling a Timing object when to start timing code and when to stop timing. We also need a method for returning the data stored in the duration data member.

As you can see, the Timing class is quite small, needing just a few methods. Here's the definition:

```
public class Timing {

  TimeSpan startingTime;
  TimeSpan duration;

  public Timing() {
    startingTime = new TimeSpan(0);
    duration = new TimeSpan(0);
  }

  public void StopTime() {
    duration =
      Process.GetCurrentProcess().Threads[0].
        UserProcessorTime.Subtract(startingTime);
```

```
  }

  public void startTime() {
    GC.Collect();
    GC.WaitForPendingFinalizers();
    startingTime =
      Process.GetCurrentProcess().Threads[0].
        UserProcessorTime;
  }

  public TimeSpan Result() {
  return duration;
}
}
```

Here's the program to test the DisplayNums subroutine, rewritten with the Timing class:

```
using System;
using System.Diagnostics;

public class Timing {

  TimeSpan startingTime;
  TimeSpan duration;

  public Timing() {
    startingTime = new TimeSpan(0);
    duration = new TimeSpan(0);
  }

  public void StopTime() {
    duration =
      Process.GetCurrentProcess().Threads[0].
        UserProcessorTime.
          Subtract(startingTime);
  }

  public void startTime() {
    GC.Collect();
    GC.WaitForPendingFinalizers();
    startingTime =
```

```
                Process.GetCurrentProcess().Threads[0].
                   UserProcessorTime;
    }
    public TimeSpan Result() {
      return duration;
    }
}
class chapter1 {
  static void Main() {
      int[] nums = new int[100000];
      BuildArray(nums);
      Timing tObj = new Timing();
      tObj.startTime();
      DisplayNums(nums);
      tObj.stopTime();
      Console.WriteLine("time (.NET): " & tObj.Result.
                          TotalSeconds);
  }
  static void BuildArray(int[] arr) {
    for(int i = 0; i < 100000; i++)
       arr[i] = I;
  }
}
```

By moving the timing code into a class, we've cut down the number of lines in the main program from 13 to 8. Admittedly, that's not a lot of code to cut out of a program, but more important than the number of lines we cut is the clutter in the main program. Without the class, assigning the starting time to a variable looks like this:

```
startTime = Process.GetCurrentProcess().Threads[0].
               UserProcessorTime;
```

With the Timing class, assigning the starting time to the class data member looks like this:

```
tObj.startTime();
```

Encapsulating the long assignment statement into a class method makes our code easier to read and less likely to have bugs.

SUMMARY

This chapter reviews three important techniques we will use often in this book. Many, though not all of the programs we will write, as well as the libraries we will discuss, are written in an object-oriented manner. The Collection class we developed illustrates many of the basic OOP concepts seen throughout these chapters. Generic programming allows the programmer to simplify the definition of several data structures by limiting the number of methods that have to be written or overloaded. The Timing class provides a simple, yet effective way to measure the performance of the data structures and algorithms we will study.

EXERCISES

1. Create a class called Test that has data members for a student's name and a number indicating the test number. This class is used in the following scenario: When a student turns in a test, they place it face down on the desk. If a student wants to check an answer, the teacher has to turn the stack over so the first test is face up, work through the stack until the student's test is found, and then remove the test from the stack. When the student finishes checking the test, it is reinserted at the end of the stack.

   Write a Windows application to model this situation. Include text boxes for the user to enter a name and a test number. Put a list box on the form for displaying the final list of tests. Provide four buttons for the following actions: 1. Turn in a test; 2. Let student look at test; 3. Return a test; and 4. Exit. Perform the following actions to test your application: 1. Enter a name and a test number. Insert the test into a collection named submittedTests; 2. Enter a name, delete the associated test from submittedTests, and insert the test in a collection named outForChecking; 3. Enter a name, delete the test from outForChecking, and insert it in submittedTests; 4. Press the Exit button. The Exit button doesn't stop the application but instead deletes all tests from outForChecking and inserts them in submittedTests and displays a list of all the submitted tests.

   Use the Collection class developed in this chapter.

2. Add to the Collection class by implementing the following methods:
   a. Insert
   b. Contains
   c. IndexOf
   d. RemoveAt
3. Use the Timing class to compare the performance of the Collection class and an ArrayList when adding 1,000,000 integers to each.
4. Build your own Collection class without deriving your class from CollectionBase. Use generics in your implementation.

CHAPTER 2

Arrays and ArrayLists

The array is the most common data structure, present in nearly all programming languages. Using an array in C# involves creating an array object of System.Array type, the abstract base type for all arrays. The Array class provides a set of methods for performing tasks such as sorting and searching that programmers had to build by hand in the past.

An interesting alternative to using arrays in C# is the ArrayList class. An arraylist is an array that grows dynamically as more space is needed. For situations where you can't accurately determine the ultimate size of an array, or where the size of the array will change quite a bit over the lifetime of a program, an arraylist may be a better choice than an array.

In this chapter, we'll quickly touch on the basics of using arrays in C#, then move on to more advanced topics, including copying, cloning, testing for equality and using the static methods of the Array and ArrayList classes.

ARRAY BASICS

Arrays are indexed collections of data. The data can be of either a built-in type or a user-defined type. In fact, it is probably the simplest just to say that array data are objects. Arrays in C# are actually objects themselves because they derive from the System.Array class. Since an array is a declared instance of the System.Array class, you have the use of all the methods and properties of this class when using arrays.

Declaring and Initializing Arrays

Arrays are declared using the following syntax:

```
type[] array-name;
```

where type is the data type of the array elements. Here is an example:

```
string[] names;
```

A second line is necessary to instantiate the array (since it is an object of System.Array type) and to determine the size of the array. The following line instantiates the names array just declared:

```
names = new string[10];
```

and reserves memory for five strings.

You can combine these two statements into one line when necessary to do so:

```
string[] names = new string[10];
```

There are times when you will want to declare, instantiate, and assign data to an array in one statement. You can do this in C# using an initialization list:

```
int[] numbers = new int[] {1,2,3,4,5};
```

The list of numbers, called the initialization list, is delimited with curly braces, and each element is delimited with a comma. When you declare an array using this technique, you don't have to specify the number of elements. The compiler infers this data from the number of items in the initialization list.

Setting and Accessing Array Elements

Elements are stored in an array either by direct access or by calling the Array class method SetValue. Direct access involves referencing an array position by index on the left-hand side of an assignment statement:

```
Names[2] = "Raymond";
Sales[19] = 23123;
```

The SetValue method provides a more object-oriented way to set the value of an array element. The method takes two arguments, an index number and the value of the element.

```
names.SetValue[2, "Raymond"];
sales.SetValue[19, 23123];
```

Array elements are accessed either by direct access or by calling the GetValue method. The GetValue method takes a single argument—an index.

```
myName = names[2];
monthSales = sales.GetValue[19];
```

It is common to loop through an array in order to access every array element using a For loop. A frequent mistake programmers make when coding the loop is to either hard-code the upper value of the loop (which is a mistake because the upper bound may change if the array is dynamic) or call a function that accesses the upper bound of the loop for each iteration of the loop:

```
(for int i = 0; i <= sales.GetUpperBound(0); i++)
  totalSales = totalSales + sales[i];
```

Methods and Properties for Retrieving Array Metadata

The Array class provides several properties for retrieving metadata about an array:

- Length: Returns the total number of elements in all dimensions of an array.
- GetLength: Returns the number of elements in specified dimension of an array.

- Rank: Returns the number of dimensions of an array.
- GetType: Returns the Type of the current array instance.

The Length method is useful for counting the number of elements in a multidimensional array, as well as returning the exact number of elements in the array. Otherwise, you can use the GetUpperBound method and add one to the value.

Since Length returns the total number of elements in an array, the GetLength method counts the elements in one dimension of an array. This method, along with the Rank property, can be used to resize an array at run-time without running the risk of losing data. This technique is discussed later in the chapter.

The GetType method is used for determining the data type of an array in a situation where you may not be sure of the array's type, such as when the array is passed as an argument to a method. In the following code fragment, we create a variable of type Type, which allows us to use call a class method, IsArray, to determine if an object is an array. If the object is an array, then the code returns the data type of the array.

```
int[] numbers;
numbers = new int[] {0,1,2,3,4};
Type arrayType = numbers.GetType();
if (arrayType.IsArray)
   Console.WriteLine("The array type is: {0}", arrayType);
else
   Console.WriteLine("Not an array");
Console.Read();
```

The GetType method returns not only the type of the array, but also lets us know that the object is indeed an array. Here is the output from the code:

```
The array type is: System.Int32[]
```

The brackets indicate the object is an array. Also notice that we use a format when displaying the data type. We have to do this because we can't convert the Type data to string in order to concatenate it with the rest of the displayed string.

Multidimensional Arrays

So far we have limited our discussion to arrays that have just a single dimension. In C#, an array can have up to 32 dimensions, though arrays with more than three dimensions are very rare (and very confusing).

Multidimensional arrays are declared by providing the upper bound of each of the dimensions of the array. The two-dimensional declaration:

```
int[,] grades = new int[4,5];
```

declares an array that consists of 4 rows and 5 columns. Two-dimensional arrays are often used to model matrices.

You can also declare a multidimensional array without specifing the dimension bounds. To do this, you use commas to specify the number of dimensions. For example,

```
double[,] Sales;
```

declares a two-dimensional array, whereas

```
double[,,] sales;
```

declares a three-dimensional array. When you declare arrays without providing the upper bounds of the dimensions, you have to later redimension the array with those bounds:

```
sales = new double[4,5];
```

Multidimensional arrays can be initialized with an initialization list. Look at the following statement:

```
Int[,] grades = new int[,] {{1, 82, 74, 89, 100},
                            {2, 93, 96, 85, 86},
                            {3, 83, 72, 95, 89},
                            {4, 91, 98, 79, 88}}
```

First, notice that the upper bounds of the array are not specified. When you initialize an array with an initialization list, you can't specify the bounds of the array. The compiler computes the upper bounds of each dimension from the data in the initialization list. The initialization list itself is demarcated with curly braces, as is each row of the array. Each element in the row is delimited with a comma.

Accessing the elements of a multidimensional array is similar to accessing the elements of a one-dimensional array. You can use the traditional array access technique,

```
grade = Grades[2,2];
Grades(2,2) = 99
```

or you can use the methods of the Array class:

```
grade = Grades.GetValue[0,2]
```

You can't use the SetValue method with a multidimensional array because the method only accepts two arguments: a value and a single index.

It is a common operation to perform calculations on all the elements of a multidimensional array, though often based on either the values stored in the rows of the array or the values stored in the columns of the array. Using the Grades array, if each row of the array is a student record, we can calculate the grade average for each student as follows:

```
int[,] grades = new int[,] {{1, 82, 74, 89, 100},
                            {2, 93, 96, 85, 86},
                            {3, 83, 72, 95, 89},
                            {4, 91, 98, 79, 88}};
int last_grade = grades.GetUpperBound(1);
double average = 0.0;
int total;
int last_student = grades.GetUpperBound(0);
for(int row = 0; row <= last_student; row++) {
  total = 0;
  for (int col = 0; col <= last_grade; col++)
    total += grades[row, col];
    average = total / last_grade;
    Console.WriteLine("Average: " + average);
  }
}
```

Parameter Arrays

Most method definitions require that a set number of parameters be provided to the method, but there are times when you want to write a method definition that allows an optional number of parameters. You can do this using a construct called a parameter array.

A parameter array is specified in the parameter list of a method definition by using the keyword ParamArray. The following method definition allows any amount of numbers to be supplied as parameters, with the total of the numbers returned from the method:

```
static int sumNums(params int[] nums) {
  int sum = 0;
  for(int i = 0; i <= nums.GetUpperBound(0); i++)
    sum += nums[i];
  return sum;
}
```

This method will work with the either of the following calls:

```
total = sumNums(1, 2, 3);
total = sumNums(1, 2, 3, 4, 5, 6, 7, 8, 9, 10);
```

When you define a method using a parameter array, the parameter array arguments have to be supplied last in the parameter list in order for the compiler to be able to process the list of parameters correctly. Otherwise, the compiler wouldn't know the ending point of the parameter array elements and the beginning of other parameters of the method.

Jagged Arrays

When you create a multidimensional array, you always create a structure that has the same number of elements in each of the rows. For example, look at the following array declaration:

```
int sales[,] = new int[12,30];   ' Sales for each day of
                                   each month
```

This array assumes each row (month) has the same number of elements (days), when we know that some months have 30 days, some have 31, and one month has 29. With the array we've just declared, there will be several empty elements in the array. This isn't much of a problem for this array, but with a much larger array we end up with a lot of wasted space.

The solution to this problem is to use a jagged array instead of a two-dimensional array. A jagged array is an array of arrays where each row of an array is made up of an array. Each dimension of a jagged array is a one-dimensional array. We call it a "jagged" array because the number of elements in each row may be different. A picture of a jagged array would not be square or rectangular, but would have uneven or jagged edges.

A jagged array is declared by putting two sets of parentheses after the array variable name. The first set of parentheses indicates the number of rows in the array. The second set of parentheses is left blank. This marks the place for the one-dimensional array that is stored in each row. Normally, the number of rows is set in an initialization list in the declaration statement, like this:

```
int[][] jagged = new int[12][];
```

This statement looks strange, but makes sense when you break it down. jagged is an Integer array of 12 elements, where each of the elements is also an Integer array. The initialization list is actually just the initialization for the rows of the array, indicating that each row element is an array of 12 elements, with each element initialized to the default value.

Once the jagged array is declared, the elements of the individual row arrays can be assigned values. The following code fragment assigns values to jaggedArray:

```
jagged[0][0] = 23;
jagged[0][1] = 13;
. . .
jagged[7][5] = 45;
```

The first set of parentheses indicates the row number and the second set indicates the element of the row array. The first statement accesses the first element of the first array, the second element access the second element of the first array, and the third statement accesses the sixth element of the eighth array.

For an example of using a jagged array, the following program creates an array named sales (tracking one week of sales for two months), assigns sales figures to its elements, and then loops through the array to calculate the average sales for one week of each of the two months stored in the array.

```
using System;
class class1 {
    static void Main[] {
  int[] Jan = new int[31];
  int[] Feb = new int[29];
  int[][] sales = new int{Jan, Feb};
  int month, day, total;
  double average = 0.0;
  sales[0][0] = 41;
  sales[0][1] = 30;
  sales[0][0] = 41;
  sales[0][1] = 30;
  sales[0][2] = 23;
  sales[0][3] = 34;
  sales[0][4] = 28;
  sales[0][5] = 35;
  sales[0][6] = 45;
  sales[1][0] = 35;
  sales[1][1] = 37;
  sales[1][2] = 32;
  sales[1][3] = 26;
  sales[1][4] = 45;
  sales[1][5] = 38;
  sales[1][6] = 42;
  for(month = 0; month <= 1; month++) {
    total = 0;
    for(day = 0; day <= 6; day++)
      total += sales[month][day];
    average = total / 7;
    Console.WriteLine("Average sales for month: " +
                    month + ": " + average);
 }
  }
}
```

The ArrayList Class

Static arrays are not very useful when the size of an array is unknown in advance or is likely to change during the lifetime of a program. One solution to this problem is to use a type of array that automatically resizes itself when the array is out of storage space. This array is called an ArrayList and it is part of the System.Collections namespace in the .NET Framework library.

An ArrayList object has a Capacity property that stores its size. The initial value of the property is 16. When the number of elements in an ArrayList reaches this limit, the Capacity property adds another 16 elements to the storage space of the ArrayList. Using an ArrayList in a situation where the number of elements in an array can grow larger, or smaller, can be more efficient than using ReDim Preserver with a standard array.

As we discussed in Chapter 1, an ArrayList stores objects using the Object type. If you need a strongly typed array, you should use a standard array or some other data structure.

Members of the ArrayList Class

The ArrayList class includes several methods and properties for working with ArrayLists. Here is a list of some of the most commonly used methods and properties:

- Add(): Adds an element to the ArrayList.
- AddRange(): Adds the elements of a collection to the end of the ArrayList.
- Capacity: Stores the number of elements the ArrayList can hold.
- Clear(): Removes all elements from the ArrayList.
- Contains(): Determines if a specified item is in the ArrayList.
- CopyTo(): Copies the ArrayList or a segment of it to an array.
- Count: Returns the number of elements currently in the ArrayList.
- GetEnumerator(): Returns an enumerator to iterate over the ArrayList.
- GetRange(): Returns a subset of the ArrayList as an ArrayList.
- IndexOf(): Returns the index of the first occurrence of the specified item.
- Insert(): Insert an element into the ArrayList at a specified index.
- InsertRange(): Inserts the elements of a collection into the ArrayList starting at the specified index.

- Item(): Gets or sets an element at the specified index.
- Remove(): Removes the first occurrence of the specified item.
- RemoveAt(): Removes an element at the specified index.
- Reverse(): Reverses the order of the elements in the ArrayList.
- Sort(): Alphabetically sorts the elements in the ArrayList.
- ToArray(): Copies the elements of the ArrayList to an array.
- TrimToSize(): Sets the capacity of the ArrayList to the number of elements in the ArrayList.

Using the ArrayList Class

ArrayLists are not used like standard arrays. Normally, items are just added to an ArrayList using the Add method, unless there is a reason why an item should be added at a particular position, in which case the Insert method should be used. In this section, we examine how to use these and the other members of the ArrayList class.

The first thing we have to do with an ArrayList is declare it, as follows:

```
ArrayList grades = new ArrayList();
```

Notice that a constructor is used in this declaration. If an ArrayList is not declared using a constructor, the object will not be available in later program statements.

Objects are added to an ArrayList using the Add method. This method takes one argument—an Object to add to the ArrayList. The Add method also returns an integer indicating the position in the ArrayList where the element was added, though this value is rarely used in a program. Here are some examples:

```
grades.Add(100);
grades.Add(84);
int position;
position = grades.Add(77);
Console.WriteLine("The grade 77 was added at position:
                " + position);
```

The objects in an ArrayList can be displayed using a For Each loop. The ArrayList has a built-in enumerator that manages iterating through all the objects in the ArrayList, one at a time. The following code fragment demonstrates how to use a For Each loop with an ArrayList:

```
int total = 0;
double average = 0.0;
foreach (Object grade in grades)
    total += (int)grade;
  average = total / grades.Count;
  Console.WriteLine("The average grade is: " + average);
```

If you want to add an element to an ArrayList at a particular position, you can use the Insert method. This method takes two arguments: the index to insert the element, and the element to be inserted. The following code fragment inserts two grades in specific positions in order to preserve the order of the objects in the ArrayList:

```
grades.Insert(1, 99);
grades.Insert(3, 80);
```

You can check the current capacity of an ArrayList by calling the Capacity property and you can determine how many elements are in an ArrayList by calling the Count property:

```
Console.WriteLine("The current capacity of grades is:
                " + grades.Capacity);
Console.WriteLine("The number of grades in grades is:
                " + grades.Count);
```

There are several ways to remove items from an ArrayList. If you know the item you want to remove, but don't know what position it is in, you can use the Remove method. This method takes just one argument—an object to remove from the ArrayList. If the object exists in the ArrayList, it is removed. If the object isn't in the ArrayList, nothing happens. When a method like Remove is used, it is typically called inside an If–Then statement using a method that can verify the object is actually in the ArrayList, such as the Contains method. Here's a sample code fragment:

```
if (grades.Contains(54))
  grades.Remove(54)
else
  Console.Write("Object not in ArrayList.");
```

If you know the index of the object you want to remove, you can use the RemoveAt method. This method takes one argument—the index of the object you want to remove. The only exception you can cause is passing an invalid index to the method. The method works like this:

```
grades.RemoveAt(2);
```

You can determine the position of an object in an ArrayList by calling the IndexOf method. This method takes one argument, an object, and returns the object's position in the ArrayList. If the object is not in the ArrayList, the method returns -1. Here's a short code fragment that uses the IndexOf method in conjunction with the RemoveAt method:

```
int pos;
pos = grades.IndexOf(70);
grades.RemoveAt(pos);
```

In addition to adding individual objects to an ArrayList, you can also add ranges of objects. The objects must be stored in a data type that is derived from ICollection. This means that the objects can be stored in an array, a Collection, or even in another ArrayList.

There are two different methods you can use to add a range to an ArrayList. These methods are AddRange and InsertRange. The AddRange method adds the range of objects to the end of the ArrayList, and the InsertRange method adds the range at a specified position in the ArrayList.

The following program demonstrates how these two methods are used:

```
using System;
using System.Collections;
class class1 {
  static void Main() {
    ArrayList names = new ArrayList();
    names.Add("Mike");
    names.Add("Beata");
    names.Add("Raymond");
    names.Add("Bernica");
    names.Add("Jennifer");
    Console.WriteLine("The original list of names: ");
```

```
      foreach (Object name in names)
        Console.WriteLine(name);
      Console.WriteLine();
      string[] newNames = new string[] {"David", "Michael"};
      ArrayList moreNames = new ArrayList();
      moreNames.Add("Terrill");
      moreNames.Add("Donnie");
      moreNames.Add("Mayo");
      moreNames.Add("Clayton");
      moreNames.Add("Alisa");
      names.InsertRange(0, newNames);
      names.AddRange(moreNames);
      Console.WriteLine("The new list of names: ");
      foreach (Object name in names)
        Console.WriteLine(name);
   }
}
```

The output from this program is:

```
David
Michael
Mike
Bernica
Beata
Raymond
Jennifer
Terrill
Donnie
Mayo
Clayton
Alisa
```

The first two names are added at the beginning of the ArrayList because the specified index is 0. The last names are added at the end because the AddRange method is used.

Two other methods that many programmers find useful are the ToArray method and the GetRange method. The GetRange method returns a range of objects from the ArrayList as another ArrayList. The ToArray method copies all the elements of the ArrayList to an array. Let's look first at the GetRange method.

The GetRange method takes two arguments: the starting index and the number of elements to retrieve from the ArrayList. GetRange is not destructive, in that the objects are just copied from the original ArrayList into the new ArrayList. Here's an example of how the method works, using the same aforementioned program:

```
ArrayList someNames = new ArrayList();
someNames = names.GetRange(2,4);
Console.WriteLine("someNames sub-ArrayList: ");
foreach (Object name in someNames)
  Console.WriteLine(name);
```

The output from this program fragment is:

```
Mike
Bernica
Beata
Raymond
```

The ToArray method allows you to easily transfer the contents of an ArrayList to a standard array. The primary reason you will use the ToArray method is because you need the faster access speed of an array.

The ToArray method takes no arguments and returns the elements of the ArrayList to an array. Here's an example of how to use the method:

```
Object[] arrNames;
arrNames = names.ToArray();
Console.WriteLine("Names from an array: ");
for(int i = 0; i <= arrNames.GetUpperBound(0); i++)
  Console.WriteLine(arrNames[i]);
```

The last part of the code fragment proves that the elements from the ArrayList have actually been stored in the array arrNames.

SUMMARY

The array is the most commonly used data structure in computer programming. Most, if not all, computer languages provide some type of built-in array.

For many applications, the array is the easiest data structure to implement and the most efficient. Arrays are useful in situations where you need direct access to "far away" elements of your data set.

The .NET Framework introduces a new type of array called an ArrayList. ArrayLists have many of the features of the array, but are somewhat more powerful because they can resize themselves when the current capacity of the structure is full. The ArrayList also has several useful methods for performing insertions, deletions, and searches. Since C# does not allow a programmer to dynamically resize an array as you can in VB.NET, the ArrayList is a useful data structure for situations where you can't know in advance the total number of items for storage.

EXERCISES

1. Design and implement a class that allows a teacher to track the grades in a single course. Include methods that calculate the average grade, the highest grade, and the lowest grade. Write a program to test your class implementation.
2. Modify Exercise 1 so that the class can keep track of multiple courses. Write a program to test your implementation.
3. Rewrite Exercise 1 using an ArrayList. Write a program to test your implementation and compare its performance to that of the array implementation in Exercise 1 using the Timing class.
4. Design and implement a class that uses an array to mimic the behavior of the ArrayList class. Include as many methods from the ArrayList class as possible. Write a program to test your implementation.

CHAPTER 3

Basic Sorting Algorithms

The two most common operations performed on data stored in a computer are sorting and searching. This has been true since the beginning of the computing industry, which means that sorting and searching are also two of the most studied operations in computer science. Many of the data structures discussed in this book are designed primarily to make sorting and/or searching easier and more efficient on the data stored in the structure.

This chapter introduces you to the fundamental algorithms for sorting and searching data. These algorithms depend on only the array as a data structure and the only "advanced" programming technique used is recursion. This chapter also introduces you to the techniques we'll use throughout the book to informally analyze different algorithms for speed and efficiency.

SORTING ALGORITHMS

Most of the data we work with in our day-to-day lives is sorted. We look up definitions in a dictionary by searching alphabetically. We look up a phone number by moving through the last names in the book alphabetically. The post office sorts mail in several ways—by zip code, then by street address, and then by name. Sorting is a fundamental process in working with data and deserves close study.

As was mentioned earlier, there has been quite a bit of research performed on different sorting techniques. Although some very sophisticated sorting algorithms have been developed, there are also several simple sorting algorithms you should study first. These sorting algorithms are the insertion sort, the bubble sort, and the selection sort. Each of these algorithms is easy to understand and easy to implement. They are not the best overall algorithms for sorting by any means, but for small data sets and in other special circumstances, they are the best algorithms to use.

An Array Class Test Bed

To examine these algorithms, we will first need a test bed in which to implement and test them. We'll build a class that encapsulates the normal operations performed with an array—element insertion, element access, and displaying the contents of the array. Here's the code:

```
class CArray {

  private int [] arr;
  private int upper;
  .private int numElements;
  public CArray(int size) {
    arr = new int[size];
    upper = size-1;
    numElements = 0;
  }

  public void Insert(int item) {
    arr[numElements] = item;
    numElements++;
  }

  public void DisplayElements() {
    for(int i = 0; i <= upper; i++)
      Console.Write(arr[i] + " ");
  }

  public void Clear() {
    for(int i = 0; i <= upper; i++)
```

```
      arr[i] = 0;
    numElements = 0;
  }
}
static void Main() {
  CArray nums = new CArray();
  for(int i = 0; i <= 49; i++)
    nums.Insert(i);
  nums.DisplayElements();
}
```

The output looks like this:

Before leaving the CArray class to begin the examination of sorting and searching algorithms, let's discuss how we're going to actually store data in a CArray class object. In order to demonstrate most effectively how the different sorting algorithms work, the data in the array needs to be in a random order. This is best achieved by using a random number generator to assign each array element to the array.

Random numbers can be created in C# using the Random class. An object of this type can generate random numbers. To instantiate a Random object, you have to pass a seed to the class constructor. This seed can be seen as an upper bound for the range of numbers the random number generator can create.

Here's another look at a program that uses the CArray class to store numbers, using the random number generator to select the data to store in the array:

```
static void Main() {
  CArray nums = new CArray();
  Random rnd = new Random(100);
  for(int i = 0; i < 10; i++)
    nums.Insert((int)(rnd.NextDouble() * 100));
  nums.DisplayElements();
}
```

The output from this program is:

Bubble Sort

The first sorting algorithm to examine is the bubble sort. The bubble sort is one of the slowest sorting algorithms available, but it is also one of the simplest sorts to understand and implement, which makes it an excellent candidate for our first sorting algorithm.

The sort gets its name because values "float like a bubble" from one end of the list to another. Assuming you are sorting a list of numbers in ascending order, higher values float to the right whereas lower values float to the left. This behavior is caused by moving through the list many times, comparing adjacent values and swapping them if the value to the left is greater than the value to the right.

Figure 3.1 illustrates how the bubble sort works. Two numbers from the numbers inserted into the array (2 and 72) from the previous example are highlighted with circles. You can watch how 72 moves from the beginning of the array to the middle of the array, and you can see how 2 moves from just past the middle of the array to the beginning of the array.

| (72) | 54 | 59 | 30 | 31 | 78 | (2) | 77 | 82 | 72 |

| 54 | 58 | 30 | 31 | (72) | (2) | 77 | 78 | 72 | 82 |

| 54 | 30 | 32 | 58 | (2) | (72) | 72 | 77 | 78 | 82 |

| 30 | 32 | 54 | (2) | 58 | (72) | 72 | 77 | 78 | 82 |

| 30 | 32 | (2) | 54 | 58 | (72) | 72 | 77 | 78 | 82 |

| 30 | (2) | 32 | 54 | 58 | (72) | 72 | 77 | 78 | 82 |

| (2) | 30 | 32 | 54 | 58 | (72) | 72 | 77 | 78 | 82 |

FIGURE 3.1. The Bubble Sort.

The code for the BubbleSort algorithm is shown as follows:

```
public void BubbleSort() {
  int temp;
  for(int outer = upper; outer >= 1; outer--) {
    for(int inner = 0; inner <= outer-1;inner++)
      if ((int)arr[inner] > arr[inner+1]) {
        temp = arr[inner];
        arr[inner] = arr[inner+1];
        arr[inner+1] = temp;
    }
  }
}
```

There are several things to notice about this code. First, the code to swap two array elements is written in line rather than as a subroutine. A swap subroutine might slow down the sorting since it will be called many times. Since the swap code is only three lines long, the clarity of the code is not sacrificed by not putting the code in its own subroutine.

More importantly, notice that the outer loop starts at the end of the array and moves toward the beginning of the array. If you look back at Figure 3.1, the highest value in the array is in its proper place at the end of the array. This means that the array indices that are greater than the value in the outer loop are already in their proper place and the algorithm doesn't need to access these values any more.

The inner loop starts at the first element of the array and ends when it gets to the next to last position in the array. The inner loop compares the two adjacent positions indicated by inner and inner +1, swapping them if necessary.

Examining the Sorting Process

One of the things you will probably want to do while developing an algorithm is viewing the intermediate results of the code while the program is running. When you're using Visual Studio.NET, it's possible to do this using the Debugging tools available in the IDE. However, sometimes, all you really want to see is a display of the array (or whatever data structure you are building, sorting, or searching). An easy way to do this is to insert a displaying method in the appropriate place in the code.

For the aforementioned BubbleSort method, the best place to examine how the array changes during the sorting is between the inner loop and the outer loop. If we do this for each iteration of the two loops, we can view a record of how the values move through the array while they are being sorted.

For example, here is the BubbleSort method modified to display intermediate results:

```
public void BubbleSort() {
  int temp;
  for(int outer = upper; outer >= 1; outer--) {
    for(int inner = 0; inner <= outer-1;inner++) {
      if ((int)arr[inner] > arr[inner+1]) {
        temp = arr[inner];
        arr[inner] = arr[inner+1];
        arr[inner+1] = temp;
      }
    }
    this.DisplayElements();
  }
}
```

The DisplayElements() method is placed between the two For loops. If the main program is modified as follows:

```
static void Main() {
  CArray nums = new CArray(10);
  Random rnd = new Random(100);
  for(int i = 0; i < 10; i++)
    nums.Insert((int)(rnd.NextDouble() * 100));
  Console.WriteLine("Before sorting: ");
  nums.DisplayElements();
  Console.WriteLine("During sorting: ");
  nums.BubbleSort();
  Console.WriteLine("After sorting: ");
  nums.DisplayElements();
}
```

the following output is displayed:

```
C:\Documents and Settings\Administrator\My Documents\Visual Studio Projects\ArrayClass\...
Before sorting:
72 54 59 30 31 78 2 77 82 72
During sorting:
54 59 30 31 72 2 77 78 72 82
54 30 31 59 2 72 77 72 78 82
30 31 54 2 59 72 72 77 78 82
30 31 2 54 59 72 72 77 78 82
30 2 31 54 59 72 72 77 78 82
2 30 31 54 59 72 72 77 78 82
2 30 31 54 59 72 72 77 78 82
2 30 31 54 59 72 72 77 78 82
After sorting:
2 30 31 54 59 72 72 77 78 82
```

Selection Sort

The next sort to examine is the Selection sort. This sort works by starting at the beginning of the array, comparing the first element with the other elements in the array. The smallest element is placed in position 0, and the sort then begins again at position 1. This continues until each position except the last position has been the starting point for a new loop.

Two loops are used in the SelectionSort algorithm. The outer loop moves from the first element in the array to the next to last element, whereas the inner loop moves from the second element of the array to the last element, looking for values that are smaller than the element currently being pointed at by the outer loop. After each iteration of the inner loop, the most minimum value in the array is assigned to its proper place in the array. Figure 3.2 illustrates how this works with the CArray data used before.

The code to implement the SelectionSort algorithm is shown as follows:

```
public void SelectionSort() {
  int min, temp;
  for(int outer = 0; outer <= upper; outer++) {
    min = outer;
    for(int inner = outer + 1; inner <= upper; inner++)
      if (arr[inner] < arr[min])
        min = inner;
    temp = arr[outer];
    arr[outer] = arr[min];
    arr[min] = temp;
  }
}
```

72	54	59	30	31	78	2	77	82	72
2	54	59	30	31	78	72	77	82	72
2	30	59	54	31	78	72	77	82	72
2	30	31	54	59	78	72	77	82	72
2	30	31	54	59	78	72	77	82	72
2	30	31	54	59	78	72	77	82	72
2	30	31	54	59	72	78	77	82	72
2	30	31	54	59	72	72	77	82	78
2	30	31	54	59	72	72	77	82	78
2	30	31	54	59	72	72	77	78	82

FIGURE 3.2. The Selection Sort.

To demonstrate how the algorithm works, place a call to the showArray() method right before the Next statement that is attached to the outer loop. The output should look something like this:

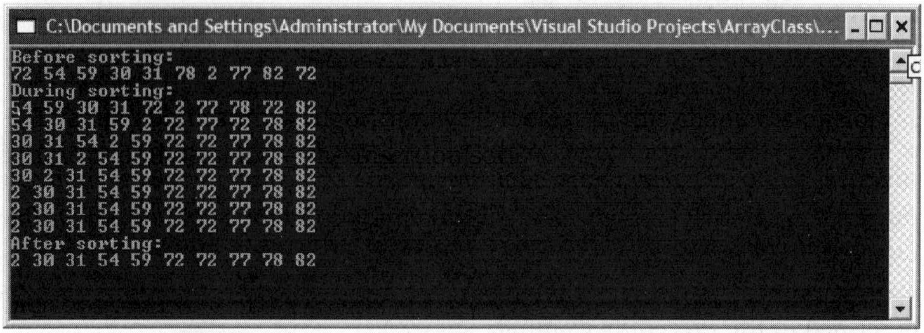

The final basic sorting algorithm we'll look at in this chapter is one of the simplest to understand—the Insertion sort.

Insertion Sort

The Insertion sort is an analog to the way we normally sort things numerically or alphabetically. Let's say that I have asked a class of students to turn in index card with their names, id numbers, and a short biographical sketch. The students return the cards in random order, but I want them to be alphabetized so I can build a seating chart.

I take the cards back to my office, clear off my desk, and take the first card. The name on the card is Smith. I place it at the top left position of the desk and take the second card. It is Brown. I move Smith over to the right and put Brown in Smith's place. The next card is Williams. It can be inserted at the right without having to shift any other cards. The next card is Acklin. It has to go at the beginning of the list, so each of the other cards must be shifted one position to the right to make room. That is how the Insertion sort works.

The code for the Insertion sort is shown here, followed by an explanation of how it works:

```
public void InsertionSort() {
   int inner, temp;
   for(int outer = 1; outer <= upper; outer++) {
      temp = arr[outer];
      inner = outer;
      while(inner > 0 && arr[inner-1] >= temp) {
         arr[inner] = arr[inner-1];
         inner -= 1;
      }
      arr[inner] = temp;
   }
}
```

The Insertion sort has two loops. The outer loop moves element by element through the array whereas the inner loop compares the element chosen in the outer loop to the element next to it in the array. If the element selected by the outer loop is less than the element selected by the inner loop, array elements are shifted over to the right to make room for the inner loop element, just as described in the preceding example.

Now let's look at how the Insertion sort works with the set of numbers sorted in the earlier examples. Here's the output:

```
■ C:\Documents and Settings\Administrator\My Documents\Visual Studio Projects\ArrayClass\...  _ □ ×
Before sorting numbers:
72 54 59 30 31 78 2 77 82 72
Now into Insertion sort:
54 72 59 30 31 78 2 77 82 72
54 59 72 30 31 78 2 77 82 72
30 54 59 72 31 78 2 77 82 72
30 31 54 59 72 78 2 77 82 72
30 31 54 59 72 78 2 77 82 72
2 30 31 54 59 72 78 77 82 72
2 30 31 54 59 72 77 78 82 72
2 30 31 54 59 72 77 78 82 72
2 30 31 54 59 72 72 77 78 82
After sorting numbers:
2 30 31 54 59 72 72 77 78 82
```

This display clearly shows that the Insertion sort works not by making exchanges, but by moving larger array elements to the right to make room for smaller elements on the left side of the array.

TIMING COMPARISONS OF THE BASIC SORTING ALGORITHMS

These three sorting algorithms are very similar in complexity and theoretically, at least, should perform similarly when compared with each other. We can use the Timing class to compare the three algorithms to see if any of them stand out from the others in terms of the time it takes to sort a large set of numbers.

To perform the test, we used the same basic code we used earlier to demonstrate how each algorithm works. In the following tests, however, the array sizes are varied to demonstrate how the three algorithms perform with both smaller data sets and larger data sets. The timing tests are run for array sizes of 100 elements, 1,000 elements, and 10,000 elements. Here's the code:

```
static void Main() {
    Timing sortTime = new Timing();
    Random rnd = new Random(100);
    int numItems = 1000;
    CArray theArray = new CArray(numItems);
    for(int i = 0; i < numItems; i++)
```

```
        theArray.Insert((int)(rnd.NextDouble() * 100));
    sortTime.startTime();
    theArray.SelectionSort();
    sortTime.stopTime();
    Console.WriteLine("Time for Selection sort: " +
                    sortTime.getResult().
                    TotalMilliseconds);
    theArray.Clear();
    for(int i = 0; i < numItems; i++)
       theArray.Insert((int)(rnd.NextDouble() * 100));
    sortTime.startTime();
    theArray.BubbleSort();
    sortTime.stopTime();
    Console.WriteLine("Time for Bubble sort: " +
                    sortTime.getResult().
                    TotalMilliseconds);
    theArray.Clear();
    for(int i = 0; i < numItems; i++)
       theArray.Insert((int)(rnd.NextDouble() * 100));
    sortTime.startTime();
    theArray.InsertionSort();
    sortTime.stopTime();
    Console.WriteLine("Time for Selection sort: " +
                    sortTime.getResult().
                    TotalMilliseconds);
}
```

The output from this program is:

```
C:\Documents and Settings\Administrator\My Documents\Visual Studio Projects\ArrayClass\...
Time for Selection sort: 10.0144
Time for Bubble sort: 10.0144
Time for Insertion sort: 20.0288
```

showing that the Selection and Bubble sorts perform at the same speed and the Insertion sort is about half as fast (or twice as slow).

Now let's compare the algorithms when the array size is 1,000 elements:

```
C:\Documents and Settings\Administrator\My Documents\Visual Studio Projects\ArrayClass\...
Time for Selection sort: 40.0576
Time for Bubble sort: 500.72
Time for Insertion sort: 871.2528
```

Here we see that the size of the array makes a big difference in the performance of the algorithm. The Selection sort is over 100 times faster than the Bubble sort and over 200 times faster than the Insertion sort.

When we increase the array size to 10,000 elements, we can really see the effect of size on the three algorithms:

```
C:\Documents and Settings\Administrator\My Documents\Visual Studio Projects\ArrayClass\...
Time for Selection sort: 2864.1184
Time for Bubble sort: 53607.0832
Time for Insertion sort: 84751.8672
```

The performance of all three algorithms degrades considerably, though the Selection sort is still many times faster than the other two. Clearly, none of these algorithms is ideal for sorting large data sets. There are sorting algorithms, though, that can handle large data sets more efficiently. We'll examine their design and use in Chapter 16.

SUMMARY

In this chapter, we discussed three algorithms for sorting data—the Selection sort, the Bubble sort, and the Insertion sort. All of these algorithms are fairly easy to implement and they all work well with small data sets. The Selection sort is the most efficient of the algorithms, followed by the Bubble sort and the Insertion sort. As we saw at the end of the chapter, none of these algorithms is well suited for larger data sets (i.e., more than a few thousand elements).

EXERCISES

1. Create a data file consisting of at least 100 string values. You can create the list yourself, or perhaps copy the values from a text file of some type, or you can even create the file by generating random strings. Sort the file using each of the sorting algorithms discussed in the chapter. Create a program that times each algorithm and outputs the times similar to the output from the last section of this chapter.
2. Create an array of 1,000 integers sorted in numerical order. Write a program that runs each sorting algorithm with this array, timing each algorithm, and compare the times. Compare these times to the times for sorting a random array of integers.
3. Create an array of 1,000 integers sorted in reverse numerical order. Write a program that runs each sorting algorithm with this array, timing each algorithm, and compare the times.

CHAPTER 4

Basic Searching Algorithms

Searching for data is a fundamental computer programming task and one that has been studied for many years. This chapter looks at just one aspect of the search problem—searching for a given value in a list (array).

There are two fundamental ways to search for data in a list: the sequential search and the binary search. Sequential search is used when the items in the list are in random order; binary search is used when the items are sorted in the list.

SEQUENTIAL SEARCHING

The most obvious type of search is to begin at the beginning of a set of records and move through each record until you find the record you are looking for or you come to the end of the records. This is called a *sequential search*.

A sequential search (also called a linear search) is very easy to implement. Start at the beginning of the array and compare each accessed array element to the value you're searching for. If you find a match, the search is over. If you get to the end of the array without generating a match, then the value is not in the array.

Here is a function that performs a sequential search:

```
bool SeqSearch(int[] arr, int sValue) {
  for (int index = 0; index < arr.Length-1; index++)
    if (arr[index] == sValue)
      return true;
  return false;
}
```

If a match is found, the function immediately returns True and exits. If the end of the array is reached without the function returning True, then the value being searched for is not in array and the function returns False.

Here is a program to test our implementation of a sequential search:

```
using System;
using System.IO;

public class Chapter4 {

  static void Main() {
    int [] numbers = new int[100];
    StreamReader numFile =
        File.OpenText("c:\\numbers.txt");
    for (int i = 0; i < numbers.Length-1; i++)
      numbers[i] =
          Convert.ToInt32(numFile.ReadLine(), 10);
    int searchNumber;
    Console.Write("Enter a number to search for: ");
    searchNumber = Convert.ToInt32(Console.ReadLine(),
                              10);
    bool found;
    found = SeqSearch(numbers, searchNumber);
    if (found)
      Console.WriteLine(searchNumber + " is in the
                        array.");
    else
      Console.WriteLine(searchNumber + " is not in the
                        array.");
```

```
    }
    static bool SeqSearch(int[] arr, int sValue) {
        for (int index = 0; index < arr.Length-1; index++)
            if (arr[index] == sValue)
            return true;
        return false;
    }
}
```

The program works by first reading in a set of data from a text file. The data consists of the first 100 integers, stored in the file in a partially random order. The program then prompts the user to enter a number to search for and calls the SeqSearch function to perform the search.

You can also write the sequential search function so that the function returns the position in the array where the searched-for value is found or a −1 if the value cannot be found. First, let's look at the new function:

```
static int SeqSearch(int[] arr, int sValue) {
    for (int index = 0; index < arr.Length-1; index++)
        if (arr[index] == sValue)
            return index;
    return -1;
}
```

The following program uses this function:

```
using System;
using System.IO;

public class Chapter4 {
    static void Main() {
        int [] numbers = new int[100];
        StreamReader numFile =_
            File.OpenText("c:\\numbers.txt");
        for (int i = 0; i < numbers.Length-1; i++)
            numbers[i] = Convert.ToInt32(numFile.ReadLine(),
                                        10);
```

```
      int searchNumber;
      Console.Write("Enter a number to search for: ");
      searchNumber = Convert.ToInt32(Console.ReadLine(),
                                10);
      int foundAt;
      foundAt = SeqSearch(numbers, searchNumber);
      if (foundAt >= 0)
        Console.WriteLine(searchNumber + " is in the_
                      array at position " + foundAt);
      else
        Console.WriteLine(searchNumber + " is not in the
                      array.");
    }

  static int SeqSearch(int[] arr, int sValue) {
    for (int index = 0; index < arr.Length-1; index++)
      if (arr[index] == sValue)
        return index;
    return -1;
  }

}
```

Searching for Minimum and Maximum Values

Computer programs are often asked to search an array (or other data structure)
for minimum and maximum values. In an ordered array, searching for these
values is a trivial task. Searching an unordered array, however, is a little more
challenging.

Let's start by looking at how to find the minimum value in an array. The
algorithm is:

1. Assign the first element of the array to a variable as the minimum value.
2. Begin looping through the array, comparing each successive array element
   with the minimum value variable.
3. If the currently accessed array element is less than the minimum value,
   assign this element to the minimum value variable.
4. Continue until the last array element is accessed.
5. The minimum value is stored in the variable.

Let's look at a function, FindMin, which implements this algorithm:

```
static int FindMin(int[] arr) {
  int min = arr[0];
  for(int i = 0; i < arr.Length-1; i++)
    if (arr[index] < min)
      min = arr[index];
  return min;
}
```

Notice that the array search starts at position 1 and not at position 0. The 0th position is assigned as the minimum value before the loop starts, so we can start making comparisons at position 1.

The algorithm for finding the maximum value in an array works in the same way. We assign the first array element to a variable that holds the maximum amount. Next we loop through the array, comparing each array element with the value stored in the variable, replacing the current value if the accessed value is greater. Here's the code:

```
static int FindMax(int[] arr) {
  int max = arr[0];
  for(int i = 0; i < arr.Length-1; i++)
    if (arr[index] > max)
      max = arr[index];
    return max;
}
```

An alternative version of these two functions could return the position of the maximum or minimum value in the array rather than the actual value.

Making Sequential Search Faster: Self-Organizing Data

The fastest successful sequential searches occur when the data element being searched for is at the beginning of the data set. You can ensure that a successfully located data item is at the beginning of the data set by moving it there after it has been found.

The concept behind this strategy is that we can minimize search times by putting frequently searched-for items at the beginning of the data set.

Eventually, all the most frequently searched-for data items will be located at the beginning of the data set. This is an example of self-organization, in that the data set is organized not by the programmer before the program runs, but by the program while the program is running.

It makes sense to allow your data to organize in this way since the data being searched probably follows the "80–20" rule, meaning that 80% of the searches conducted on your data set are searching for 20% of the data in the data set. Self-organization will eventually put that 20% at the beginning of the data set, where a sequential search will find them quickly.

Probability distributions such as this are called Pareto distributions, named for Vilfredo Pareto, who discovered these distributions studying the spread of income and wealth in the late nineteenth century. See Knuth (1998, pp. 399–401) for more on probability distributions in data sets.

We can modify our SeqSearch method quite easily to include self-organization. Here's a first stab at the method:

```
static bool SeqSearch(int sValue) {
  for(int index = 0; i < arr.Length-1; i++)
    if (arr[index] == sValue) {
      swap(index, index-1);
      return true;
    }
  return false;
}
```

If the search is successful, the item found is switched with the element at the first of the array using a swap function, shown as follows:

```
static void swap(ref int item1, ref int item2) {
  int temp = arr[item1];
  arr[item1] = arr[item2];
  arr[item2] = temp;
}
```

The problem with the SeqSearch method as we've modified it is that frequently accessed items might be moved around quite a bit during the course of many searches. We want to keep items that are moved to the first of the data set there and not moved farther back when a subsequent item farther down in the set is successfully located.

There are two ways we can achieve this goal. First, we can only swap found items if they are located away from the beginning of the data set. We only have to determine what is considered to be far enough back in the data set to warrant swapping. Following the "80–20" rule again, we can make a rule that a data item is relocated to the beginning of the data set only if its location is outside the first 20% of the items in the data set. Here's the code for this first rewrite:

```
static int SeqSearch(int sValue) {
   for(int index = 0; i < arr.Length-1; i++)
     if (arr[index] == sValue && index > (arr.Length *_
        0.2)) {
       swap(index, index-1);
       return index;
     } else
         if (arr[index] == sValue)
            return index;
   return -1;
}
```

The If–Then statement is short-circuited because if the item isn't found in the data set, there's no reason to test to see where the index is in the data set.

The other way we can rewrite the SeqSearch method is to swap a found item with the element that precedes it in the data set. Using this method, which is similar to how data is sorted using the Bubble sort, the most frequently accessed items will eventually work their way up to the front of the data set. This technique also guarantees that if an item is already at the beginning of the data set, it won't move back down.

The code for this new version of SeqSearch is shown as follows:

```
static int SeqSearch(int sValue) {
   for(int index = 0; i < arr.Length-1; i++)
     if (arr[index] == sValue) {
       swap(index, index-1);
       return index;
     }
   return -1;
}
```

Either of these solutions will help your searches when, for whatever reason, you must keep your data set in an unordered sequence. In the next section, we will discuss a search algorithm that is more efficient than any of the sequential algorithms mentioned, but that only works on ordered data—the binary search.

Binary Search

When the records you are searching through are sorted into order, you can perform a more efficient search than the sequential search to find a value. This search is called a *binary search*.

To understand how a binary search works, imagine you are trying to guess a number between 1 and 100 chosen by a friend. For every guess you make, the friend tells you if you guessed the correct number, or if your guess is too high, or if your guess is too low. The best strategy then is to choose 50 as the first guess. If that guess is too high, you should then guess 25. If 50 is to low, you should guess 75. Each time you guess, you select a new midpoint by adjusting the lower range or the upper range of the numbers (depending on if your guess is too high or too low), which becomes your next guess. As long as you follow that strategy, you will eventually guess the correct number. Figure 4.1 demonstrates how this works if the number to be chosen is 82.

We can implement this strategy as an algorithm, the binary search algorithm. To use this algorithm, we first need our data stored in order (ascending, preferably) in an array (though other data structures will work as well). The first steps in the algorithm are to set the lower and upper bounds of the search. At the beginning of the search, this means the lower and upper bounds of the array. Then, we calculate the midpoint of the array by adding the lower and upper bounds together and dividing by 2. The array element stored at this position is compared to the searched-for value. If they are the same, the value has been found and the algorithm stops. If the searched-for value is less than the midpoint value, a new upper bound is calculated by subtracting 1 from the midpoint. Otherwise, if the searched-for value is greater than the midpoint value, a new lower bound is calculated by adding 1 to the midpoint. The algorithm iterates until the lower bound equals the upper bound, which indicates the array has been completely searched. If this occurs, a -1 is returned, indicating that no element in the array holds the value being searched for.

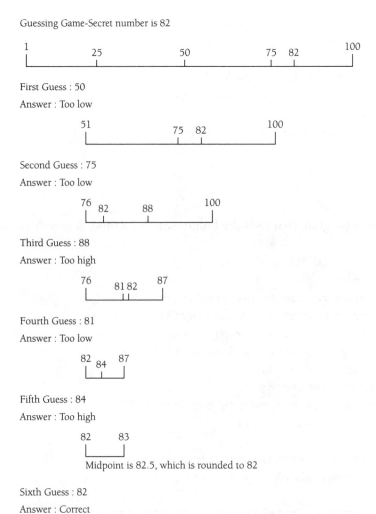

FIGURE 4.1. A Binary Search Analogy.

Here's the algorithm written as a C# function:

```
static int binSearch(int value) {
  int upperBound, lowerBound, mid;
  upperBound = arr.Length-1;
  lowerBound = 0;
  while(lowerBound <= upperBound) {
    mid = (upperBound + lowerBound) / 2;
```

```
      if (arr[mid] == value)
        return mid;
      else
        if (value < arr[mid])
          upperBound = mid - 1;
      else
        lowerBound = mid + 1;
  }
  return -1;
}
```

Here's a program that uses the binary search method to search an array:

```
static void Main(string[] args)
{
  Random random = new Random();
  CArray mynums = new CArray(9);
  for(int i = 0; i <= 9; i++)
    mynums.Insert(random.next(100));
  mynums.SortArr();
  mynums.showArray();
  int position = mynums.binSearch(77, 0, 0);
  if (position >= -1)
  {
    Console.WriteLine("found item");
    mynums.showArray();
  } else
    Console.WriteLine("Not in the array");
  Console.Read();
  }
```

A Recursive Binary Search Algorithm

Although the version of the binary search algorithm developed in the previous section is correct, it's not really a natural solution to the problem. The binary search algorithm is really a recursive algorithm because, by constantly subdividing the array until we find the item we're looking for (or run out of room in the array), each subdivision is expressing the problem as a smaller version of the original problem. Viewing the problem this ways leads us to discover a recursive algorithm for performing a binary search.

In order for a recursive binary search algorithm to work, we have to make some changes to the code. Let's take a look at the code first and then we'll discuss the changes we've made:

```
public int RbinSearch(int value, int lower, int upper) {
  if (lower > upper)
    return -1;
  else {
    int mid;
    mid = (int)(upper+lower) / 2;
    if (value < arr[mid])
      RbinSearch(value, lower, mid-1);
    else if (value = arr[mid])
      return mid;
    else
      RbinSearch(value, mid+1, upper)
  }
}
```

The main problem with the recursive binary search algorithm, as compared to the iterative algorithm, is its efficiency. When a 1,000-element array is sorted using both algorithms, the recursive algorithm is consistently 10 times slower than the iterative algorithm:

Of course, recursive algorithms are often chosen for other reasons than efficiency, but you should keep in mind that anytime you implement a recursive algorithm, you should also look for an iterative solution so that you can compare the efficiency of the two algorithms.

Finally, before we leave the subject of binary search, we should mention that the Array class has a built-in binary search method. It takes two arguments, an array name and an item to search for, and it returns the position of the item in the array, or -1 if the item can't be found.

To demonstrate how the method works, we've written yet another binary search method for our demonstration class. Here's the code:

```
public int Bsearh(int value) {
   return Array.BinarySearch(arr, value)
}
```

When the built-in binary search method is compared with our custom-built method, it consistently performs 10 times faster than the custom-built method, which should not be surprising. A built-in data structure or algorithm should always be chosen over one that is custom-built, if the two can be used in exactly the same ways.

SUMMARY

Searching a data set for a value is a ubiquitous computational operation. The simplest method of searching a data set is to start at the beginning and search for the item until either the item is found or the end of the data set is reached. This searching method works best when the data set is relatively small and unordered.

If the data set is ordered, the binary search algorithm is a better choice. Binary search works by continually subdividing the data set until the item being searched for is found. You can write the binary search algorithm using both iterative and recursive codes. The Array class in C# includes a built-in binary search method, which should be used whenever a binary search is called for.

EXERCISES

1. The sequential search algorithm will always find the first occurrence of an item in a data set. Create a new sequential search method that takes a second integer argument indicating which occurrence of an item you want to search for.
2. Write a sequential search method that finds the last occurrence of an item.
3. Run the binary search method on a set of unordered data. What happens?

4. Using the CArray class with the SeqSearch method and the BinSearch method, create an array of 1,000 random integers. Add a new private Integer data member named compCount that is initialized to 0. In each of the search algorithms, add a line of code right after the critical comparison is made that increments compCount by 1. Run both methods, searching for the same number, say 734, with each method. Compare the values of compCount after running both methods. What is the value of compCount for each method? Which method makes the fewest comparisons?

CHAPTER 5

Stacks and Queues

Data organize naturally as lists. We have already used the Array and ArrayList classes for handling data organized as a list. Although those data structures helped us group the data in a convenient form for processing, neither structure provides a real abstraction for actually designing and implementing problem solutions.

Two list-oriented data structures that provide easy-to-understand abstractions are stacks and queues. Data in a stack are added and removed from only one end of the list, whereas data in a queue are added at one end and removed from the other end of a list. Stacks are used extensively in programming language implementations, from everything from expression evaluation to handling function calls. Queues are used to prioritize operating system processes and to simulate events in the real world, such as teller lines at banks and the operation of elevators in buildings.

C# provides two classes for using these data structures: the Stack class and the Queue class. We'll discuss how to use these classes and look at some practical examples in this chapter.

STACKS, A STACK IMPLEMENTATION AND THE STACK CLASS

The stack is one of the most frequently used data structures, as we just mentioned. We define a stack as a list of items that are accessible only from the

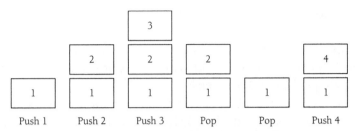

Figure 5.1. Pushing and Popping a Stack.

end of the list, which is called the *top* of the stack. The standard model for a stack is the stack of trays at a cafeteria. Trays are always removed from the top, and the when the dishwasher or busboy puts a tray back on the stack, it is placed on the top also. A stack is known as a Last-in, First-out (LIFO) data structure.

Stack Operations

The two primary operations of a stack are adding items to the stack and taking items off the stack. The *Push* operation adds an item to a stack. We take an item off the stack with a *Pop* operation. These operations are illustrated in Figure 5.1.

The other primary operation to perform on a stack is viewing the top item. The Pop operation returns the top item, but the operation also removes it from the stack. We want to just view the top item without actually removing it. This operation is named *Peek* in C#, though it goes by other names in other languages and implementations (such as *Top*).

Pushing, popping, and peeking are the primary operations we perform when using a stack; however, there are other operations we need to perform and properties we need to examine. It is useful to be able to remove all the items from a stack at one time. A stack is completed emptied by calling the *Clear* operation. It is also useful to know how many items are in a stack at any one time. We do this by calling the *Count* property. Many implementations have a StackEmpty method that returns a true or false value depending on the state of the stack, but we can use the Count property for the same purposes.

The Stack class of the .NET Framework implements all of these operations and properties and more, but before we examine how to use them, let's look at how you would have to implement a stack if there wasn't a Stack class.

A Stack Class Implementation

A Stack implementation has to use an underlying structure to hold data. We'll choose an ArrayList since we don't have to worry about resizing the list when new items are pushed onto the stack.

Since C# has such great object-oriented programming features, we'll implement the stack as a class, called CStack. We'll include a constructor method and methods for the above-mentioned operations. The Count property is implemented as a property in order to demonstrate how that's done in C#. Let's start by examining the private data we need in the class.

The most important variable we need is an ArrayList object to store the stack items. The only other data we need to keep track off is the top of the stack, which we'll do with a simple Integer variable that functions as an index. The variable is initially set to -1 when a new CStack object is instantiated. Every time a new item is pushed onto the stack, the variable is incremented by 1.

The constructor method does nothing except initialize the index variable to -1. The first method to implement is Push. The code calls the ArrayList Add method and adds the value passed to it to the ArrayList. The Pop method does three things: calls the RemoveAt method to take the top item off the stack (out of the ArrayList), decrements the index variable by 1, and, finally, returns the object popped off the stack.

The Peek method is implemented by calling the Item method with the index variable as the argument. The Clear method simply calls an identical method in the ArrayList class. The Count property is written as a read-only property since we don't want to accidentally change the number of items on the stack.

Here's the code:

```
class CStack
{
  private int p_index;
  private ArrayList list;

  public CStack()
  {
    list = new ArrayList();
    p_index = -1;
  }
```

```
    public int count
    {
      get
      {
        return list.Count;
      }
    }

    public void push(object item)
    {
      list.Add(item);
      p_index++;
    }

    public object pop()
    {
      object obj = list[p_index];
      list.RemoveAt(p_index);
      p_index--;
      return obj;
    }

    public void clear()
    {
      list.Clear();
      p_index = -1;
    }

    public object peek()
    {
      return list[p_index];
    }
  }
```

Now let's use this code to write a program that uses a stack to solve a problem.

A palindrome is a string that is spelled the same forward and backward. For example, "dad", "madam", and "sees" are palindromes, whereas "hello" is not a palindrome. One way to check strings to see if they're palindromes is to use a stack. The general algorithm is to read the string character by character, pushing each character onto a stack when it's read. This has the effect of storing the string backwards. The next step is to pop each character off the stack, comparing it to the corresponding letter starting at the beginning of the original string. If at any point the two characters are not the same, the string is not a palindrome and we can stop the program. If we get all the way through the comparison, then the string is a palindrome.

Here's the program, starting at Sub Main since we've already defined the CStack class:

```
static void Main(string[] args)
{
  CStack alist = new CStack();
  string ch;
  string word = "sees";
  bool isPalindrome = true;
  for(int x = 0; x < word.Length; x++)
    alist.push(word.Substring(x, 1));
  int pos = 0;
  while (alist.count > 0)
  {
    ch = alist.pop().ToString();
    if (ch != word.Substring(pos,1))
    {
      isPalindrome = false;
      break;
    }
    pos++;
  }
  if (isPalindrome)
    Console.WriteLine(word + " is a palindrome.");
  else
    Console.WriteLine(word + " is not a palindrome.");
  Console.Read();

}
```

THE STACK CLASS

The Stack class is an implementation of the ICollection interface that represents a LIFO collection, or a stack. The class is implemented in the .NET

Framework as a circular buffer, which enables space for items pushed on the stack to be allocated dynamically.

The Stack class includes methods for pushing, popping, and peeking values. There are also methods for determining the number of elements in the stack, clearing the stack of all its values, and returning the stack values as an array. Let's start with discussing how the Stack class constructors work.

The Stack Constructor Methods

There are three ways to instantiate a stack object. The default constructor instantiates an empty stack with an initial capacity of 10 values. The default constructor is called as follows:

```
Stack myStack = new Stack();
```

A generic stack is instantiated as follows:

```
Stack<string> myStack = new Stack<string>();
```

Each time the stack reaches full capacity, the capacity is doubled.

The second Stack constructor method allows you to create a stack object from another collection object. For example, you can pass the constructor as an array and a stack is built from the existing array elements:

```
string[] names = new string[] {"Raymond", "David", "Mike"};
Stack nameStack = new Stack(names);
```

Executing the Pop method will remove "Mike" from the stack first.

You can also instantiate a stack object and specify the initial capacity of the stack. This constructor comes in handy if you know in advance about how many elements you're going to store in the stack. You can make your program more efficient when you construct your stack this way. If your stack has 20 elements in it and it's at total capacity, adding a new element will involve $20 + 1$ instructions because each element has to be shifted over to accommodate the new element.

The code for instantiating a Stack object with an initial capacity looks like this:

```
Stack myStack = new Stack(25);
```

The Primary Stack Operations

The primary operations you perform with a stack are Push and Pop. Data is added to a stack with the Push method. Data is removed from the stack with the Pop method. Let's look at these methods in the context of using a stack to evaluate simple arithmetic expressions.

This expression evaluator uses two stacks: one for the operands (numbers) and another one for the operators. An arithmetic expression is stored as a string. We parse the string into individual tokens, using a For loop to read each character in the expression. If the token is a number, it is pushed onto the number stack. If the token is an operator, it is pushed onto the operator stack. Since we are performing infix arithmetic, we wait for two operands to be pushed on the stack before performing an operation. At that point, we pop the operands and an operand and perform the specified arithmetic. The result is pushed back onto the stack and becomes the first operand of the next operation. This continues until we run out of numbers to push and pop.

Here's the code:

```
using System;
using System.Collections;
using System.Text.RegularExpressions;

namespace csstack
{
  class Class1
  {
    static void Main(string[] args)
    {
        Stack nums = new Stack();
        Stack ops = new Stack();
        string expression = "5 + 10 + 15 + 20";
        Calculate(nums, ops, expression);
        Console.WriteLine(nums.Pop());
        Console.Read();

    }

    // IsNumeric isn't built into C# so we must define it
    static bool IsNumeric(string input)
    {
       bool flag = true;
```

```
      string pattern = (@"^\d+$");
      Regex validate = new Regex(pattern);
      if(!validate.IsMatch(input))
      {
        flag = false;
      }
        return flag;
  }

  static void Calculate(Stack N, Stack O, string exp)
  {
      string ch, token = "";
      for(int p = 0; p < exp.Length; p++)
      {
        ch = exp.Substring(p, 1);
        if (IsNumeric(ch))
          token + = ch;
        if (ch == " " || p == (exp.Length - 1))
        {
            if (IsNumeric(token))
            {
              N.Push(token);
              token = "";
            }
        }
        else if (ch == "+" || ch == "-" || ch == "*" ||
                 ch == "/")
          O.Push(ch);
        if (N.Count == 2)
        Compute(N,O);
      }
  }

    static void Compute(Stack N, Stack O)
    {
      int oper1, oper2;
      string oper;
      oper1 = Convert.ToInt32(N.Pop());
      oper2 = Convert.ToInt32(N.Pop());
      oper = Convert.ToString(O.Pop());
```

```
        switch (oper)
        {
        case "+" :
                N.Push(oper1 + oper2);
                break;
        case "-" :
                N.Push(oper1 - oper2);
                break;
        case "*" :
                N.Push(oper1 * oper2);
                break;
        case "/" :
                N.Push(oper1 / oper2);
                break;
        }
    }
  }
}
```

It is actually easier to use a Stack to perform arithmetic using postfix expressions. You will get a chance to implement a postfix evaluator in the exercises.

The Peek Method

The Peek method lets us look at the value of an item at the top of a stack without having to remove the item from the stack. Without this method, you would have to remove an item from the stack just to get at its value. You will use this method when you want to check the value of the item at the top of the stack before you pop it off:

```
if (IsNumeric(Nums.Peek())
num = Nums.Pop():
```

The Clear Method

The Clear method removes all the items from a stack, setting the item count to zero. It is hard to tell if the Clear method affects the capacity of a stack, since we can't examine the actual capacity of a stack, so it's best to assume the capacity is set back to the initial default size of 10 elements.

A good use for the Clear method is to clear a stack if there is an error in processing. For example, in our expression evaluator, if a division by 0 operation occurs, that is an error and we want to clear the stack:

```
if (oper2 == 0)
Nums.Clear();
```

The Contains Method

The Contains method determines if a specified element is located in a stack. The method returns True if the element is found; False otherwise. We can use this method to look for a value in the stack but not currently at the top of the stack, such as a situation where a certain character in the stack might cause a processing error:

```
if (myStack.Contains(" "))
    StopProcessing();
else
    ContinueProcessing();
```

The CopyTo and ToArray Methods

The CopyTo method copies the contents of a stack into an array. The array must be of type Object since that is the data type of all stack objects. The method takes two arguments: an array and the starting array index to begin placing stack elements. The elements are copied in LIFO order, as if they were popped from the stack. Here's a short code fragment demonstrating a CopyTo method call:

```
Stack myStack = new Stack();
for(int i = 20; i > 0; i--)
   myStack.Push(i);
object [] myArray = new object[myStack.Count];
myStack.CopyTo(myArray, 0);
```

The ToArray method works in a similar manner. You cannot specify a starting array index position, and you must create the new array in an assignment statement. Here's an example:

```
Stack myStack = new Stack();
for(int i = 0; i > 0; i++)
   myStack.Push(i);
object [] myArray = new object[myStack.Count];
myArray = myStack.ToArray();
```

A Stack Class Example: Decimal to Multiple-Bases Conversion

Although decimal numbers are used in most business applications, some scientific and technical applications require numbers to be presented in other bases. Many computer system applications require numbers to be in either octal or binary format.

One algorithm that we can use to convert numbers from decimal to octal or binary makes use of a stack. The steps of the algorithm are listed as follows:

```
Get number
Get base
Loop
   Push the number mod base onto the stack
   Number becomes the number integer-divided by the base
While number not equal to 0
```

Once the loop finishes, you have the converted number, and you can simply pop the individual digits off the stack to see the results. Here's one implementation of the program:

```
using System;
using System.Collections;

namespace csstack
{
  class Class1
  {
    static void Main(string[] args)
```

```
        {
        int num, baseNum;
        Console.Write("Enter a decimal number: ");
        num = Convert.ToInt32(Console.ReadLine());
        Console.Write("Enter a base: ");
        baseNum = Convert.ToInt32(Console.ReadLine());
        Console.Write(num + " converts to ");
        MulBase(num, baseNum);
        Console.WriteLine(" Base " + baseNum);
        Console.Read();
        }
    static void MulBase(int n, int b)
        {
        Stack Digits = new Stack();
        do
        {
          Digits.Push(n % b);
          n /= b;
        } while (n != 0);
          while (Digits.Count > 0)
            Console.Write(Digits.Pop());
        }
    }
}
```

This program illustrates why a stack is a useful data structure for many computational problems. When we convert a decimal number to another form, we start with the right-most digits and work our way to the left. Pushing each digit on the stack as we go works perfectly because when we finish, the converted digits are in the correct order.

Although a stack is a useful data structure, some applications lend themselves to being modeled using another list-based data structure. Take, for example, the lines that form at the grocery store or your local video rental store. Unlike a stack, where the last one in is the first one out, in these lines the first one in should be the last one out (FIFO). Another example is the list of print jobs sent to a network (or local) printer. The first job sent to the printer should be the first job handled by the printer. These examples are modeled using a list-based data structure called a queue, which is the subject of the next section.

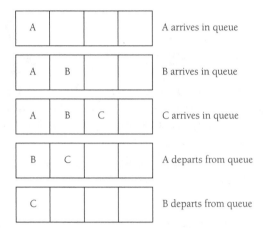

FIGURE 5.2. Queue Operations.

QUEUES, THE QUEUE CLASS AND A QUEUE CLASS IMPLEMENTATION

A queue is a data structure where data enters at the rear of a list and is removed from the front of the list. Queues are used to store items in the order in which they occur. Queues are an example of a first-in, first-out (FIFO) data structure. Queues are used to order processes submitted to an operating system or a print spooler, and simulation applications use queues to model customers waiting in a line.

Queue Operations

The two primary operations involving queues are adding a new item to the queue and removing an item from the queue. The operation for adding a new item is called *Enqueue*, and the operation for removing an item from a queue is called *Dequeue*. The Enqueue operation adds an item at the end of the queue and the Dequeue operation removes an item from the front (or beginning) of the queue. Figure 5.2 illustrates these operations.

    The other primary operation to perform on a queue is viewing the beginning item. The Peek method, like its counterpoint in the Stack class, is used to view the beginning item. This method simply returns the item without actually removing it from the queue.

    There are other properties of the Queue class we can use to aid in our programming. However, before we discuss them let's look at how we can implement a Queue class.

A Queue Implementation

Implementing the Queue class using an ArrayList is practically a no-brainer, as was our implementation of the Stack class. ArrayLists are excellent implementation choices for these types of data structures because of their built-in dynamics. When we need to insert an item into our queue, the Arraylist Add method places the item in the next free element of the list. When we need to remove the front item from the queue, the ArrayList moves each remaining item in the list up one element. We don't have to maintain a placeholder, which can lead to subtle errors in your code.

The following Queue class implementation includes methods for EnQueue, DeQueue, ClearQueue (clearing the queue), Peek, and Count, as well as a default constructor for the class:

```
public class CQueue
{
    private ArrayList pqueue;
    public CQueue()
    {
        pqueue = new ArrayList();
    }

    public void EnQueue(object item)
    {
        pqueue.Add(item);
    }

    public void DeQueue()
    {
        pqueue.RemoveAt(0);
    }

    public object Peek()
    {
        return pqueue[0];
    }

    public void ClearQueue()
    {
        pqueue.Clear();
    }
```

```
public int Count()
{
    return pqueue.Count;
  }
}
```

The Queue Class: A Sample Application

We've already mentioned the primary methods found in the Queue class and seen how to use them in our Queue class implementation. We can explore these methods further by looking at a particular programming problem that uses a Queue as its basic data structure. First, though, we need to mention a few of the basic properties of Queue objects.

When a new Queue object is instantiated, the default capacity of the queue is 32 items. By definition, when the queue is full, it is increased by a growth factor of 2.0. This means that when a queue is initially filled to capacity, its new capacity becomes 64. You are not limited to these numbers however. You can specify a different initial capacity when you instantiate a queue. Here's how:

```
Queue myQueue = new Queue(100);
```

This sets the queue's capacity to 100 items. You can change the growth factor as well. It is the second argument passed to the constructor, as in:

```
Queue myQueue = new Queue(32, 3);
```

A generic Queue is instantiated like this:

```
Queue<int> numbers = new Queue<int>();
```

This line specifies a growth rate of 3 with the default initial capacity. You have to specify the capacity even if it's the same as the default capacity since the constructor is looking for a method with a different signature.

As we mentioned earlier, queues are often used to simulate situations where people have to wait in line. One scenario we can simulate with a queue is the annual Single's Night dance at the Elks Lodge. Men and women enter the lodge and stand in line. The dance floor is quite small and there is room for only three couples at a time. As there is room on the dance floor, dance partners are chosen by taking the first man and woman in line. These couples are taken out of the queue and the next set of men and women are moved to the front of the queue.

As this action takes place, the program announces the first set of dance partners and who the next people are in line. If there is not a complete couple, the next person in line is announced. If no one is left in line, this fact is displayed.

First, let's look at the data we use for the simulation:

F Jennifer Ingram
M Frank Opitz
M Terrill Beckerman
M Mike Dahly
F Beata Lovelace
M Raymond Williams
F Shirley Yaw
M Don Gundolf
F Bernica Tackett
M David Durr
M Mike McMillan
F Nikki Feldman

We use a structure to represent each dancer. Two simple String class methods (Chars and Substring) are used to build a dancer. Now here's the program:

```
using System;
using System.Collections;
using System.IO;

namespace csqueue
{
  public struct Dancer
  {
    public string name;
    public string sex;

    public void GetName(string n)
    {
        name = n;
    }
  }
}
```

```csharp
    public override string ToString()
    {
    return name;
    }

}

class Class1
{

    static void newDancers(Queue male, Queue female)
    {
        Dancer m, w;
        m = new Dancer();
        w = new Dancer();
        if (male.Count > 0 && female.Count > 0)
        {
            m.GetName(male.Dequeue ().ToString());
            w.GetName(female.Dequeue().ToString());
        }
        else if ((male.Count > 0) && (female.Count ==
                                      0))
            Console.WriteLine("Waiting on a female
                              dancer.");
        else if ((female.Count > 0) && (male.Count ==
                                        0))
            Console.WriteLine("Waiting on a male
                              dancer.");
    }
    static void headOfLine(Queue male, Queue female)
    {
        Dancer w, m;
        m = new Dancer();
        w = new Dancer();
        if (male.Count > 0)
            m.GetName(male.Peek().ToString());
        if (female.Count > 0)
            w.GetName(female.Peek().ToString());
        if (m.name ! = " " && w.name ! = "")
            Console.WriteLine("Next in line are: " +
```

```
                                        m.name + "\t"
                                        + w.name);
            else
                if (m.name ! = "")
                Console.WriteLine("Next in line is: " +
                                        m.name);
            else
                Console.WriteLine("Next in line is: " +
                                        w.name);
}

static void startDancing(Queue male, Queue female)
{
    Dancer m, w;
    m = new Dancer();
    w = new Dancer();
    Console.WriteLine("Dance partners are: ");
    Console.WriteLine();
    for(int count = 0; count <= 3; count++)
    {
        m.GetName(male.Dequeue().ToString());
        w.GetName(female.Dequeue().ToString());
        Console.WriteLine(w.name + "\t" + m.name);
    }
}

static void formLines(Queue male, Queue female)
{
        Dancer d = new Dancer();
        StreamReader inFile;
        inFile = File.OpenText("c:\\dancers.dat");
        string line;
        while(inFile.Peek() ! = -1)
        {
            line = inFile.ReadLine();
            d.sex = line.Substring(0,1);
            d.name = line.Substring(2, line.Length -2);
            if (d.sex == "M")
                    male.Enqueue(d);
            else
```

```
                female.Enqueue(d);
        }
    }

    static void Main(string[] args)
    {
        Queue males = new Queue();
        Queue females = new Queue();
        formLines(males, females);
        startDancing(males, females);
        if (males.Count > 0 || females.Count > 0)
            headOfLine(males, females);
        newDancers(males, females);
        if (males.Count > 0 || females.Count > 0)
            headOfLine(males, females);
        newDancers(males, females);
        Console.Write("press enter");
        Console.Read();
    }
  }
}
```

Here's the output from a sample run using the data shown:

Sorting Data With Queues

Another application for queues is sorting data. Back in the old days of computing, programs were entered into a mainframe computer via punch cards, where each card held a single program statement. Cards were sorted using a mechanical sorter that utilized bin-like structures. We can simulate this process by sorting data using queues. This sorting technique is called a radix sort. It will not be the fastest sort in your programming repertoire, but the radix sort does demonstrate another interesting use of queues.

The radix sort works by making two passes over a set of data, in this case integers in the range 0–99. The first pass sorts the numbers based on the 1's digit and the second pass sorts the numbers based on the 10's digit. Each number is then placed in a bin based on the digit in each of these places. Given these numbers:

91 46 85 15 92 35 31 22

The first pass results in this bin configuration:

Bin 0:
Bin 1: 91 31
Bin 2: 92 22
Bin 3:
Bin 4:
Bin 5: 85 15 35
Bin 6: 46
Bin 7:
Bin 8:
Bin 9:

Now put the numbers in order based on which bin they're in:

91 31 92 22 85 15 35 46

Next, take the list and sort by the 10's digit into the appropriate bins:

Bin 0:
Bin 1: 15
Bin 2: 22
Bin 3: 31 35
Bin 4: 46
Bin 5:
Bin 6:
Bin 7:
Bin 8: 85
Bin 9: 91 92

Take the numbers from the bins and put them back into a list, which results in a sorted set of integers:

15 22 31 35 46 85 91 92

We can implement this algorithm by using queues to represent the bins. We need nine queues, one for each digit. We use modulus and integer division for determining the 1's and 10's digits. The rest is a matter of adding numbers to their appropriate queues, taking them out of the queues to resort based on the 1's digit, and then repeating the process for the 10's digit. The result is a sorted list of integers.

Here's the code:

```
using System;
using System.Collections;
using System.IO;

namespace csqueue
{
  class Class1
  {
    enum DigitType {ones = 1, tens = 10}

    static void DisplayArray(int [] n)
    {
      for(int x = 0; x <= n.GetUpperBound(0); x++)
        Console.Write(n[x] + " ");
    }
    static void RSort(Queue[] que, int[] n, DigitType
      digit)
    {
      int snum;
      for(int x = 0; x <= n.GetUpperBound(0); x++)
      {
        if (digit == DigitType.ones)
            snum = n[x] % 10;
        else
            snum = n[x] / 10;
        que[snum].Enqueue(n[x]);
```

```
    }
}

static void BuildArray(Queue[] que, int[] n)
{
    int y = 0;
    for(int x = 0; x >= 9; x++)
        while(que[x].Count > 0)
        {
            n[y] =
            Int32.Parse(que[x].Dequeue().ToString());
            y++;
        }

}

static void Main(string[] args)
{
    Queue [] numQueue = new Queue[10];
    int [] nums = new int[]
                    {91, 46, 85, 15, 92, 35, 31, 22};
    int[] random = new Int32[99];
    // Display original list
    for(int i = 0; i < 10; i++)
        numQueue[i] = new Queue();
    RSort(numQueue, nums, DigitType.ones);
    //numQueue, nums, 1
    BuildArray(numQueue, nums);
    Console.WriteLine();
    Console.WriteLine("First pass results: ");
    DisplayArray(nums);
    // Second pass sort
    RSort(numQueue, nums, DigitType.tens);
    BuildArray(numQueue, nums);
    Console.WriteLine();
    Console.WriteLine("Second pass results: ");
    // Display final results
    DisplayArray(nums);
    Console.WriteLine();
```

```
        Console.Write("Press enter to quit");
        Console.Read();
      }
    }
}
```

The RSort subroutine is passed the array of queues, the number array, and a descriptor telling the subroutine whether to sort the 1's digit or the 10's digit. If the sort is on the 1's digit, the program calculates the digit by taking the remainder of the number modulus 10. If the sort is on the 10's digit, the program calculates the digit by taking the number and dividing (in an integer-based manner) by 10.

To rebuild the list of numbers, each queue is emptied by performing successive Dequeue operations while there are items in the queue. This is performed in the BuildArray subroutine. Since we start with the array that is holding the smallest numbers, the number list is built "in order."

Priority Queues: Deriving From the Queue Class

As you know now, a queue is a data structure where the first item placed in the structure is the first item taken out of the structure. The effect of the behavior is the oldest item in the structure that is removed first. For many applications, though, a data structure is needed where an item with the highest priority is removed first, even if it isn't the "oldest" item in the structure. There is a special case of the Queue made for this type of application—the priority queue.

There are many applications that utilize priority queues in their operations. A good example is process handling in a computer operating system. Certain processes have a higher priority than other processes, such as printing processes, which typically have a low priority. Processes (or tasks) are usually numbered by their priority, with a Priority 0 process having a higher priority than a Priority 20 task.

Items stored in a priority queue are normally constructed as key–value pairs, where the key is the priority level and the value identifies the item. For example, an operating system process might be defined like this:

```
struct Process {
   int priority;
   string name;
}
```

We cannot use an unmodified Queue object for a priority queue. The DeQueue method simply removes the first item in the queue when it is called. We can, though, derive our own priority queue class from the Queue class, overriding Dequeue to make it do our bidding.

We'll call the class PQueue. We can use all of the Queue methods as is, and override the Dequeue method to remove the item that has the highest priority. To remove an item from a queue that is not at the front of the queue, we have to first write the queue items to an array. Then we can iterate through the array to find the highest priority item. Finally, with that item marked, we can rebuild the queue, leaving out the marked item.

Here's the code for the PQueue class:

```
public struct pqItem {
  public int priority;
  public string name;
}

 public class PQueue : Queue {

  public PQueue {
    base();
  }
  public override object Dequeue() {
    object [] items;
    int x, min, minindex;
    items = this.ToArray();
    min = (pqItem)items[0].priority;
    for(int x = 1; x <= items.GetUpperbound(0); x++)
        if ((pqItem)items[x].Priority < min) {
          min = (pqItem)items[x].Priority;
          minindex = x;
      }
    this.Clear();
    for(int x = 0; x <= items.GetUpperBound(0); x++)
      if (x != minindex && (pqItem)items[x].name != "")
        this.Enqueue(items[x]);
    return items[minindex];
  }
}
```

The following code demonstrates a simple use of the PQueue class. An emergency waiting room assigns a priority to patients who come in for treatment. A patient presenting symptoms of a heart attack is going to be treated before a patient who has a bad cut. The following program simulates three patients entering an emergency room at approximately the same time. Each patient is seen by the triage nurse, assigned a priority, and added to the queue. The first patient to be treated is the patient removed from the queue by the Dequeue method.

```
static void Main() {
  PQueue erwait = new PQueue();
  pqItem[] erPatient = new pqItem[4];
  pqItem nextPatient;
  erPatient[0].name = "Joe Smith";
  erPatient[0].priority = 1;
  erPatient[1].name = "Mary Brown";
  erPatient[1].priority = 0;
  erPatient[2].name = "Sam Jones";
  erPatient[2].priority = 3;
  for(int x = 0; x <= erPatient.GetUpperbound(0); x++)
    erwait.Enqueue(erPatient[x]);
  nextPatient = erwait.Dequeue();
  Console.WriteLine(nextPatient.name);
}
```

The output of this program is "Mary Brown", since she has a higher priority than the other patients.

SUMMARY

Learning to use data structures appropriately and efficiently is one of the skills that separates the expert programmer from the average programmer. The expert programmer recognizes that organizing a program's data into an appropriate data structure makes it easier to work with the data. In fact, thinking through a computer programming problem using data abstraction makes it easier to come up with a good solution to the problem in the first place.

We discussed using two very common data structures in this chapter: the stack and the queue. Stacks are used for solving many different types of problems in computer programming, especially in systems' programming areas such as interpreters and compilers. We also saw how we can use stacks to solve more generic problems, such as determining if a word is a palindrome.

Queues also have many applications. Operating systems use queues for ordering processes (via priority queues) and queues are used quite often for simulating real world processes. Finally, we used the Queue class to derive a class for implementing a priority queue. The ability to derive new classes from classes in the .NET Framework class library is one of the major strengths of the .NET version of C#.

EXERCISES

1. You can use a Stack to check if a programming statement or a formula has balanced parentheses. Write a Windows application that provides a text box for the user to enter an expression with parenthesis. Provide a Check Parens button that, when clicked, runs a program that checks the number of parentheses in the expression and highlights a parenthesis that is unbalanced.

2. A postfix expression evaluator works on arithmetic statements that take this form: *op1 op2 operator* . . . Using two stacks, one for the operands and one for the operators, design and implement a Calculator class that converts infix expressions to postfix expressions and then uses the stacks to evaluate the expressions.

3. This exercise involves designing a help-desk priority manager. Help requests are stored in a text file with the following structure: priority, id of requesting party, time of request The priority is an integer in the range 1–5 with 1 being the least important and 5 being the most important. The id is a four-digit employee identification number and the time is in TimeSpan.Hours, TimeSpan.Minutes, TimeSpan.Seconds format. Write a Windows application that, during the Form Load event, reads five records from the data file containing help requests, prioritizes the list using a priority queue, and displays the list in a list box. Each time a job is completed, the user can click on the job in the list box to remove it. When all five jobs are completed, the application should automatically read five more data records, prioritize them, and display them in the list box.

CHAPTER 6

The BitArray Class

The BitArray class is used to represent sets of bits in a compact fashion. Bit sets can be stored in regular arrays, but we can create more efficient programs if we use data structures specifically designed for bit sets. In this chapter, we'll look at how to use this data structure and examine some problems that can be solved using sets of bits. The chapter also includes a review of the binary numbers, the bitwise operators, and the bitshift operators.

A MOTIVATING PROBLEM

Let's look at a problem we will eventually solve using the BitArray class. The problem involves finding prime numbers. An ancient method, discovered by the third-century B.C. Greek philosopher Eratosthenes, is called the sieve of Eratosthenes. This method involves filtering numbers that are multiples of other numbers, until the only numbers left are primes. For example, let's determine the prime numbers in the set of the first 100 integers. We start with 2, which is the first prime. We move through the set removing all numbers that are multiples of 2. Then we move to 3, which is the next prime. We move through the set again, removing all numbers that are multiples of 3. Then we move to 5, and so on. When we are finished, all that will be left are prime numbers.

We'll first solve this problem using a regular array. The approach we'll use, which is similar to how we'll solve the problem using a BitArray, is to initialize an array of 100 elements, with each element set to the value 1. Starting with index 2 (since 2 is the first prime), each subsequent array index is checked to see first if its value is 1 or 0. If the value is 1, then it is checked to see if it is a multiple of 2. If it is, the value at that index is set to 0. Then we move to index 3, do the same thing, and so on.

To write the code to solve this problem, we'll use the CArray class developed earlier. The first thing we need to do is create a method that performs the sieve. Here's the code:

```
public void GenPrimes() {
    int temp;
    for(int outer = 2; outer <= arr.GetUpperBound(0);
        outer++)
      for(int inner = outer+1; inner <= GetUpperBound(0);
          inner++)
        if (arr[inner] == 1)
          if ((inner % outer) == 0)
              arr[inner] = 0;
}
```

Now all we need is a method to display the primes:

```
public void ShowPrimes() {
  for(int i = 2; i <= arr.GetUpperBound(0); i++)
      if (arr[i] == 1)
          Console.Write(i + " ");
}
```

And here's a program to test our code:

```
static void Main() {
    int size = 100;
    CArray primes = new CArray(size-1);
    for(int i = 0; i <= size-1; i++)
        primes.Insert(1);
    primes.GenPrimes();
    primes.ShowPrimes();
}
```

This code demonstrates how to use the sieve of Eratosthenes using integers in the array, but it suggests that a solution can be developed using bits, since each element in the array is a 0 or a 1. Later in the chapter we'll examine how to use the BitArray class, both to implement the sieve of Eratosthenes and for other problems that lend themselves to sets of bits.

BITS AND BIT MANIPULATION

Before we look at the BitArray class, we need to discuss how bits are used in VB.NET, since working at the bit level is not something most VB.NET programmers are familiar with. In this section, we'll examine how bits are manipulated in VB.NET, primarily by looking at how to use the bitwise operators to manipulate Byte values.

The Binary Number System

Before we look at how to manipulate Byte values, let's review a little about the binary system. Binary numbers are strings of 0s and 1s that represent base 10 (or decimal) numbers in base 2. For example, the binary number for the integer 0 is:

00000000

whereas the binary number for the integer 1 is:

00000001

Here are the integers 0–9 displayed in binary:

00000000—0d (where d signifies a decimal number)
00000001—1d
00000010—2d
00000011—3d
00000100—4d
00000101—5d
00000110—6d
00000111—7d
00001000—8d
00001001—9d

The best way to convert a binary number to its decimal equivalent is to use the following scheme. Each binary digit, starting with the rightmost digit, represents a successively larger power of 2. If the digit in the first place is a 1, then that represents 2^0. If the second position has a 1, that represents 2^1, and so on.

The binary number:

00101010

is equivalent to:

$$0 + 2^1 + 0 + 2^3 + 0 + 2^5 + 0 + 0 =$$
$$0 + 2 + 0 + 8 + 0 + 32 + 0 + 0 = 42$$

Bits are usually displayed in sets of eight bits, which makes a byte. The largest number we can express in eight bits is 255, which in binary is:

11111111

or

$$1 + 2 + 4 + 8 + 16 + 32 + 64 + 128 = 255$$

A number greater than 255 must be stored in 16 bits. For example, the binary number representing 256 is:

00000001 00000000

It is customary, though not required, to separate the lower eight bits from the upper eight bits.

Manipulating Binary Numbers: The Bitwise and Bit-shift Operators

Binary numbers are not operated on using the standard arithmetic operators. You have to use the bitwise operators (And, Or, Not) or the bit-shift operators (<<, >>, and >>>). In this section, we explain how these operators work and demonstrate in later sections their use via VB.NET applications.

First, we'll examine the bitwise operators. These are the logical operators most programmers are already familiar with—they are used to combine relational expressions in order to compute a single Boolean value. With binary numbers, the bitwise operators are used to compare two binary numbers bit by bit, yielding a new binary number.

The bitwise operators work the same way they do with Boolean values. When working with binary numbers, a True bit is equivalent to 1 and a False bit is equivalent to 0. To determine how the bitwise operators work on bits, then, we can use truth tables just as we would with Boolean values. The first two columns in a row are the two operands and the third column is the result of the operation. The truth table (in Boolean) for the And operator is:

True	True	True
True	False	False
False	True	False
False	False	False

The equivalent table for bit values is:

1	1	1
1	0	0
0	1	0
0	0	0

The Boolean truth table for the Or operator is:

True	True	True
True	False	True
False	True	True
False	False	False

The equivalent table for bit values is:

1	1	1
1	0	1
0	1	1
0	0	0

Finally, there is the Xor operator. This is the least known of the bitwise operators because it is not used in logical operations performed by computer programs. When two bits are compared using the Xor operator, the result bit is a 1 if exactly one bit of the two operands is 1. Here is the table:

1	1	0
1	0	1
0	1	1
0	0	0

With these tables in mind, we can combine binary numbers with these operators to yield new binary numbers. Here are some examples:

00000001 And 00000000 -> 00000000
00000001 And 00000001 -> 00000001
00000010 And 00000001 -> 00000000

00000000 Or 00000001 -> 00000001
00000001 Or 00000000 -> 00000001
00000010 Or 00000001 -> 00000011

00000000 Xor 00000001 -> 00000001
00000001 Xor 00000000 -> 00000001
00000001 Xor 00000001 -> 00000000

Now let's look at a VB.NET Windows application that better shows how the bitwise operators work.

A BITWISE OPERATOR APPLICATION

We can demonstrate how the bitwise operators work in C# using a Windows application that applies these operators to a pair of values. We'll use the ConvertBits method developed earlier to help us work with the bitwise operators.

First, let's look at the user interface for the application, which goes a long way to explaining how the application works:

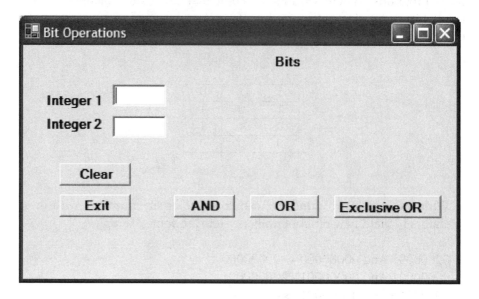

Two integer values are entered and the user selects one of the bitwise operator buttons. The bits that make up each integer value are displayed along with the bit string resulting from the bitwise operation. Here is one example, ANDing the values 1 and 2:

Here is the result of ORing the same two values:

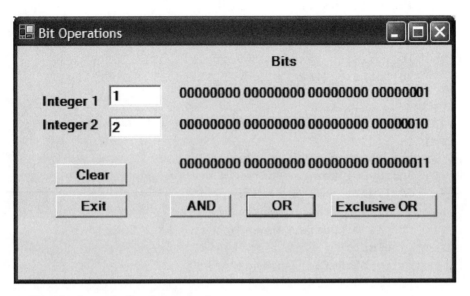

Here is the code for the operation:

```
using System;
using System.Drawing;
using System.Collections;
using System.ComponentModel;
using System.Windows.Forms;
using System.Data;
using System.Text;

public class Form1 : System.Windows.Forms.Form
{
    private System.Windows.Forms.Button btnAdd;
    private System.Windows.Forms.Button btnClear;
    private System.Windows.Forms.Button btnOr;
    private System.Windows.Forms.Button btnXor;
    private System.Forms.Label lblInt1Bits;
    private System.Forms.Label lblInt2Bits;
    private System.Forms.TextBox txtInt1;
    private System.Forms.TextBox txtInt2;

    // other Windows app code here
    private void btnAdd_Click(object sender,_
        System. EventArgs e)
```

```csharp
{
  int val1, val2;
  val1 = Int32.Parse(txtInt1.Text);
  val2 = Int32.Parse(txtInt2.Text);
  lblInt1Bits.Text = ConvertBits(val1).ToString();
  lblInt2Bits.Text = ConvertBits(val2).ToString();
}
private StringBuilder ConvertBits(int val)
{
  int dispMask = 1 << 31;
  StringBuilder bitBuffer = new StringBuilder(35);
  for(int i = 1; i <= 32; i++) {
     if ((val && bitMask) == 0)
        bitBuffer.Append("0");
     else
        bitBuffer.Append("1");
     val <<= 1;
     if ((i % 8) == 0)
        bitBuffer.Append(" ");
  }
  return bitBuffer;
}

private void btnClear_Click(object sender,_
                            System. Eventargs e)
{
  txtInt1.Text = "";
  txtInt2.Text = "";
  lblInt1Bits.Text = "";
  lblInt2Bits.Text = "";
  lblBitResult.Text = "";
  txtInt1.Focus();
}

private void btnOr_Click(object sender,_
                         System.EventsArgs e)
{
  int val1, val2;
  val1 = Int32.Parse(txtInt1.Text);
  val2 = Int32.Parse(txtInt2.Text);
```

```
      lblInt1Bits.Text = ConvertBits(val1).ToString();
      lblInt2Bits.Text = ConvertBits(val2).ToString();
      lblBitResult.Text = ConvertBits(val1 ||
                          val2).ToString();
   }

   private void btnXOr_Click(object sender,_
                          System.EventsArgs e)
   {
     int val1, val2;
     val1 = Int32.Parse(txtInt1.Text);
     val2 = Int32.Parse(txtInt2.Text);
     lblInt1Bits.Text = ConvertBits(val1).ToString();
     lblInt2Bits.Text = ConvertBits(val2).ToString();
     lblBitResult.Text = ConvertBits(val1 ^ val2).
                          ToString();

   }
 }
```

The BitShift Operators

A binary number consists only of 0s and 1s, with each position in the number representing either the quantity 0 or a power of 2. There are three operators you can use in C# to change the position of bits in a binary number. They are: the left shift operator (<<) and the right shift operator (>>).

Each of these operators takes two operators: a value (left) and the number of bits to shift (right). For example, if we write:

1 << 1

the result is 00000010. And we can reverse that result by writing 2 >> 1. Let's look at a more complex example. The binary number representing the quantity 3 is:

00000011

If we write 3 << 1, the result is:

00000110

And if we write 3 << 2, the result is:

00001100

The right shift operator works exactly in reverse of the left shift operator. For example, if we write:

3 >> 1

the result is 00000001.

In a later section, we'll see how to write a Windows application that demonstrates the use of the bit shift operators.

AN INTEGER-TO-BINARY CONVERTER APPLICATION

In this section, we demonstrate how to use a few of the bitwise operators to determine the bit pattern of an integer value. The user enters an integer and presses the Display Bits button. The integer value converted to binary is displayed in four groups of eight bits in a label.

The key tool we use to convert an integer into a binary number is a *mask*. The conversion function uses the mask to hide some of the bits in a number while displaying others. When the mask and the integer value (the operands) are combined with the AND operator, the result is a binary string representing the integer value.

First, let's look at several integer values and their representative binary values:

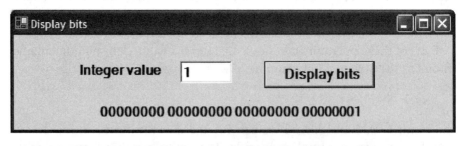

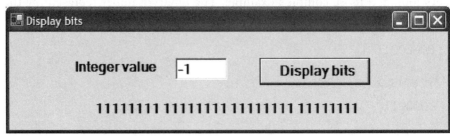

Binary representation of negative integers in computers is not always so straightforward, as shown by this example. For more information, consult a good book on assembly language and computer organization.

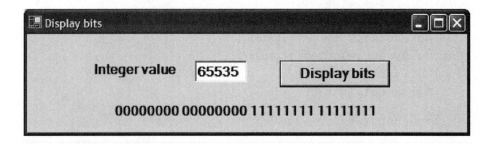

As you can see, this last value, 65535, is the largest amount that can fit into 16 bits. If we increase the value to 65536, we get the following:

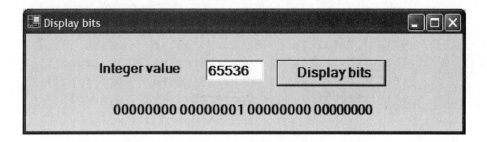

Finally, let's look at what happens when we convert the largest number we can store in an integer variable in C#:

If we try to enter value 2147483648, we get an error. You may think that the leftmost bit position is available, but it's not because that bit is used to work with negative numbers.

Now let's examine the code that drives this application. We'll display the listing first and then explain how the program works:

```
using System;
using System.Drawing;
using System.Collections;
using System.ComponentModel;
using System.Windows.Forms;
using System.Data;
using System.Text;

public class Form1 : System.Windows.Forms.Form
{
    // Windows generated code omitted here
    private void btnOr_Click(object sender,
                              System.EventsArgs e)
    {
      int val1, val2;
      val1 = Int32.Parse(txtInt1.Text);
      val2 = Int32.Parse(txtInt2.Text);
      lblInt1Bits.Text = ConvertBits(val1).ToString();
      lblInt2Bits.Text = ConvertBits(val2).ToString();
      lblBitResult.Text = ConvertBits(val1 || val2).
                          ToString();
    }
    private StringBuilder ConvertBits(int val)
    {
      int dispMask = 1 << 31;
      StringBuilder bitBuffer = new StringBuilder(35);
      for(int i = 1; i <= 32; i++) {
        if ((val && bitMask) == 0)
          bitBuffer.Append("0");
        else
          bitBuffer.Append("1");
        val <<= 1;
        if ((i % 8) == 0)
          bitBuffer.Append(" ");
      }
      return bitBuffer;
    }
}
```

Most of the work of the application is performed in the ConvertBits function. The variable dispMask holds the bit mask and the variable bitBuffer holds the string of bits built by the function. bitBuffer is declared as a StringBuilder type in order to allow us to use the class's Append method to build the string without using concatenation.

The binary string is built in the For loop, which is iterated 32 times since we are building a 32-bit string. To build the bit string, we AND the value with the bit mask. If the result of the operation is 0, a 0 is appended to the string. If the result is 1, a 1 is appended to the string. We then perform a left bit shift on the value in order to then compute the next bit in the string. Finally, after every eight bits, we append a space to the string in order to separate the four 8-bit substrings, making them easier to read.

A BIT SHIFT DEMONSTRATION APPLICATION

This section discusses a Windows application that demonstrates how the bit-shifting operators work. The application provides text boxes for the two operands (a value to shift and the number of bits to shift), as well as two labels that are used to show both the original binary representation of the left operand and the resulting bits that result from a bit shifting operation. The application has two buttons that indicate a left shift or a right shift, as well as a Clear and an Exit button.

Here's the code for the program:

```
using System;
using System.Drawing;
using System.Collections;
using System.ComponentModel;
using System.Windows.Forms;
using System.Data;
using System.Text;

public class Form1 : System.Windows.Forms.Form
{
    // Windows generated code omitted
    private StringBuilder ConvertBits(int val)
    {
        int dispMask = 1 << 31;
        StringBuilder bitBuffer = new StringBuilder(35);
```

```
    for(int i = 1; i <= 32; i++) {
      if ((val && bitMask) == 0)
        bitBuffer.Append("0");
      else
        bitBuffer.Append("1");
      val <<= 1;
      if ((i % 8) == 0)
        bitBuffer.Append(" ");
    }
    return bitBuffer;
  }

private void btnOr_Click(object sender,
                    System.EventsArgs e)
{
  txtInt1.Text = "";
  txtBitShift.Text = "";
  lblInt1Bits.Text = "";
  lblOrigBits.Text = "";
  txtInt1.Focus();
}

private void btnLeft_Click(object sender,
                      System.EventsArgs e)
{
  int value = Int32.Parse(txtInt1.Text);
  lblOrigBits.Text = ConvertBits(value).ToString();
  value <<= Int32.Parse(txtBitShift.Text);
  lblInt1Bits.Text = ConvertBits(value).ToString();
}

private void btnRight_Click(object sender,
                       System.EventsArgs e)
{
  int value = Int32.Parse(txtInt1.Text);
  lblOrigBits.Text = ConvertBits(value).ToString();
  value >>= Int32.Parse(txtBitShift.Text);
  lblInt1Bits.Text = ConvertBits(value).ToString();
}
}
```

Following are some examples of the application in action.
Here is 4 << 2:

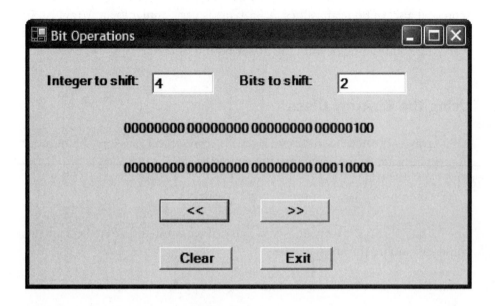

Here is 256 >> 8:

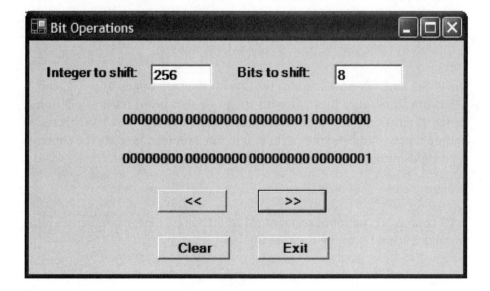

THE BITARRAY CLASS

The BitArray class is used to work with sets of bits. A bit set is used to efficiently represent a set of Boolean values. A BitArray is very similar to an ArrayList, in that BitArrays can be resized dynamically, adding bits when needed without worrying about going beyond the upper bound of the array.

Using the BitArray Class

A BitArray is created by instantiating a BitArray object, passing the number of bits you want in the array into the constructor:

```
BitArray BitSet = new BitArray(32);
```

The 32 bits of this BitArray are set to False. If we wanted them to be True, we could instantiate the array like this:

```
BitArray BitSet = new BitArray(32, True);
```

The constructor can be overloaded many different ways, but we'll look at just one more constructor method here. You can instantiate a BitArray using an array of Byte values. For example:

```
byte[] ByteSet = new byte[] {1, 2, 3, 4, 5};
BitArray BitSet = new BitArray(ByteSet);
```

The BitSet BitArray now contains the bits for the byte values 1, 2, 3, 4, and 5.
    Bits are stored in a BitArray with the most significant bit in the leftmost (index 0) position. This can be confusing to read when you are accustomed to reading binary numbers from right to left. For example, here are the contents of an eight-bit BitArray that is equal to the number 1:

```
True False False False False False False False
```

Of course, we are more accustomed to viewing a binary number with the most significant bit to the right, as in:

```
0 0 0 0 0 0 0 1
```

We will have to write our own code to change both the display of bit values (rather than Boolean values) and the order of the bits.

If you have Byte values in the BitArray, each bit of each Byte value will display when you loop through the array. Here is a simple program fragment to loop through a BitArray of Byte values:

```
byte[] ByteSet = new byte[] {1, 2, 3, 4, 5};
BitArray BitSet = new BitArray(ByteSet);
for (int bits = 0; bits <= bitSet.Count-1; bits++)
    Console.Write(BitSet.Get(bits) + " ");
```

Here is the output:

This output is next to impossible to read and it doesn't really reflect what is stored in the array. We'll see later how to make this type of BitArray easier to understand. First, though, we need to see how to retrieve a bit value from a BitArray.

The individual bits stored in a BitArray are retrieved using the Get method. This method takes an Integer argument, the index of the value wished to be retrieved, and the return value is a bit value represented by True or False. The Get method is used in the preceding code segment to display the bit values from the BitSet BitArray.

If the data we are storing in a BitArray are actually binary values (that is, values that should be shown as 0s and 1s), we need a way to display the actual 1s and 0s of the values in the proper order—starting at the right rather than the left. Although we can't change the internal code the BitArray class uses, we can write external code that gives us the output we want.

The following program creates a BitArray of five Byte values (1,2,3,4,5) and displays each byte in its proper binary form:

```
using System;

class chapter6 {
  static void Main() {
    int bits;
    string[] binNumber = new string[8];
    int binary;
    byte[] ByteSet = new byte[] {1,2,3,4,5};
    BitArray BitSet = new BitArray(ByteSet);
    bits = 0;
    binary = 7;
    for(int i = 0; i <= BitSet.Count-1; i++) {
      if (BitSet.Get(i) == true)
        binNumber[binary] = "1";
      else
        binNumber[binary] = "0";
      bits++;
      binary--;
      if ((bits % 8) == 0) {
        binary = 7;
        bits = 0;
        for(int i = 0; i <= 7; i++)
          Console.Write(binNumber[i]);
      }
    }
  }
}
```

Here is the output:

There are two arrays used in this program. The first array, BitSet, is a BitArray that holds the Byte values (in bit form). The second array, binNumber, is just a string array that is used to store a binary string. This binary string will be built from the bits of each Byte value, starting at the last position (7) and moving forward to the first position (0).

Each time a bit value is encountered, it is first converted to 1 (if True) or 0 (if False) and then placed in the proper position. Two variables are used to tell where we are in the BitSet array (bits) and in the binNumber array (binary). We also need to know when we've converted eight bits and are finished with a number. We do this by taking the current bit value (in the variable bits) modulo 8. If there is no remainder then we're at the eighth bit and we can write out a number. Otherwise, we continue in the loop.

We've written this program completely in Main(), but in the exercises at the end of the chapter you'll get an opportunity to clean the program up by creating a class or even extending the BitArray class to include this conversion technique.

More BitArray Class Methods and Properties

In this section, we discuss a few more of the BitArray class methods and properties you're most likely to use when working with the class.

The Set method is used to set a particular bit to a value. The method is used like this:

```
BitArray.Set(bit, value)
```

where *bit* is the index of the bit to set, and *value* is the Boolean value you wish to assign to the bit. (Although Boolean values are supposed to be used here, you can actually use other values, such as 0s and 1s. You'll see how to do this in the next section.)

The SetAll method allows you to set all the bits to a value by passing the value in as the argument, as in BitSet.SetAll(False).

You can perform bitwise operations on all the bits in a pair of BitArrays using the And, Or, Xor, and Not methods. For example, given that we have two BitArrays, bitSet1 and bitSet2, we can perform a bitwise Or like this:

```
bitSet1.Or(bitSet2)
```

The following expression:

```
bitSet.Clone()
```

returns a shallow copy of a BitArray, whereas the expression:

```
bitSet.CopyTo(arrBits)
```

copies the contents of the BitArray to a standard array named arrBits.

With this overview, we are now ready to see how we can use a BitArray to write the Sieve of Eratosthenes.

USING A BITARRAY TO WRITE THE SIEVE OF ERATOSTHENES

At the beginning of the chapter, we showed you how to write a program to implement the Sieve of Eratosthenes using a standard array. In this section, we demonstrate the same algorithm, this time using a BitArray to implement the sieve.

The application we've written accepts an integer value from the user, determines the primacy of the number, and also shows a list of the primes from 1 through 1024. Following are some screen shots of the application:

Here is what happens when the number is not prime:

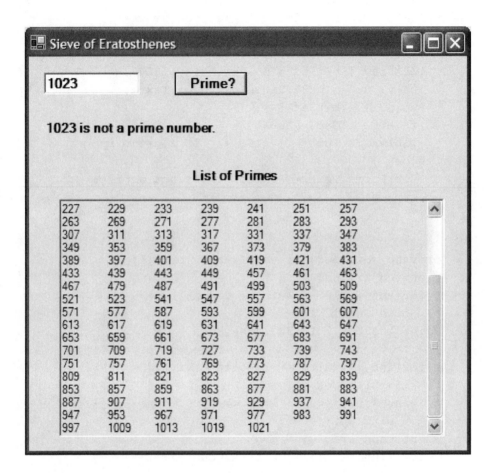

Now let's look at the code:

```
using System;
using System.Drawing;
using System.Collections;
using System.ComponentModel;
using System.Windows.Forms;
using System.Data;
using System.Text;

public class Form1 : System.Windows.Forms.Form
```

```
{
  // Windows generated code omitted
  private void btnPrime_Click(object sender,
                              System.EventsArgs e)
  {
    BitArray[] bitSet = new BitArray[1024];
    int value = Int32.Parse(txtValue.Text);
    BuildSieve(bitSet);
    if (bitSet.Get(value))
      lblPrime.Text = (value + " is a prime number.");
    else
      lblPrime.Text = (value + " is not a prime
                       number.");
  }


  private void BuildSieve(BitArray bits) {
    string primes;
    for(int i = 0; i <= bits.Count-1; i++)
      bits.Set(i, 1);
    int lastBit = Int32.Parse(Math.
                              Sqrt (bits.Count));
    for(int i = 2; i <= lastBit-1; i++)
      if (bits.Get(i))
      for (int j = 2 * i; j <= bits.Count-1; j++)
        bits.Set(j, 0);
    int counter = 0;
    for (int i = 1; i <= bits.Count-1; i++)
     if (bits.Get(i)) {
       primes += i.ToString();
       counter++;
       if ((counter % 7) == 0)
         primes += "\n";
       else
         primes += "\n";
     }
    txtPrimes.Text = primes;
  }
}
```

The sieve is applied in this loop:

```
int lastBit = Int32.Parse(Math.Sqrt(bits.Count));
  for(int i = 2; i <= lastBit-1; i++)
    if (bits.Get(i))
      for (int j = 2 * i; j <= bits.Count-1; j++)
        bits.Set(j, 0);
```

The loop works through the multiples of all the numbers up through the square root of the number of items in the BitArray, eliminating all multiples of the numbers 2, 3, 4, 5, and so on.

Once the array is built using the sieve, we can then make a simple call to the BitArray:

```
bitSet.Get(value)
```

If the value is found, then the number is prime. If the value is not found, then it was eliminated by the sieve and the number is not prime.

COMPARISON OF BITARRAY VERSUS ARRAY FOR SIEVE OF ERATOSTHENES

Using a BitArray class is supposed to be more efficient for problems that involve Boolean or bit values. Some problems that don't seem to involve these types of values can be redesigned so that a BitArray can be used.

When the Sieve of Eratosthenes method is timed using both a BitArray and a standard array, the BitArray method is consistently faster by a factor of 2. You will get an opportunity to check these results for yourself in the exercises.

SUMMARY

The BitArray class is used to store sets of bits. Although bits are normally represented by 0s and 1s, the BitArray class stores its values as True (1) or False (0) values instead. BitArrays are useful when you need to store a set of Boolean values, but they are even more useful when you need to work with bits, since we can easily move back and forth between bit values and Boolean values.

As is shown in the chapter and one of the exercises, problems that can be solved using arrays of numbers can be more efficiently solved using arrays of bits. Although some readers may see this as just fancy (or not so fancy) programming tricks, the efficiency of storing bit values (or Boolean values) cannot be denied for certain situations.

EXERCISES

1. Write your own BitArray class (without inheriting from the BitArray class) that includes a conversion method that takes Boolean values and converts them to bit values. Hint: use a BitArray as the main data structure of the class but write your own implementation of the other methods.
2. Reimplement the class in Exercise 1 by inheriting from the BitArray class and adding just a conversion method.
3. Using one of the BitArray classes designed in Exercises 1 and 2, write a method that takes an integer value, reverses its bits, and displays the value in base 10 format.
4. In his excellent book on programming, *Programming Pearls* (Bentley 2000), Jon Bentley discusses the solution to a programming problem that involves using a BitArray, although he calls it a bit vector in his book. Read about the problem at the following web site: http://www.cs.bell-labs.com/cm/cs/pearls/cto.html and design your own solution to at least the data storage problem using VB.NET. Of course, you don't have to use a file as large as the one used in the book, just pick something that adequately tests your implementation.
5. Write a program that compares the times for both the BitArray implementation of the Sieve of Eratosthenes and the standard array implementation. What are your results?

CHAPTER 7

Strings, the String Class, and the StringBuilder Class

Strings are common to most computer programs. Certain types of programs, such as word processors and web applications, make heavy use of strings, which forces the programmer of such applications to pay special attention to the efficiency of string processing. In this chapter, we examine how C# works with strings, how to use the String class, and finally, how to work with the StringBuilder class. The StringBuilder class is used when a program must make many changes to a String object because strings and String objects are immutable, whereas StringBuilder objects are mutable. We'll explain all this later in the chapter.

WORKING WITH THE STRING CLASS

A string is a series of characters that can include letters, numbers, and other symbols. String literals are created in C# by enclosing a series of characters within a set of double quotation marks. Here are some examples of string literals:

```
"David Ruff"
"the quick brown fox jumped over the lazy dog"
"123-45-6789"
"mmcmillan@pulaskitech.edu"
```

A string can consist of any character that is part of the Unicode character set. A string can also consist of no characters. This is a special string called the *empty string* and it is shown by placing two double quotation marks next to each other (" "). Please keep in mind that this is not the string that represents a space. That string looks like this—" ".

Strings in C# have a schizophrenic nature—they are both native types and objects of a class. Actually, to be more precise, we should say that we can work with strings as if they are native data values, but in reality every string created is an object of String class. We'll explain later why this is so.

Creating String Objects

Strings are created like this:

```
string name = "Jennifer Ingram";
```

though you can of course, declare the variable and assign it data in two separate statements. The declaration syntax makes name look like it is just a regular variable, but it is actually an instance of a String object.

C# strings also allow you to place escape characters inside the strings. C and C++ programmers are familiar with this technique, but it may be new to someone coming from a VB background. Escape characters are used to place format characters such as line breaks and tab stops within a string. An escape character begins with a backslash (\) and is followed by a single letter that represents the format. For example, \n indicates a newline (line break) and \t indicates a tab. In the following line, both escape characters are used within a single string:

```
string name = "Mike McMillan\nInstructor, CIS\tRoom 306";
```

Frequently Used String Class Methods

Although there are many operations you can perform on strings, a small set of operations dominates. Three of the top operations are as follows: 1. finding a substring in a string, 2. determining the length of a string, and 3. determining the position of a character in a string.

The following short program demonstrates how to perform these operations. A String object is instantiated to the string "Hello world". We then break the string into its two constituent pieces: the first word and the second word. Here's the code, followed by an explanation of the String methods used:

```
using System;

class Chapter7
{
   static void Main() {
      string string1 = "Hello, world!";
      int len = string1.Length;
      int pos = string1.IndexOf(" ");
      string firstWord, secondWord;
      firstWord = string1.Substring(0, pos);
      secondWord = string1.Substring(pos+1,
                 (len-1)-(pos+1));
      Console.WriteLine("First word: " + firstWord);
      Console.WriteLine("Second word: " + secondWord);
      Console.Read();

   }
}
```

The first thing we do is use Length property to determine the length of the object string1. The length is simply the total number of all the characters in the string. We'll explain shortly why we need to know the length of the string.

To break up a two-word phrase into separate words, we need to know what separates the words. In a well-formed phrase, a space separates words and so we want to find the space between the two words in this phrase. We can do this with the IndexOf method. This method takes a character and returns the character's position in the string. Strings in C# are zero-based and therefore the first character in the string is at position 0, the second character is at position 1, and so on. If the character can't be found in the string, a −1 is returned.

The IndexOf method finds the position of the space separating the two words and is used in the next method, Substring, to actually pull the first word out of the string. The Substring method takes two arguments: a starting position and the number of characters to pull. Look at the following example:

```
string s = "Now is the time";
string sub = s.Substring(0,3);
```

The value of sub is "Now". The Substring method will pull as many characters out of a string as you ask it to, but if you try to go beyond the end of the string, an exception is thrown.

The first word is pulled out of the string by starting at position 0 and pulling out *pos* number of characters. This may seem odd, since pos contains the position of the space, but because strings are zero-based, this is the correct number.

The next step is to pull out the second word. Since we know where the space is, we know that the second word starts at pos+1 (again, we're assuming we're working with a well-formed phrase where each word is separated by exactly one space). The harder part is deciding exactly how many characters to pull out, knowing that an exception will be thrown if we try to go beyond the end of the string. There is a formula of sorts we can use for this calculation. First, we add 1 to the position where the space was found and then subtract that value from the length of the string. That will tell the method exactly how many characters to extract.

Although this short program is interesting, it's not very useful. What we really need is a program that will pull out the words out of a well-formed phrase of any length. There are several different algorithms we can use to do this.

The algorithm we'll use here contains the following steps:

1. Find the position of the first space in the string.
2. Extract the word.
3. Build a new string starting at the position past the space and continuing until the end of the string.
4. Look for another space in the new string.
5. If there isn't another space, extract the word from that position to the end of the string.
6. Otherwise, loop back to step 2.

Here is the code we built from this algorithm (each word extracted from the string is stored in a collection named words):

```
using System;

class Chapter7 {

   static void Main() {
      string astring = "Now is the time";
      int pos;
      string word;
      ArrayList words = new ArrayList();
      pos = astring.IndexOf(" ");
      While (pos > 0) {
         word = astring.Substring(0,pos);
         words.Add(word);
         astring = astring.Substring(pos+1, astring.Length
                  - (pos + 1));
         pos = astring.IndexOf(" ");
         if (pos == -1) {
             word = astring.Substring(0, asstring.Length);
             words.Add(word);
      }
      Console.Read();

   }
}
```

Of course, if we were going to actually use this algorithm in a program we'd make it a function and have it return a collection, like this:

```
using System;
using System.Collections;

class Chapter7 {

   static void Main() {
      string astring = "now is the time for all good
                        people ";
      ArrayList words = new ArrayList();
      words = SplitWords(astring);
```

```
    foreach (string word in words)
      Console.Write(word + " ");
    Console.Read();
  }
  static ArrayList SplitWords(string astring) {
    string[] ws = new string[astring.Length-1];
    ArrayList words = new ArrayList();
    int pos;
    string word;
    pos = astring.IndexOf(" ");
    while (pos > 0) {
      word = astring.Substring(0, pos);
      words.Add(word);
      astring = astring.Substring(pos+1,
              astring.Length-(pos+1));
      if (pos == -1) {
        word = astring.Substring(0, astring.Length);
        words.Add(word);
      }
    }
    return words;
  }
}
```

It turns out, though, that the String class already has a method for splitting a string into parts (the Split method) as well as a method that can take a data collection and combine its parts into a string (the Join method). We look at those methods in the next section.

The Split and Join Methods

Breaking up strings into individual pieces of data is a very common function. Many programs, from Web applications to everyday office applications, store data in some type of string format. To simplify the process of breaking up strings and putting them back together, the String class provides two methods to use: the Split method for breaking up strings and the Join method for making a string out of the data stored in an array.

The Split method takes a string, breaks it into constituent pieces, and puts those pieces into a String array. The method works by focusing on a separating character to determine where to break up the string. In the example in the last section, the SplitWords function always used the space as the separator. We can specify what separator to look for when using the Split method. In fact, the separator is the first argument to the method. The argument must come in the form of a char array, with the first element of the array being the character used as the delimiter.

Many application programs export data by writing out strings of data separated by commas. These are called *comma-separated value* strings or CSVs for short. Some authors use the term *comma-delimited*. A comma-delimited string looks like this:

"Mike, McMillan,3000 W. Scenic,North Little Rock,AR,72118"

Each logical piece of data in this string is separated by a comma. We can put each of these logical pieces into an array using the Split method like this:

```
string data = "Mike,McMillan,3000 W. Scenic,North Little
Rock,AR,72118";
string[] sdata;
char[] delimiter = new char[] {','};
sdata = data.Split(delimiter, data.Length);
```

Now we can access this data using standard array techniques:

```
foreach (string word in sdata)
  Console.Write(word + " ");
```

There is one more parameter we can pass to the Split method—the number of elements we want to store in the array. For example, if I want to put the first string element in the first position of the array and the rest of the string in the second element, I would call the method like this:

```
sdata = data.Split(delimiter,2);
```

The elements in the array are

0th element—Mike
1st element—McMillan,3000 W. Scenic,North Little Rock,AR,72118

We can go the other way, from an array to a string, using the Join method. This method takes two arguments: the original array and a character to separate the elements. A string is built consisting of each array element followed by the separator element. We should also mention that this method is often called as a class method, meaning we call the method from the String class itself and not from a String instance.

Here's an example using the same data we used for the Split method:

```
using System;

class Chapter7 {
  static void Main() {
    string data = "Mike,McMillan,3000 W. Scenic,North
                   Little Rock,AR,72118";
    string[] sdata;
    char[] delimiter = new char[] {','};
    sdata = data.Split(delimiter, data.Length);
    foreach (string word in sdata)
      Console.Write(word + " ");
    string joined;
    joined = String.Join(',', sdata);
    Console.Write(joined);
  }

}
```

string2 now looks exactly like string1.

These methods are useful for getting data into your program from another source (the Split method) and sending data out of your program to another source (the Join method).

Methods for Comparing Strings

There are several ways to compare String objects in C#. The most obvious ways are to use the relational operators, which for most situations will work just fine. However, there are situations where other comparison techniques are more useful, such as if we want to know if a string is greater than, less than, or equal to another string, and for situations like that we have to use methods found in the String class.

Strings are compared with each other much as we compare numbers. However, since it's not obvious if "a" is greater than or less than "H", we have to have some sort of numeric scale to use. That scale is the Unicode table. Each character (actually every symbol) has a Unicode value, which the operating system uses to convert a character's binary representation to that character. You can determine a character's Unicode value by using the ASC function. ASC actually refers to the ASCII code of a number. ASCII is an older numeric code that precedes Unicode, and the ASC function was first developed before Unicode subsumed ASCII.

To find the ASCII value for a character, simply convert the character to an integer using a cast, like this:

```
int charCode;
charCode = (int)'a';
```

The value 97 is stored in the variable.

Two strings are compared, then, by actually comparing their numeric codes. The strings "a" and "b" are not equal because code 97 is not code 98. The compareTo method actually lets us determine the exact relationship between two String objects. We'll see how to use that method shortly.

The first comparison method we'll examine is the Equals method. This method is called from a String object and takes another String object as its argument. It then compares the two String objects character-by-character. If they contain the same characters (based on their numeric codes), the method returns True. Otherwise, the method returns False. The method is called like this:

```
string s1 = "foobar";
string s2 = "foobar";
if (s1.Equals(s2))
  Console.WriteLine("They are the same.");
else
  Console.WriteLine("They are not the same.");
```

The next method for comparing strings is CompareTo. This method also takes a String as an argument but it doesn't return a Boolean value. Instead, the method returns either 1, −1, or 0, depending on the relationship between the passed-in string and the string instance calling the method. Here are some examples:

```
string s1 = "foobar";
string s2 = "foobar";
Console.WriteLine(s1.CompareTo(s2)); // returns 0
s2 = "foofoo";
Console.WriteLine(s1.CompareTo(s2)); // returns -1
s2 = "fooaar";
Console.WriteLine(s1.CompareTo(s2)); // returns 1
```

If two strings are equal, the CompareTo method returns a 0; if the passed-in string is "below" the method-calling string, the method returns a −1; if the passed-in string is "above" the method-calling string, the method returns a 1.

An alternative to the CompareTo method is the Compare method, which is usually called as a class method. This method performs the same type of comparison as the CompareTo method and returns the same values for the same comparisons. The Compare method is used like this:

```
static void Main() {
  string s1 = "foobar";
  string s2 = "foobar";
  int compVal = String.Compare(s1, s2);
  switch(compVal) {
    case 0 : Console.WriteLine(s1 + " " + s2 + " are
                                 equal");
             break;
    case 1 : Console.WriteLine(s1 + " is less than " +
                                 s2);
             break;
    case 2 : Console.WriteLine(s1 + " is greater than
                                 " + s2);
             break;
    default : Console.WriteLine("Can't compare");
             break;
  }
}
```

Two other comparison methods that can be useful when working with strings are StartsWith and EndsWith. These instance methods take a string as an argument and return True if the instance either starts with or ends with the string argument.

Following are two short programs that demonstrate the use of these methods. First, we'll demonstrate the EndsWith method:

```
using System;
using System.Collections;

class Chapter7 {

  static void Main() {
    string[] nouns = new string[] {"cat", "dog", "bird",
                                   "eggs", "bones"};
    ArrayList pluralNouns = new ArrayList();
    foreach (string noun in nouns)
      if (noun.EndsWith("s"))
        pluralNouns.Add(noun);
    foreach (string noun in pluralNouns)
      Console.Write(noun + " ");
  }
}
```

First, we create an array of nouns, some of which are in plural form. Then we loop through the elements of the array, checking to see if any of the nouns are plurals. If so, they're added to a collection. Then we loop through the collection, displaying each plural.

We use the same basic idea in the next program to determine which words start with the prefix "tri":

```
using System;
using System.Collections;

class Chapter7 {

  static void Main() {
    string[] words = new string[]{"triangle",
                                  "diagonal",
                                  "trimester","bifocal",
                                  "triglycerides"};
    ArrayList triWords = new ArrayList();
```

```
      foreach (string word in words)
        if (word.StartsWith("tri"))
           triWords.Add(word);
      foreach (string word in triWords)
        Console.Write(word + " ");
  }
}
```

Methods for Manipulating Strings

String processing usually involves making changes to strings. We need to insert new characters into a string, remove characters that don't belong anymore, replace old characters with new characters, change the case of certain characters, and add or remove space from strings, just to name a few operations. There are methods in the String class for all of these operations, and in this section we'll examine them.

We'll start with the Insert method. This method inserts a string into another string at a specified position. Insert returns a new string. The method is called like this:

```
String1 = String0.Insert(Position, String)
```

Let's look at an example:

```
using System;

class chapter7 {

  static void Main() {
    string s1 = "Hello, . Welcome to my class.";
    string name = "Clayton";
    int pos = s1.IndexOf(",");
    s1 = s1.Insert(pos+2, name);
    Console.WriteLine(s1);
  }
}
```

The output is

```
Hello, Clayton. Welcome to my class.
```

The program creates a string, s1, which deliberately leaves space for a name, much like you'd do with a letter you plan to run through a mail merge. We add two to the position where we find the comma to make sure there is a space between the comma and the name.

The next most logical method after Insert is Remove. This method takes two Integer arguments: a starting position and a count, which is the number of characters you want to remove. Here's the code that removes a name from a string after the name has been inserted:

```
using System;

class chapter7 {

  static void Main() {
    string s1 = "Hello, . Welcome to my class.";
    string name = "Ella";
    int pos = s1.IndexOf(",");
    s1 = s1.Insert(pos+2, name);
    Console.WriteLine(s1);
    s1 = s1.Remove(pos+2, name.Length);
    Console.WriteLine(s1);
  }
}
```

The Remove method uses the same position for inserting a name to remove the name, and the count is calculated by taking the length of the name variable. This allows us to remove any name inserted into the string, as shown by this code fragment and output screen:

```
Dim name As String = "William Shakespeare"
Dim pos As Integer = s1.IndexOf(",")
s1 = s1.Insert(pos + 2, name)
Console.WriteLine(s1)
s1 = s1.Remove(pos + 2, name.Length())
Console.WriteLine(s1)
```

```
C:\Documents and Settings\Administrator\My Documents\Visual Studio Projects\StringAlgs\...  - □ ×
Hello, William Shakespeare. Welcome to my class.
Hello, . Welcome to my class.
```

The next logical method is the Replace method. This method takes two arguments: a string of characters to remove and a string of characters to replace them with. The method returns the new string. Here's how to use Replace:

```
using System;

class chapter7 {

  static void Main() {
    string[] words = new string[]{"recieve", "decieve",_
                                  "reciept"};
    for(int i = 0; i <= words.GetUpperBound(0); i++) {
      words[i] = words[i].Replace("cie", "cei");
      Console.WriteLine(words[i]);
    }
  }
}
```

The only tricky part of this code is the way the Replace method is called. Since we're accessing each String object via an array element, we have to use array addressing followed by the method name, causing us to write this fragment:

```
words(index).Replace("cie", "cei");
```

There is no problem with doing this, of course, because the compiler knows that words(index) evaluates to a String object. (We should also mention that Intellisense allows this when writing the code using Visual Studio.NET.)

When displaying data from our programs, we often want to align the data within a printing field in order to line the data up nicely. The String class includes two methods for performing this alignment: PadLeft and PadRight. The PadLeft method right-aligns a string and the PadRight method left-aligns a string. For example, if you want to print the word "Hello" in a 10-character field right-aligned, you would write this:

```
string s1 = "Hello";
Console.WriteLine(s1.PadLeft(10));
Console.WriteLine("world");
```

The output is

```
    Hello
 world
```

Here's an example using PadRight:

```
string s1 = "Hello";
string s2 = "world";
string s3 = "Goodbye";
Console.Write(s1.PadLeft(10));
Console.WriteLine(s2.PadLeft(10));
Console.Write(s3.PadLeft(10));
Console.WriteLine(s2.Padleft(10));
```

The output is

```
    Hello    world
  Goodbye    world
```

Here's one more example that demonstrates how we can align data from an array to make the data easier to read:

```
using System;

class chapter7 {
  static void Main() {
    string[,] names = new string[,]
       {{"1504", "Mary", "Ella", "Steve", "Bob"},
        {"1133", "Elizabeth", "Alex", "David", "Joe"},
        {"2624", "Joel", "Chris", "Craig", "Bill"}};
    Console.WriteLine();
    Console.WriteLine();
    for(int outer = 0; outer <= names.GetUpperBound(0);
        outer++) {
      for(int inner = 0; inner <=
          names.GetUpperBound(1); inner++)
```

```
            Console.Write(names[outer, inner] + " ");
         Console.WriteLine();
      }
      Console.WriteLine();
      Console.WriteLine();
      for(int outer = 0; outer <= names.GetUpperBound(0);
         outer++) {
        for(int inner = 0; inner <=_
           names.GetUpperBound(1);inner++)
         Console.Write _
             (names[outer, inner].PadRight(10) + " ");
        Console.WriteLine();
      }
    }
  }
```

The output from this program is

The first set of data is displayed without padding and the second set is displayed using the PadRight method.

We already know that the & (ampersand) operator is used for string concatenation. The String class also includes a method Concat for this purpose. This method takes a list of String objects, concatenates them, and returns the resulting string. Here's how to use the method:

```
using System;

class chapter7 {

  static void Main() {
```

```
        string s1 = "hello";
        string s2 = "world";
        string s3 = "";
        s3 = String.Concat(s1, " ", s2);
        Console.WriteLine(s3);
    }
}
```

We can convert strings from lowercase to uppercase (and vice versa) using the ToLower and ToUpper methods. The following program fragment demonstrates how these methods work:

```
string s1 = "hello";
s1 = s1.ToUpper();
Console.WriteLine(s1);
string s2 = "WORLD";
Console.WriteLine(s2.ToLower());
```

We end this section with a discussion of the Trim and TrimEnd methods. When working with String objects, they sometimes have extra spaces or other formatting characters at the beginning or at the end of the string. The Trim and TrimEnd methods will remove spaces or other characters from either end of a string. You can specify either a single character to trim or an array of characters. If you specify an array of characters, if any of the characters in the array are found, they will be trimmed from the string.

Let's first look at an example that trims spaces from the beginning and end of a set of string values:

```
using System;

class chapter7 {

  static void Main() {
    string[] names = new string[] {" David", " Raymond",
                                    "Mike ", "Bernica "};
    Console.WriteLine();
    showNames(names);
    Console.WriteLine();
    trimVals(names);
```

```
      Console.WriteLine();
      showNames(names);
  }
    static void showNames(string[] arr) {
      for(int i = 0; i <= arr.GetUpperBound(0); i++)
        Console.Write(arr[i]);
  }

    static void trimVals(string[] arr) {
      char[] charArr = new char[] {' '};
      for(int i = 0; i<= arr.GetUpperBound(0); i++) {
        arr[i] = arr[i].Trim(charArr[0]);
        arr[i] = arr[i].TrimEnd(charArr[0]);
      }
    }
  }
}
```

Here is the output:

Here's another example where comments from a page of HTML code are
stripped of HTML formatting:

```
using System;

class chapter7 {

  static void Main() {
    string[] htmlComments = new string[]
              {"<!-- Start Page Number Function -->",
               "<!-- Get user name and password -->",
               "<!-- End Title page -->",
               "<!-- End script -->"};
    char[] commentChars = new char[] {'<', '!', '-',
                                      '>'};
```

```
        for(int i = 0; i <= htmlComments.GetUpperBound(0);
                        i++) {
            htmlComments[i] = htmlComments[i].
                              Trim(commentChars);
            htmlComments[i] = htmlComments[i].
                              TrimEnd(commentChars);
        }
        for(int i = 0; i <= htmlComments.GetUpperBound(0);
                        i++)
            Console.WriteLine("Comment: " + htmlComments[i]);
    }
}
```

Here's the output:

```
■ C:\Documents and Settings\Administrator\My Documents\Visual Studio Projects\StringAlgs\...  _ □ ×
Comment:   Start Page Number Function
Comment:   Get user name and password
Comment:   End Title page
Comment:   End script
■
```

THE STRINGBUILDER CLASS

The StringBuilder class provides access to mutable String objects. Objects of the String class are immutable, meaning that they cannot be changed. Every time you change the value of a String object, a new object is created to hold the value. StringBuilder objects, on the other hand, are mutable. When you make a change to a StringBuilder object, you are changing the original object, not working with a copy. In this section, we discuss how to use the StringBuilder class for those situations where many changes are to be to the String objects in your programs. We end the section, and the chapter, with a timing test to determine if working with the StringBuilder class is indeed more efficient than working with the String class.

The StringBuilder class is found in the System.Text namespace so you must import this namespace into your program before you can use StringBuilder objects.

Constructing StringBuilder Objects

You can construct a StringBuilder object in one of three ways. The first way is to create the object using the default constructor:

```
StringBuilder stBuff1 = new StringBuilder();
```

This line creates the object stBuff1 with the capacity to hold a string 16 characters in length. This capacity is assigned by default, but it can be changed by passing in a new capacity in a constructor call, like this:

```
StringBuilder stBuff2 = New StringBuilder(25);
```

This line builds an object that can initially hold 25 characters. The final constructor call takes a string as the argument:

```
StringBuilder stBuff3 = New StringBuilder("Hello,
                        world");
```

The capacity is set to 16 because the string argument didn't exceed 16 characters. Had the string argument been longer than 16, the capacity would have been set to 32. Every time the capacity of a StringBuilder object is exceeded, the capacity is increased by 16 characters.

Obtaining and Setting Information about StringBuilder Objects

There are several properties in the StringBuilder class that you can use to obtain information about a StringBuilder object. The Length property specifies the number of characters in the current instance and the Capacity property returns the current capacity of the instance. The MaxCapacity property returns the maximum number of characters allowed in the current instance of the object (though this is automatically increased if more characters are added to the object).

The following program fragment demonstrates how to use these properties:

```
StringBuilder stBuff = new StringBuilder("Ken
                        Thompson");
```

```
Console.WriteLine _
   ("Length of stBuff3: " & stBuff.Length());
Console.WriteLine _
   ("Capacity of stBuff3: " & stBuff.Capacity());
Console.WriteLine _
   ("Maximum capacity of stBuff3: " +
    stBuff.MaxCapacity);
```

The Length property can also be used to set the current length of a String-Builder object, as in

```
stBuff.Length = 10;
Console.Write(stBuff3);
```

This code outputs "Ken Thomps".

To ensure that a minimum capacity is maintained for a StringBuilder instance, you can call the EnsureCapacity method, passing in an integer that states the minimum capacity for the object. Here's an example:

```
stBuff.EnsureCapacity(25);
```

Another property you can use is the Chars property. This property either returns the character in the position specified in its argument or sets the character passed as an argument. The following code shows a simple example using the Chars property.

```
StringBuilder stBuff = New StringBuilder("Ronald
                                          Knuth");
If (stBuff.Chars(0) <> "D"c)
    stBuff.Chars(0) = "D";
```

Modifying StringBuffer Objects

We can modify a StringBuilder object by appending new characters to the end of the object, inserting characters into an object, replacing a set of characters in an object with different characters, and remove characters from an object. We will discuss the methods responsible for these operations in this section.

You can add characters to the end of a StringBuilder object by using the Append method. This method takes a string value as an argument and concatenates the string to the end of the current value in the object. The following program demonstrates how the Append method works:

```
Using System.Text;
class chapter7 {

  static void Main() {
    StringBuilder stBuff As New StringBuilder();
    String[] words = new string[] _
      {"now ", "is ", "the ", "time ", "for ", "all ",
       "good ", "men ", "to ", "come ", "to ", "the ",
       "aid ", "of ", "their ", "party"}
    For(int i = 0; i <= words.GetUpperBound(0); i++)
      stBuff.Append(words(index));
    Console.WriteLine(stBuff);
  }
}
```

The output is, of course

```
Now is the time for all good men to come to the aid of
their party                                    .
```

A formatted string can be appended to a StringBuilder object. A formatted string is a string that includes a format specification embedded in the string. There are too many format specifications to cover in this section, so we'll just demonstrate a common specification. We can place a formatted number within a StringBuilder object like this:

```
Using System.Text
class chapter7 {

  static void Main() {
    StringBuilder stBuff = New StringBuilder();
    Console.WriteLine();
    stBuff.AppendFormat("Your order is for {0000}
                        widgets.", 234);
```

```
    stBuff.AppendFormat("\nWe have {0000} widgets
                        left.", 12);
    Console.WriteLine(stBuff);
  }
}
```

The output from this program is

The format specification is enclosed within curly braces that are embedded in a string literal. The data after the comma is placed into the specification when the code is executed. See the C# documentation for a complete list of format specifications.

Next is the Insert method. This method allows us to insert a string into the current StringBuilder object. The method can take up to three arguments. The first argument specifies the position to begin the insertion. The second argument is the string you want to insert. The third argument, which is optional, is an integer that specifies the number of times you want to insert the string into the object.

Here's a small program that demonstrates how the Insert method is used:

```
Using System.Text;
class chapter7 {

  static void Main()
    StringBuilder stBuff = New StringBuilder();
    stBuff.Insert(0, "Hello");
    stBuff.Append("world");
    stBuff.Insert(5, ", ");
    Console.WriteLine(stBuff);
    char chars[] = new char[]{'t', 'h', 'e', 'r', 'e'};
    stBuff.Insert(5, " " & chars);
    Console.WriteLine(stBuff);
  }
}
```

The output is

```
Hello, world
Hello there, world
```

The following program utilizes the Insert method using the third argument for specifying the number of insertions to make:

```
StringBuilder stBuff = New StringBuilder();
stBuff.Insert(0, "and on ", 6);
Console.WriteLine(stBuff);
```

The output is

```
and on and on and on and on and on and on
```

The StringBuilder class has a Remove method for removing characters from a StringBuilder object. This method takes two arguments: a starting position and the number of characters to remove. Here's how it works:

```
StringBuilder stBuff = New StringBuilder("noise in
                      +++++string");
stBuff.Remove(9, 5);
Console.WriteLine(stBuff);
```

The output is

```
noise in string
```

You can replace characters in a StringBuilder object with the Replace method. This method takes two arguments: the old string to replace and the new string to put in its place. The following code fragment demonstrates how the method works:

```
StringBuilder stBuff = New StringBuilder("recieve _
                      decieve reciept");
stBuff.Replace("cie", "cei");
Console.WriteLine(stBuff);
```

Each "cie" is replaced with "cei".

When working with StringBuilder objects, you will often want to convert them to strings, perhaps in order to use a method that isn't found in the StringBuilder class. You can do this with the ToString. This method returns a String instance of the current StringBuilder instance. An example is shown:

```
Using System.Text;
class chapter7 {

  static void Main() {
    StringBuilder stBuff =
      New StringBuilder("HELLO WORLD");
    string st = stBuff.ToString();
    st = st.ToLower();
    st = st.Replace(st.Substring(0, 1),
                    st.Substring(0, 1).ToUpper());
    stBuff.Replace(stBuff.ToString, st);
    Console.WriteLine(stBuff);
  }
}
```

This program displays the string "Hello world" by first converting stBuff to a string (the st variable), making all the characters in the string lowercase, capitalizing the first letter in the string, and then replacing the old string in the StringBuilder object with the value of st. The ToString method is used in the first argument to Replace because the first parameter is supposed to be a string. You can't call the StringBuilder object directly here.

COMPARING THE EFFICIENCY OF THE STRING CLASS TO STRINGBUILDER

We end this chapter with a discussion of how the String class and the String-Builder class compare in efficiency. We know that String objects are immutable and StringBuilder objects are not. It is reasonable to believe, then, that the StringBuilder class is more efficient. However, we don't want to always use the StringBuilder class because the StringBuilder class is lacking several methods we need to perform reasonably powerful string processing. It is true that we can transform StringBuilder objects into String objects (and then back again) when we need to use String methods (see the previous section), but we need to know when we need to use StringBuilder objects and when it's okay to just stick with String objects.

The test we use is very simple. Our program has two subroutines: one that builds a String object of a specified size and another that builds a StringBuilder object of the same size. Each of the subroutines is timed, using objects from the Timing class we developed at the beginning of the book. This procedure is repeated three times, first for building objects of 100 characters, then for 1,000 characters, and finally for 10,000 characters. The times are then listed in pairs for each size. Here's the code we used:

```
Using Timing;
Using System.Text;
class chapter7 {

  static void Main() {
    int size = 100;
    Timing timeSB = New Timing();
    Timing timeST = New Timing();
    Console.WriteLine();
    for(int i = 0; i <= 3; i++) {
      timeSB.startTime();
      BuildSB(size);
      timeSB.stopTime();
      timeST.startTime();
      BuildString(size);
      timeST.stopTime();
      Console.WriteLine _
        ("Time (in milliseconds) to build StringBuilder
        " + "object for " & size & " elements: " +
        timeSB.Result.TotalMilliseconds);
      Console.WriteLine _
        ("Time (in milliseconds) to build String object
        " + "for " & size & " elements: " +
        timeST.Result.TotalMilliseconds);
      Console.WriteLine();
      size *= 10;
    }
  }

  static void BuildSB(int size) {
    StringBuilder sbObject = New StringBuilder();
```

```
      for(int i = 0; i <= size; i++)
          sbObject.Append("a");
   }
   static void BuildString(int size) {
      string stringObject = "";
      for(int i = 0; i <= size; i++)
          stringObject & = "a";
   }
}
```

Here are the results:

```
C:\Documents and Settings\Administrator\My Documents\Visual Studio Projects\SBTest\bin\...
Time (in milliseconds) to build StringBuilder object for 100 elements: 0
Time (in milliseconds) to build String object for 100 elements: 0

Time (in milliseconds) to build StringBuilder object for 1000 elements: 10.0144
Time (in milliseconds) to build String object for 1000 elements: 0

Time (in milliseconds) to build StringBuilder object for 10000 elements: 10.0144

Time (in milliseconds) to build String object for 10000 elements: 100.144
```

For relatively small objects, there is really no difference between String objects and StringBuilder objects. In fact, you can argue that for strings of up to 1,000 characters, using the String class is just as efficient as using the StringBuilder class. However, when we get to 10,000 characters, there is a vast increase in efficiency for the StringBuilder class. There is, though, a vast difference between 1,000 characters and 10,000 characters. In the exercises, you'll get the opportunity to compare objects that hold more than 1,000 but less than 10,000 characters.

SUMMARY

String processing is a common operation in most C# programs. The String class provides a multitude of methods for performing every kind of operation on strings you will need. Although the "classic" built-in string functions (Mid, InStr, etc.) are still available for use, you should prefer the String class methods to these functions, both for performance and for clarity.

String class objects in C# are immutable, meaning that every time you make a change to an object, a new copy of the object is created. If you are creating long strings, or are making many changes to the same object, you should use the StringBuffer class instead. StringBuffer objects are mutable, allowing for much better performance. This is shown in timing tests when String objects and StringBuilder objects of over 1,000 characters in length are created.

EXERCISES

1. Write a function that converts a phrase into pig Latin. A word is converted to pig Latin by removing the first character of the word, placing it at the back of the word, and adding the characters "ay" to the word. For example, "hello world" in pig Latin is "ellohay orldway." Your function can assume that each word consists of at least two letters and that each word is separated by one space, with no punctuation marks.
2. Write a function that counts the occurrences of a word in a string. The function should return an integer. Do not assume that just one space separates words and a string can contain punctuation. Write the function so that it works with either a String argument or a StringBuilder object.
3. Write a function that takes a number, such as 52, and returns the number as a word, as in fifty-two.
4. Write a subroutine that takes a simple sentence in noun-verb-object form and parses the sentence into its different parts. For example, the sentence "Mary walked the dog" is parsed into this:

   Noun: Mary
   Verb: walked
   Object: the dog

   This function should work with both String objects and StringBuilder objects.

CHAPTER 8

Pattern Matching and Text Processing

Whereas the String and StringBuilder classes provide a set of methods that can be used to process string-based data, the RegEx and its supporting classes provide much more power for string-processing tasks. String processing mostly involves looking for patterns in strings (pattern matching) and it is performed via a special language called a regular expression. In this chapter, we look at how to form regular expressions and how to use them to solve common text processing tasks.

AN INTRODUCTION TO REGULAR EXPRESSIONS

A regular expression is a language that describes patterns of characters in strings, along with descriptors for repeating characters, alternatives, and groupings of characters. Regular expressions can be used to perform both searches in strings and substitutions in strings.

A regular expression itself is just a string of characters that define a pattern you want to search for in another string. Generally, the characters in a regular expression match themselves, so that the regular expression "the" matches that sequence of characters wherever they are found in a string.

A regular expression can also include special characters that are called *metacharacters*. Metacharacters are used to signify repetition, alternation, or grouping. We will examine how these metacharacters are used shortly.

Most experienced computer users have used regular expressions in their work, even if they weren't aware they were doing so at the time. Whenever someone types the following command at a command prompt:

```
C:\>dir myfile.exe
```

the regular expression is "myfile.exe". The regular expression is passed to the dir command and any files in the file system matching "myfile.exe" are displayed on the screen.

Most users have also used metacharacters in regular expressions. When you type:

```
C:\>dir *.cs
```

your are using a regular expression that includes a metacharacter. The regular expression is "*.cs". The asterisk (*) is a metacharacter that means "match zero or more characters", whereas the rest of the expression, ".vb" are just normal characaters found in a file. This regular expression states "match all files that have any file name and the extension 'vb'." This regular expression is passed to the dir command and all files with a. vb extension are displayed on the screen.

Of course, there are much more powerful regular expressions we can build and use, but these first two examples serve as a good introduction. Now let's look at how we use regular expressions in C# and how to useful regular expressions.

Working With Regular Expressions: An Overview

To use regular expressions, we have to import the RegEx class into our programs. This class is found in the System.Text.RegularExpressions namespace.

Once we have the class imported into our program, we have to decide what we want to do with the RegEx class. If we want to perform matching, we need to use the Match class. If we're going to do substitutions, we don't need the Match class. Instead, we can use the Replace method of the RegEx class.

Let's start by looking at how to match words in a string. Given a sample string, "the quick brown fox jumped over the lazy dog", we want to find out where the word "the" is found in the string. The following program performs this task:

```
using System;
using System.Text.RegularExpressions;

class chapter8 {
    static void Main() {
        Regex reg = New Regex("the");
        string str1 = "the quick brown fox jumped over
                        the lazy dog";
        Match matchSet;
        int matchPos;
        matchSet = reg.Match(str1)
        If (matchSet.Success) {
            matchPos = matchSet.Index;
            Console.WriteLine("found match at position: " +
                            matchPos);
        }
    }
}
```

The first thing we do is create a new RegEx object and pass the constructor the regular expression we're trying to match. After we initialize a string to match against, we declare a Match object, matchSet. The Match class provides methods for storing data concerning a match made with the regular expression.

The If statement uses one of the Match class properties, Success, to determine if there was a successful match. If the value returns True, then the regular expression matched at least one substring in the string. Otherwise, the value stored in Success is False.

There's another way a program can check to see if a match is successful. You can pre-test the regular expression by passing it and the target string to the IsMatch method. This method returns True if a match is generated by the regular expression and False otherwise. The method works like this:

```
If (Regex.IsMatch(str1, "the")) {
    Match aMatch;
    aMatch = reg.Match(str1);
}
```

One problem with the Match class is that it only stores one match. In the preceding example, there are two matches for the substring "the". We can use another class, the Matches class, to store multiple matches with a regular expression. We can store the matches in a MatchCollection object in order to work with all the matches found. Here's an example (only the code inside the Main function is included):

```
using System;
using System.Text.RegularExpressions;

class chapter8
{
    static void Main()
    {
      Regex reg = new Regex("the");
      string str1 = "the quick brown fox jumped over
                    the lazy dog";
      MatchCollection matchSet;
      matchSet = reg.Matches(str1);
      if (matchSet.Count > 0)
          foreach (Match aMatch in matchSet)
          Console.WriteLine("found a match at: " +
                            aMatch.Index);
      Console.Read();
    }
}
```

Next, we examine how to use the Replace method to replace one string with another string. The Replace method can be called as a class method with three arguments: a target string, a substring to replace, and the substring to use as the replacement. Here's a code fragment that uses the Replace method:

```
string s = "the quick brown fox jumped over the brown
            dog";
s = Regex.Replace(s, "brown", "black");
```

The string now reads, "the quick black fox jumped over the black dog".

There are many more uses of the RegEx and supporting classes for pattern matching and text processing. We will examine them as we delve deeper into how to form and use more complex regular expressions.

QUANTIFIERS

When writing regular expressions, we often want to add quantity data to a regular expression, such as "match exactly twice" or "match one or more times". We can add this data to our regular expressions using quantifiers.

The first quantifier we'll look at is the plus sign (+). This quantifier indicates that the regular expression should match one or more of the immediately preceding character. The following program demonstrates how to use this quantifier:

```
using System;
using System.Text.RegularExpressions;

class chapter8 {
  static void Main() {
    string[] words = new string[] {"bad", "boy", "baaad",
                                   "bear", "bend"};
    foreach (string word in words)
      if (Regex.IsMatch(word, "ba+"))
        Console.WriteLine(word);
  }
}
```

The words matched are "bad" and "baaad". The regular expression specifies that a match is generated for each string that starts with the letter "b" and includes one or more of the letter "a" in the string.

A less restrictive quantifier is the asterisk (*). This quantifier indicates that the regular expression should match zero or more of the immediately preceding character. This quantifier is very hard to use in practice because the asterisk usually ends up matching almost everything. For example, using the preceding code, if we change the regular expression to read "ba*", every word in array is matched.

The question mark (?) is a quantifier that matches exactly zero or one time. If we change the regular expression in the preceding code to "ba?d", the only word that matches is "bad".

A more definite number of matches can be specified by placing a number inside a set of curly braces, as in {n}, where n is the number of matches to find. The following program demonstrates how this quantifier works:

```
using System;
using System.Text.RegularExpressions;

class chapter8 {
  static void Main() {
    string[] words = new string[] {"bad", "boy", "baad",
                                   "baaad", "bear", "bend"};
    foreach (string word in words)
      if (Regex.IsMatch(word, "ba{2}d"))
        Console.WriteLine(word);
  }
}
```

This regular expression matches only the string "baad".

You can specify a minimum and a maximum number of matches by providing two digits inside the curly braces: {n,m}, where n is the minimum number of matches and m is the maximum. The following regular expression will match "bad", "baad", and "baaad" in the string above:

```
"ba{1,3}d"
```

We could have also matched the same number of strings here by writing "ba{1,}d", which specifies at least one match, but without specifying a maximum number.

The quantifiers we've discussed so far exhibit what is called *greedy* behavior. They try to make as many matches as possible, and this behavior often leads to matches that you didn't really mean to make. Here's an example:

```
using System;
using System.Text.RegularExpressions;

class chapter8 {
  static void Main() {
    string[] words = new string[]{"Part", "of", "this",
                  "<b>string</b>", "is", "bold"};
    string regExp = "<.*>";
    MatchCollection aMatch;
    foreach (string word in words) {
```

```
        if (Regex.IsMatch(word, regExp)) {
            aMatch = Regex.Matches(word, regExp);
            for(int i = 0; i < aMatch.Count; i++)
                Console.WriteLine(aMatch[i].Value);
        }
      }
    }
}
```

We expect this program to return just the two tags: and. Instead, because of greediness, the regular expression matches string. We can solve this problem using the lazy quantifier: the question mark (?), which is also a quantifier. When the question mark is placed directly after a quantifier, it makes the quantifier lazy. Being lazy means the regular expression the lazy quantifier is used in will try to make as few matches as possible, instead of as many as possible.

Changing the regular expression to read "< .+ >" doesn't help either. We need to use the lazy quantifier, and once we do, "< .+? >", we get the right matches: and. The lazy quantifier can be used with all the quantifiers, including the quantifiers enclosed in curly braces.

USING CHARACTER CLASSES

In this and the following sections, we examine how to use the major elements that make up regular expressions. We start with character classes, which allow us to specify a pattern based on a series of characters.

The first character class we discuss is the period (.). This is a very easy character class to use but it is also very problematic. The period matches any character in a string. Here's an example:

```
using System;
using System.Text.RegularExpressions;

class chapter8 {
  static void Main() {
    string str1 = "the quick brown fox jumped over the
                   lazy dog";
    MatchCollection matchSet;
    matchSet = Regex.Matches(str1, ".");
```

```
    foreach (Match aMatch in matchSet)
      Console.WriteLine("matches at: " + aMatch.Index);
  }
}
```

The output from this program illustrates how the period works:

The period matches every single character in the string.

A better way to use the period is to use it to define a range of characters within a string that are bound by a beginning and/or an ending character. Here's one example, using the same string:

```
using System;
using System.Text.RegularExpressions;

class chapter8 {
  static void Main() {
    string str1 = "the quick brown fox jumped over the
                    lazy dog one time";
    MatchCollection matchSet;
    matchSet = Regex.Matches(str1, "t.e");
    foreach (Match aMatch in matchSet)
      Console.WriteLine("Matches at: " + aMatch.Index);
  }
}
```

The output from this program is:

```
matches: the at: 0
matches: the at: 32
```

When using regular expressions, we often want to check for patterns that include groups of characters. We can write a regular expression that consists of such a group by enclosing the group in brackets ([]). The characters inside the brackets are called a *character class*. If we wanted to write a regular expression that matched any lowercase alphabetic character, we would write the expression like this: [abcdefghijklmnopqrstuvwxyz]. But that's fairly hard to write, so we can write a shorter version by indicating a range of letters using a hyphen: [a-z].

Here's how we can use this regular expression to match a pattern:

```
using System;
using System.Text.RegularExpressions;

class chapter8 {
  static void Main() {
    string str1 = "THE quick BROWN fox JUMPED over THE
                  lazy DOG";
    MatchCollection matchSet;
    matchSet = Regex.Matches(str1, "[a-z]");
    foreach (Match aMatch in matchSet)
      Console.WriteLine("Matches at: " + aMatch.Index);
  }
}
```

The letters matched are those that make up the words "quick", "fox", "over", and "lazy".

Character classes can be formed using more than one group. If we want to match both lowercase letters and uppercase letters, we can write this regular expression: "[A-Za-z]". You can also write a character class consisting of digits, like this: [0–9], if you want to include all ten digits.

We can create the reverse, or negation, of a character class by placing a caret (^) before the character class. For example, if we have the character class [aeiou] representing the class of vowels, we can write [^aeiou] to represent the consonants, or nonvowels.

If we combine these three character classes, we form what is called a *word* in regular expression parlance. The regular expression looks like this: [A-Za-z0–9]. There is also a shorter character class we can use to express this same class: \w. The negation of \w, or the regular expression to express a nonword character (such as a mark of punctuation) is expressed by \W.

The character class for digits ([0–9]) can also be written as \d (note that because a backslash followed by another character can be an escape sequence in C#, codes such as \d are written \\d in C# code to indicate a regular expression and not an escape code) the first backslash), and the character class for nondigits ([^0–9]) can be written as \D. Finally, because a white space plays such an important role in text processing, \s is used to represent white space characters whereas \S represents non-white-space characters. We will examine using the white space character classes later when we examine the grouping constructs.

MODIFYING REGULAR EXPRESSIONS USING ASSERTIONS

C# includes a set of operators you can add to a regular expression that change the behavior of the expression without causing the regular expression engine to advance through the string. These operators are called *assertions*.

The first assertion we'll examine causes a regular expression to find matches only at the beginning of a string or a line. This assertion is made using the caret symbol (^). In the following program, the regular expression matches strings that have the letter "h" only as the first character in the string. An "h" in other places is ignored. Here's the code:

```
using System;
using System.Text.RegularExpressions;

class chapter8 {
  static void Main() {
    string[] words = new string[]{"heal", "heel",
                                  "noah", "techno"};
    string regExp = "^h";
    Match aMatch;
    foreach (string word in words)
      if (Regex.IsMatch(word, regExp)) {
        aMatch = Regex.Match(word, regExp);
```

```
        Console.WriteLine("Matched: " + word + " at
                       position: " + aMatch.Index);
    }
  }
}
```

The output of this code shows that just the strings "heal" and "heel" match.

There is also an assertion that causes a regular expression to find matches only at the end of the line. This assertion is the dollar sign ($). If we modify the previous regular expression as:

```
string regExp = "h$";
```

"noah" is the only match found.

Another assertion you can make in a regular expression is to specify that all matches can occur only at word boundaries. This means that a match can only occur at the beginning or end of a word that is separated by spaces. This assertion is made with \b. Here's how the assertion works:

```
string words = "hark, what doth thou say, Harold? ";
string regExp = "\\bh";
```

This regular expression matches the words "hark" and "Harold" in the string.

There are other assertions you can use in regular expressions, but these are three of the most commonly used.

USING GROUPING CONSTRUCTS

The RegEx class has a set of grouping constructs you can use to put successful matches into groups, which make it easier to parse a string into related matches. For example, you are given a string of birthday dates and ages and you want to identify just the dates. By grouping the dates together, you can identify them as a group and not just as individual matches.

Anonymous Groups

There are several different grouping constructs you can use. The first construct is formed by surrounding the regular expression in parentheses. You can think of this as an anonymous group, since groups can also be named, as we'll see shortly. As an example, look at the following string:

```
"08/14/57 46 02/25/29 45 06/05/85 18 03/12/88 16
 09/09/90 13"
```

This string is a combination of birthdates and ages. If we want to match just the ages, not the birthdates, we can write the regular expression as an anonymous group:

```
(\\s\\d{2}\\s)
```

By writing the regular expression this way, each match in the string is identified by a number, starting at one. Number zero is reserved for the entire match, which will usually include much more data. Here is a little program that uses an anonymous group:

```
using System;
using System.Text.RegularExpressions;

class chapter8 {
  static void Main() {
    string words = "08/14/57 46 02/25/59 45 06/05/85 18" +
                   "03/12/88 16 09/09/90 13";
    string regExp1 = "(\\s\\d{2}\\s)";
    MatchCollection matchSet = Regex.Matches(words,
                                             regExp1);
    foreach (Match aMatch in matchSet)
      Console.WriteLine(aMatch.Groups[0].Captures[0]);
  }
}
```

Named Groups

Groups are more commonly built using names. A named group is easier to work with because we can refer to the group by name when retrieving matches. A named group is formed by prefixing the regular expression with a question mark and a name enclosed in angle brackets. For example, to name the group in the previous program code "ages", we write the regular expression like this:

```
(?<ages>\\s\\d{2}\\s)
```

The name can also be surrounded by single quotes instead of angle brackets.

Now let's modify this program to search for dates instead of ages, and use a grouping construct to organize the dates. Here's the code:

```
using System;
using System.Text.RegularExpressions;

class chapter8 {
  static void Main() {
    string words = "08/14/57 46 02/25/59 45 06/05/85 18 " +
                   "03/12/88 16 09/09/90 13";
    string regExp1 = "(?<dates>(\\d{2}/\\d{2}/\\d{2}))\\s";
    MatchCollection matchSet = Regex.Matches(words,
                                             regExp1);
    foreach (Match aMatch in matchSet)
      Console.WriteLine("Date: {0}", _
                        aMatch.Groups["dates"]);
  }
}
```

Here's the output:

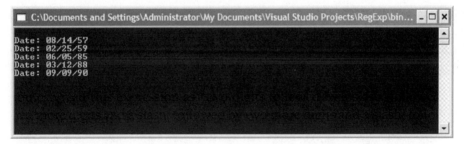

Let's focus on the regular expression used to generate the output:

```
(\\d{2}/\\d{2}/\\d{2}))\\s
```

You can read this expression as "two digits followed by a slash, followed by two more digits and a slash, followed by two more digits and a slash, followed by a space." To make the regular expression a group, we make the following additions:

```
(?<dates>(\\d{2}/\\d{2}/\\d{2}))\\s
```

For each match found in the string, we pull out the group by using the Groups method of the Match class:

```
Console.WriteLine("Date: {0}", aMatch.Groups("dates"));
```

Zero-Width Lookahead and Lookbehind Assertions

Assertions can also be made that determine how far into a match a regular expression will look for matches, going either forward or backward. These assertions can be either positive or negative, meaning that the regular expression is looking for either a particular pattern to match (positive) or a particular pattern not to match (negative). This will be clearer when we see some examples.

The first of these assertions we examine is the positive lookahead assertion. This assertion is stated like this:

```
(?= reg-exp-char)
```

where *reg-exp-char* is a regular expression character or metacharacter. This assertion states that a match is continued only if the current subexpression being checked matches at the specified position on the right. Here's a code fragment that demonstrates how this assertion works:

```
string words = "lions lion tigers tiger bears,bear";
string regExp1 = "\\w+(?=\\s)";
```

The regular expression indicates that a match is made on each word that is followed by a space. The words that match are "lions", "lion", "tigers", and "tiger". The regular expression matches the words but does not match the space. That is very important to remember.

The next assertion is the negative lookahead assertion. This assertion continues a match only if the current subexpression being checked does not match at the specified position on the right. Here's an example code fragment:

```
string words = "subroutine routine subprocedure
                procedure";
string regExp1 = "\\b(?!sub)\\w+\\b";
```

This regular expression indicates that a match is made on each word that does not begin with the prefix "sub". The words that match are "routine" and "procedure".

The next assertions are called lookbehind assertions. These assertions look for positive or negative matches to the left instead of to the right. The following code fragment demonstrates how to write a positive lookbehind assertion:

```
string words = "subroutines routine subprocedures
                procedure";
string regExp1 = "\\b\\w+(?<=s)\\b";
```

This regular expression looks for word boundaries that occur after an "s". The words that match are "subroutines" and "subprocedures".

A negative lookbehind assertion continues a match only if the subexpression does not match at the position on the left. We can easily modify the above-mentioned regular expression just to match only words that don't end with the letter "s" like this:

```
string regExp1 = "\\b\\w+(?<!s)\\b";
```

THE CAPTURESCOLLECTION CLASS

When a regular expression matches a subexpression, an object called a Capture is created and is added to a collection called a CapturesCollection. When you use a named group in a regular expression, that group has its own collection of captures.

To retrieve the captures collected from a regular expression that uses a named group, you call the Captures property from a Match objects Groups property. This is easier to see in an example. Using one of the regular expressions from the previous section, the following code returns all the dates and ages found in a string, properly grouped:

```
using System;
using System.Text.RegularExpressions;

class chapter8 {
  static void Main() {
    string dates = "08/14/57 46 02/25/59 45 06/05/85 18 " +
                   "03/12/88 16 09/09/90 13";
    string regExp =
        "(?<dates>(\\d{2}/\\d{2}/\\d{2}))\\s(?<ages>
               (\\d{2}))\\s";
    MatchCollection matchSet;
    matchSet = Regex.Matches(dates, regExp);
    Console.WriteLine();
    foreach (Match aMatch in matchSet) {
      foreach (Capture aCapture in aMatch.Groups
               ["dates"].Captures)
        Console.WriteLine("date capture: " +
                          aCapture.ToString());
        foreach (Capture aCapture in_
                 aMatch.Groups["ages"].Captures)
        Console.WriteLine("age capture: " +
                          aCapture.ToString());
    }
  }
}
```

The output from this program is:

The outer loop moves through each match, whereas the two inner loops move through the different Capture collections, one for the dates and one for the ages. Using the CapturesCollection in this way ensures that each group match is captured and not just the last match.

REGULAR EXPRESSION OPTIONS

There are several options you can set when specifying a regular expression. These options range from specifying the multiline mode so that a regular expression will work properly on more than one line of text to compiling a regular expression so that it will execute faster. The following table lists the different options you can set.

Before we view the table, we need to mention how these options are set. Generally, you can set an option by specifying the options constant value as the third argument to one of the RegEx class's methods, such as Match as Matches. For example, if we want to set the Multiline option for a regular expression, the line of code looks like this:

```
matchSet = Regex.Matches(dates, regexp,_
                    RegexOptions.Multiline);
```

This option, along with the other options, can either be typed in directly or be selected with Intellisense.

Here are the options available:

RegexOption member	Inline character	Description
None	N/A	Specifies that no options are set.
IgnoreCase	I	Specifies case-insensitive matching.
Multiline	M	Specifies multi-line mode.
ExplicitCapture	N	Specifies that the only valid captures are explicitly named or numbered groups.
Compiled	N/A	Specifies that the regular expression will be compiled to assembly.
Singleline	S	Specifies single-line mode.
IgnorePatternWhiteSpace	X	Specifies that unescaped white space is excluded from the pattern and enables comments following a pound sign (#)
RightToLeft	N/A	Specifies that the search is from right to left instead of from left to right.
ECMAScript	N/A	Specifies that ECMAScript-compliant behavior is enabled for the expression.

SUMMARY

Regular expressions present powerful options for performing text processing and pattern matching. Regular expressions can run the gamut from ridiculously simple ("a") to complex combinations that look more like line noise than executable code. Nonetheless, learning to use regular expressions will allow you to perform text processing on texts you would not even consider using tools such as the methods of the String class.

This chapter is only able to hint at the power of regular expressions. To learn more about regular expressions, consult Friedel (1997).

EXERCISES

1. Write regular expressions to match the following:
   - a string consists of an "x", followed by any three characters, and then a "y"
   - a word ending in "ed"
   - a phone number
   - an HTML anchor tag
2. Write a regular expression that finds all the words in a string that contain double letters, such as "deep" and "book".
3. Write a regular expression that finds all the header tags (<h1>, <h2>, etc.) in a Web page.
4. Write a function, using a regular expression that performs a simple search and replace in a string.

CHAPTER 9

Building Dictionaries:
The DictionaryBase Class
and the SortedList Class

A *dictionary* is a data structure that stores data as a *key–value* pair. The DictionaryBase class is used as an abstract class to implement different data structures that all store data as key–value pairs. These data structures can be hash tables, linked lists, or some other data structure type. In this chapter, we examine how to create basic dictionaries and how to use the inherited methods of the DictionaryBase class. We will use these techniques later when we explore more specialized data structures.

One example of a dictionary-based data structure is the SortedList. This class stores key–value pairs in sorted order based on the key. It is an interesting data structure because you can also access the values stored in the structure by referring to the value's index position in the data structure, which makes the structure behave somewhat like an array. We examine the behavior of the SortedList class at the end of the chapter.

THE DICTIONARYBASE CLASS

You can think of a dictionary data structure as a computerized word dictionary. The word you are looking up is the key, and the definition of the word is the value. The DictionaryBase class is an abstract (MustInherit) class that is used as a basis for specialized dictionary implementations.

The key–value pairs stored in a dictionary are actually stored as DictionaryEntry objects. The DictionaryEntry structure provides two fields, one for the key and one for the value. The only two properties (or methods) we're interested in with this structure are the Key and Value properties. These methods return the values stored when a key–value pair is entered into a dictionary. We explore DictionaryEntry objects later in the chapter.

Internally, key–value pairs are stored in a hash table object called InnerHashTable. We discuss hash tables in more detail in Chapter 12, so for now just view it as an efficient data structure for storing key–value pairs.

The DictionaryBase class actually implements an interface from the System.Collections namespace, IDictionary. This interface is actually the basis for many of the classes we'll study later in this book, including the ListDictionary class and the Hashtable class.

Fundamental DictionaryBase Class Methods and Properties

When working with a dictionary object, there are several operations you want to perform. At a minimum, you need an Add method to add new data, an Item method to retrieve a value, a Remove method to remove a key–value pair, and a Clear method to clear the data structure of all data.

Let's begin the discussion of implementing a dictionary by looking at a simple example class. The following code shows the implementation of a class that stores names and IP addresses:

```
public class IPAddresses : DictionaryBase {

  public IPAddresses() {

  }

  public void Add(string name, string ip) {
    base.InnerHashtable.Add(name, ip);
```

```
  }
  public string Item(string name) {
    return base.InnerHashtable[name].ToString();

  }

  public void Remove(string name) {
    base.InnerHashtable.Remove(name);
  }
}
```

As you can see, these methods were very easy to build. The first method implemented is the constructor. This is a simple method that does nothing but call the default constructor for the base class. The Add method takes a name/IP address pair as arguments and passes them to the Add method of the InnerHashTable object, which is instantiated in the base class.

The Item method is used to retrieve a value given a specific key. The key is passed to the corresponding Item method of the InnerHashTable object. The value that is stored with the associated key in the inner hash table is returned.

Finally, the Remove method receives a key as an argument and passes the argument to the associated Remove method of the inner hash table. The method then removes both the key and its associated value from the hash table.

There are two methods we can use without implementing them: Count and Clear. The Count method returns the number of DictionaryEntry objects stored in the inner hash table, whereas Clear removes all the DictionaryEntry objects from the inner hash table.

Let's look at a program that utilizes these methods:

```
class chapter9 {
  static void Main() {
    IPAddresses myIPs = new IPAddresses();
    myIPs.Add("Mike", "192.155.12.1");
    myIPs.Add("David", "192.155.12.2");
    myIPs.Add("Bernica", "192.155.12.3");
    Console.WriteLine("There are " + myIPs.Count +
                      " IP addresses");
    Console.WriteLine("David's ip address: " +
                      myIPs.Item("David"));
    myIPs.Clear();
```

```
Console.WriteLine("There are " + myIPs.Count +
                " IP addresses");

    }
}
```

The output from this program is:

```
C:\Documents and Settings\Administrator\My Documents\Visual Studio Projects\DictBase\bi...

There are 3 IP addresses
David's IP address: 192.155.12.2
There are 0 IP addresses
```

One modification we might want to make to the class is to overload the constructor so that we can load data into a dictionary from a file. Here's the code for the new constructor, which you can just add into the IPAddresses class definition:

```
public IPAddresses(string txtFile) {
    string line;
    string[] words;
    StreamReader inFile;
    inFile = File.OpenText(txtFile);
    while(inFile.Peek() != -1) {
        line = inFile.ReadLine();
        words = line.Split(',');
        this.InnerHashtable.Add(words[0], words[1]);
    }
    inFile.Close();
}
```

Now here's a new program to test the constructor:

```
class chapter9 {
    static void Main() {
        for(int i = 0; i < 4; i++)
            Console.WriteLine();
```

```
    IPAddresses myIPs = _
      new IPAddresses("c:\\data\\ips.txt");
    Console.WriteLine("There are {0} IP addresses",
                      myIPs.Count);
    Console.WriteLine("David's IP address: " +
                      myIPs.Item("David"));
    Console.WriteLine("Bernica's IP address: " +
                      myIPs.Item("Bernica"));
    Console.WriteLine("Mike's IP address: " +
                      myIPs.Item("Mike"));
  }

}
```

The output from this program is:

Other DictionaryBase Methods

There are two other methods that are members of the DictionaryBase class: CopyTo and GetEnumerator. We discuss these methods in this section.

The CopyTo method copies the contents of a dictionary to a one-dimensional array. The array should be declared as a DictionaryEntry array, though you can declare it as Object and then use the CType function to convert the objects to DictionaryEntry.

The following code fragment demonstrates how to use the CopyTo method:

```
IPAddresses myIPs = new IPAddresses("c:\ips.txt");
DictionaryEntry[] ips = _
  new DictionaryEntry[myIPs.Count-1];
myIPs.CopyTo(ips, 0);
```

The formula used to size the array takes the number of elements in the dictionary and then subtracts one to account for a zero-based array. The CopyTo method takes two arguments: the array to copy to and the index position to start copying from. If you want to place the contents of a dictionary at the end of an existing array, for example, you would specify the upper bound of the array plus one as the second argument.

Once we get the data from the dictionary into an array, we want to work with the contents of the array, or at least display the values. Here's some code to do that:

```
for(int i = 0; i <= ips.GetUpperBound(0); i++)
  Console.WriteLine(ips[i]);
```

The output from this code is:

Unfortunately, this is not what we want. The problem is that we're storing the data in the array as DictionaryEntry objects, and that's exactly what we see. If we use the ToString method:

```
Console.WriteLine(ips[ndex]ToString())
```

we get the same thing. In order to actually view the data in a DictionaryEntry object, we have to use either the Key property or the Value property, depending on if the object we're querying holds key data or value data. So how do we know which is which? When the contents of the dictionary are copied to the array, the data is copied in key–value order. So the first object is a key, the second object is a value, the third object is a key, and so on.

Now we can write a code fragment that allows us to actually see the data:

```
for(int i = 0; i <= ips.GetUpperBound(0); i++) {
  Console.WriteLine(ips[index].Key);
  Console.WriteLine(ips[index].Value);
}
```

The output is:

THE GENERIC KEYVALUEPAIR CLASS

C# provides a small class that allows you to create dictionary-like objects that store data based on a key. This class is called the KeyValuePair class. Each object can only hold one key and one value, so its use is limited.

A KeyValuePair object is instantiated like this:

```
KeyValuePair<string, int> mcmillan =
  new KeyValuePair<string, int>("McMillan", 99);
```

The key and the value are retrieved individually:

```
Console.Write(mcmillan.Key);
Console.Write(" " + mcmillan.Value);
```

The KeyValuePair class is better used if you put the objects in an array. The following program demonstrates how a simple grade book might be implemented:

```
using System;
using System.Collections.Generic;
using System.Text;

namespace Generics
{
  class Program
  {
    static void Main(string[] args)
```

```
    {
      KeyValuePair<string, int>[] gradeBook = new
        KeyValuePair<string, int>[10];
      gradeBook[0] = new KeyValuePair<string,
        int>("McMillan", 99);
      gradeBook[1] = new KeyValuePair<string,
        int>("Ruff", 64);
  for (int i = 0; i <= gradeBook.GetUpperBound(0); i++)
      if (gradeBook[i].Value != 0)
        Console.WriteLine(gradeBook[i].Key + ": " +
          gradeBook[i].Value);
      Console.Read();
    }
  }
}
```

THE SORTEDLIST CLASS

As we mentioned in the Introduction section of this chapter, a SortedList is a
data structure that stores key–value pairs in sorted order based on the key. We
can use this data structure when it is important for the keys to be sorted, such
as in a standard word dictionary, where we expect the words in the dictionary
to be sorted alphabetically. Later in the chapter, we'll also see how the class
can be used to store a list of single, sorted values.

Using the SortedList Class

We can use the SortedList class in much the same way we used the classes
in the previous sections, since the SortedList class is a specialization of the
DictionaryBase class.

To demonstrate this, the following code creates a SortedList object that
contains three names and IP addresses:

```
SortedList myips = New SortedList();
myips.Add("Mike", "192.155.12.1");
myips.Add("David", "192.155.12.2");
myips.Add("Bernica", "192.155.12.3");
```

The name is the key and the IP address is the stored value.

The generic version of the SortedList class allows you to decide the data type of both the key and the value:

```
SortedList<Tkey, TValue>
```

For this example, we could instantiate myips like this:

```
SortedList<string, string> myips =
  new SortedList<string, string>();
```

A grade book sorted list might be instantiated as follows:

```
SortedList<string, int> gradeBook =
  new SortedList<string, int>();
```

We can retrieve the values by using the Item method with a key as the argument:

```
Foreach(Object key In myips.Keys)
  Console.WriteLine("Name: " & key + "\n" +
                    "IP: " & myips.Item(key))
```

This fragment produces the following output:

```
C:\Documents and Settings\Administrator\My Documents\Visual Studio Projects\slist\bin\sli...
Name: Bernica    IP: 192.155.12.3
Name: David      IP: 192.155.12.2
Name: Mike       IP: 192.155.12.1
```

Alternatively, we can also access this list by referencing the index numbers where these values (and keys) are stored internally in the arrays, which actually store the data. Here's how:

```
for(int i = 0; i < myips.Count; i++)
  Console.WriteLine("Name: " + myips.GetKey(i) + "\n" +
                    "IP: " & myips.GetByIndex(i));
```

This code fragment produces the exact same sorted list of names and IP addresses:

```
C:\Documents and Settings\Administrator\My Documents\Visual Studio Projects\slist\bin\sli...
Name: Bernica    IP: 192.155.12.3
Name: David      IP: 192.155.12.2
Name: Mike       IP: 192.155.12.1

Name: Bernica    IP: 192.155.12.3
Name: David      IP: 192.155.12.2
Name: Mike       IP: 192.155.12.1
```

A key–value pair can be removed from a SortedList by either specifying a key or specifying an index number, as in the following code fragment, which demonstrates both removal methods:

```
myips.Remove("David");
myips.RemoveAt(1);
```

If you want to use index-based access into a SortedList but don't know the indexes where a particular key or value is stored, you can use the following methods to determine those values:

```
int indexDavid = myips.GetIndexOfKey("David");
int indexIPDavid = _
   myips.GetIndexOfValue(myips.Item("David"));
```

The SortedList class contains many other methods and you are encouraged to explore them via VS.NET's online documentation.

SUMMARY

The DictionaryBase class is an abstract class used to create custom dictionaries. A dictionary is a data structure that stores data in key–value pairs, using a hash table (or sometimes a singly linked list) as the underlying data structure. The key–value pairs are stored as DictionaryEntry objects and you must use the Key and Value methods to retrieve the actual values in a DictionaryEntry object.

The DictionaryBase class is often used when the programmer wants to create a strongly typed data structure. Normally, data added to a dictionary is stored as Object, but with a custom dictionary, the programmer can cut down on the number of type conversions that must be performed, making the program more efficient and easier to read.

The SortedList class is a particular type of Dictionary class, one that stores the key–value pairs in order sorted by the key. You can also retrieve the values stored in a SortedList by referencing the index number where the value is stored, much like you do with an array. There is also a SortedDictionary class in the System.Collections.Generic namespace that works in the same as the generic SortedList class.

EXERCISES

1. Using the implementation of the IPAddresses class developed in this chapter, write a method that displays the IP addresses stored in the class in ascending order. Use the method in a program.
2. Write a program that stores names and phone numbers from a text file in a dictionary, with the name being the key. Write a method that does a reverse lookup, that is, finds a name given a phone number. Write a Windows application to test your implementation.
3. Using a dictionary, write a program that displays the number of occurrences of a word in a sentence. Display a list of all the words and the number of times they occur in the sentence.
4. Rewrite Exercise 3 to work with letters rather than words.
5. Rewrite Exercise 2 using the SortedList class.
6. The SortedList class is implemented using two internal arrays, one that stores the keys and one that stores the values. Create your own SortedList class implementation using this scheme. Your class should include all the methods discussed in this chapter. Use your class to solve the problem posed in Exercise 2.

CHAPTER 10

Hashing and the Hashtable Class

*H*ashing is a very common technique for storing data in such a way the data can be inserted and retrieved very quickly. Hashing uses a data structure called a *hash table*. Although hash tables provide fast insertion, deletion, and retrieval, operations that involve searching, such as finding the minimum or maximum value, are not performed very quickly. For these types of operations, other data structures are preferred (see, for example, Chapter 12 on binary search trees).

The .NET Framework library provides a very useful class for working with hash tables, the Hashtable class. We will examine this class in the chapter, but we will also discuss how to implement a custom hash table. Building hash tables is not very difficult and the programming techniques used are well worth knowing.

AN OVERVIEW OF HASHING

A hash table data structure is designed around an array. The array consists of elements 0 through some predetermined size, though we can increase the size later if necessary. Each data item is stored in the array based on some piece of the data, called the *key*. To store an element in the hash table, the key is mapped into a number in the range of 0 to the hash table size using a function called a *hash function*.

The ideal goal of the hash function is to store each key in its own cell in the array. However, because there are an unlimited number of possible keys and a finite number of array cells, a more realistic goal of the hash function is to attempt to distribute the keys as evenly as possible among the cells of the array.

Even with a good hash function, as you have probably guessed by now, it is possible for two keys to hash to the same value. This is called a *collision* and we have to have a strategy for dealing with collisions when they occur. We'll discuss this in detail in the following.

The last thing we have to determine is how large to dimension the array used as the hash table. First, it is recommended that the array size be a prime number. We will explain why when we examine the different hash functions. After that, there are several different strategies for determining the proper array size, all of them based on the technique used to deal with collisions, so we'll examine this issue in the following discussion also.

CHOOSING A HASH FUNCTION

Choosing a hash function depends on the data type of the key you are using. If your key is an integer, the simplest function is to return the key modulo the size of the array. There are circumstances when this method is not recommended, such as when the keys all end in zero and the array size is 10. This is one reason why the array size should always be prime. Also, if the keys are random integers then the hash function should more evenly distribute the keys.

In many applications, however, the keys are strings. Choosing a hash function to work with keys is more difficult and should be chosen carefully. A simple function that at first glance seems to work well is to add the ASCII values of the letters in the key. The hash value is that value modulo the array size. The following program demonstrates how this function works:

```
using System;

class chapter10 {
  static void Main() {
    string[] names = new string[99];
    string name;
```

```csharp
        string[] someNames = new string[]{"David",
          "Jennifer", "Donnie", "Mayo", "Raymond",
          "Bernica", "Mike", "Clayton", "Beata", "Michael"};
        int hashVal;
        for(int i = 0; i < 10; i++) {
          name = someNames[i];
          hashVal = SimpleHash(name, names);
          names[hashVal] = name;
        }
        ShowDistrib(names);
      }

      static int SimpleHash(string s, string[] arr) {
        int tot = 0;
        char[] cname;
        cname = s.ToCharArray();
        for(int i = 0; i <= cname.GetUpperBound(0); i++)
          tot += (int)cname[i];
        return tot % arr.GetUpperBound(0);
      }

      static void ShowDistrib(string[] arr) {
        for(int i = 0; i <= arr.GetUpperBound(0); i++)
          if (arr[i] != null)
            Console.WriteLine(i + " " + arr[i]);
      }
    }
```

The output from this program is:

The showDistrib subroutine shows us where the names are actually placed into the array by the hash function. As you can see, the distribution is not particularly even. The names are bunched at the beginning of the array and at the end.

There is an even bigger problem lurking here, though. Not all of the names are displayed. Interestingly, if we change the size of the array to a prime number, even a prime lower than 99, all the names are stored properly. Hence, one important rule when choosing the size of your array for a hash table (and when using a hash function such as the one we're using here) is to choose a number that is prime.

The size you ultimately choose will depend on your determination of the number of records stored in the hash table, but a safe number seems to be 10,007 (given that you're not actually trying to store that many items in your table). The number 10,007 is prime and it is not so large that enough memory is used to degrade the performance of your program.

Sticking with the basic idea of using the computed total ASCII value of the key in the creation of the hash value, this next algorithm provides for a better distribution in the array. First, let's look at the code, followed by an explanation:

```
static int BetterHash(string s, string[] arr) {
    long tot = 0;
    char[] cname;
    cname = s.ToCharArray();
    for(int i = 0; i <= cname.GetUpperBound(0); i++)
      tot += 37 * tot + (int)cname[i];
    tot = tot % arr.GetUpperBound(0);
    if (tot < 0)
      tot += arr.GetUpperBound(0);
    return (int)tot;
    }
```

This function uses Horner's rule to computer the polynomial function (of 37). See (Weiss 1999) for more information on this hash function.

Now let's look at the distribution of the keys in the hash table using this new function:

```
■ C:\Documents and Settings\Administrator\My Documents\Visual Studio Projects\Hash\bin\H...  _ □ ×
3288 David
3646 Bernica
5181 Donnie
5381 Beata
5750 Jennifer
6869 Mayo
7872 Mike
7913 Raymond
9043 Clayton
9230 Michael
```

These keys are more evenly distributed though it's hard to tell with such a small data set.

Searching for Data in a Hash Table

To search for data in a hash table, we need to compute the hash value of the key and then access that element in the array. It is that simple. Here's the function:

```
static bool InHash(string s, string[] arr) {
  int hval = BetterHash(s, arr);
  if (arr[hval] == s)
    return true;
  else
    return false;
}
```

This function returns True if the item is in the hash table and False otherwise. We don't even need to compare the time this function runs versus a sequential search of the array since this function clearly runs in less time, unless of course the data item is somewhere close to the beginning of the array.

Handling Collisions

When working with hash tables, it is inevitable that you will encounter situations where the hash value of a key works out to a value that is already storing another key. This is called a collision and there are several techniques you can use when a collision occurs. These techniques include bucket hashing, open addressing, and double hashing (among others). In this section, we will briefly cover each of these techniques.

Bucket Hashing

When we originally defined a hash table, we stated that it is preferred that only one data value resides in a hash table element. This works great if there are no collisions, but if a hash function returns the same value for two data items, we have a problem.

One solution to the collision problem is to implement the hash table using *buckets*. A bucket is a simple data structure stored in a hash table element that can store multiple items. In most implementations, this data structure is an array, but in our implementation we'll make use of an arraylist, which will allow us not to worry about running out of space and to allocate more space. In the end, this will make our implementation more efficient.

To insert an item, we first use the hash function to determine which arraylist to store the item. Then we check to see if the item is already in the arraylist. If it is we do nothing, if it's not, then we call the Add method to insert the item into the arraylist.

To remove an item from a hash table, we again first determine the hash value of the item to be removed and go to that arraylist. We then check to make sure the item is in the arraylist, and if it is, we remove it.

Here's the code for a BucketHash class that includes a Hash function, an Add method, and a Remove method:

```
public class BucketHash {

  private const int SIZE = 101;
  ArrayList[] data;

  public BucketHash() {
    data = new ArrayList[SIZE];
    for(int i = 0; i <= SIZE-1; i++)
      data[i] = new ArrayList(4);
  }

  public int Hash(string s) {
  long tot = 0;
```

```
      char[] charray;
      charray = s.ToCharArray();
      for(int i = 0; i <= s.Length-1; i++)
        tot += 37 * tot + (int)charray[i];
      tot = tot % data.GetUpperBound(0);
      if (tot < 0)
        tot += data.GetUpperBound(0);
      return (int)tot;
    }

    public void Insert(string item) {
      int hash_value;
      hash_value = Hash(value);
      if (data[hash_value].Contains(item))
        data[hash_value].Add(item);
    }

    public void Remove(string item) {
      int hash_value;
      hash_value = Hash(item);
      if (data[hash_value].Contains(item))
          data[hash_value].Remove(item);
    }
}
```

When using bucket hashing, the most important thing you can do is keep the number of arraylist elements used as low as possible. This minimizes the extra work that has to be done when adding items to or removing items from the hash table. In the preceding code, we minimize the size of the arraylist by setting the initial capacity of each arraylist to 1 in the constructor call. Once we have a collision, the arraylist capacity becomes 2, and then the capacity continues to double every time the arraylist fills up. With a good hash function, though, the arraylist shouldn't get too large.

The ratio of the number of elements in the hash table to the table size is called the *load factor*. Studies have shown that hash table performance is best when the load factor is 1.0, or when the table size exactly equals the number of elements.

Open Addressing

Separate chaining decreases the performance of your hash table by using arraylists. An alternative to separate chaining for avoiding collisions is *open addressing*. An open addressing function looks for an empty cell in the hash table array to place an item. If the first cell tried is full, the next empty cell is tried, and so on until an empty cell is eventually found. We will look at two different strategies for open addressing in this section: linear probing and quadratic probing.

Linear probing uses a linear function to determine the array cell to try for an insertion. This means that cells will be tried sequentially until an empty cell is found. The problem with linear probing is that data elements will tend to cluster in adjacent cells in the array, making successive probes for empty cells longer and less efficient.

Quadratic probing eliminates the clustering problem. A quadratic function is used to determine which cell to attempt. An example of such a function is:

```
2 * collNumber - 1
```

where collNumber is the number of collisions that have occurred during the current probe. An interesting property of quadratic probing is that an empty cell is guaranteed to be found if the hash table is less than half empty.

Double Hashing

This simple collision-resolution strategy is exactly what it says it is—if a collision is found, the hash function is applied a second time and then probe at the distance sequence hash(item), 2hash(item), 4hash(item), etc. until an empty cell is found.

To make this probing technique work correctly, a few conditions must be met. First, the hash function chosen must not ever evaluate to zero, which would lead to disastrous results (since multiplying by zero produces zero). Second, the table size must be prime. If the size isn't prime, then all the array cells will not be probed, again leading to chaotic results.

Double hashing is an interesting collision resolution strategy, but it has been shown in practice that quadratic probing usually leads to better performance.

We are now finished examining custom hash table implementations. For most applications using C#, you are better off using the built-in Hashtable class that is part of the .NET Framework library. We begin our discussion of this class in the next section.

THE HASHTABLE CLASS

The Hashtable class is a special type of Dictionary object, storing key–value pairs, where the values are stored based on the hash code derived from the key. You can specify a hash function or use the one built in (we'll discuss it later) for the data type of the key. The Hashtable class is very efficient and should be used in place of custom implementations whenever possible.

The strategy the class uses to avoid collisions is the concept of a bucket. A bucket is a virtual grouping of objects together that have the same hash code, much like we used an ArrayList to handle collisions when we discussed separate chaining. If two keys have the same hash code, they are placed in the same bucket. Otherwise, each key with a unique hash code is placed in its own bucket.

The number of buckets used in a Hashtable objects is called the *load factor*. The load factor is the ratio of the elements to the number of buckets. Initially, the factor is set to 1.0. When the actual factor reaches the initial factor, the load factor is increased to the smallest prime number that is twice the current number of buckets. The load factor is important because the smaller the load factor, the better the performance of the Hashtable object.

Instantiating and Adding Data to a Hashtable Object

The Hashtable class is part of the System.Collections namespace, so you must import System.Collections at the beginning of your program.

A Hashtable object can be instantiated in one of three ways (actually there are several more, including different types of copy constructors, but we stick to the three most common constructors here). You can instantiate the hash table with an initial capacity or by using the default capacity. You can also specify both the initial capacity and the initial load factor. The following code demonstrates how to use these three constructors:

```
Hashtable symbols = new Hashtable();
HashTable symbols = new Hashtable(50);
HashTable symbols = new Hashtable(25, 3.0);
```

The first line creates a hash table with the default capacity and the default load factor. The second line creates a hash table with a capacity of 50 elements and the default load factor. The third line creates a hash table with an initial capacity of 25 elements and a load factor of 3.0.

Key–value pairs are entered into a hash table using the Add method. This method takes two arguments: the key and the value associated with the key. The key is added to the hash table after computing its hash value. Here is some example code:

```
Hashtable symbols = new Hashtable(25);
symbols.Add("salary", 100000);
symbols.Add("name", "David Durr");
symbols.Add("age", 43);
symbols.Add("dept", "Information Technology");
```

You can also add elements to a hash table using an indexer, which we discuss more completely later in this chapter. To do this, you write an assignment statement that assigns a value to the key specified as the index (much like an array index). If the key doesn't already exist, a new hash element is entered into the table; if the key already exists, the existing value is overwritten by the new value. Here are some examples:

```
Symbols["sex"] = "Male";
Symbols["age"] = 44;
```

The first line shows how to create a new key–value pair using the Item method, whereas the second line demonstrates that you can overwrite the current value associated with an existing key.

Retrieving the Keys and the Values Separately From a Hash Table

The Hashtable class has two very useful methods for retrieving the keys and values separately from a hash table: Keys and Values. These methods create an Enumerator object that allows you to use a For Each loop, or some other technique, to examine the keys and the values.

The following program demonstrates how these methods work:

```
using System;
using System.Collections;

class chapter10 {
  static void Main() {
    Hashtable symbols = new Hashtable(25);
    symbols.Add("salary", 100000);
    symbols.Add("name", "David Durr");
    symbols.Add("age", 45);
    symbols.Add("dept", "Information Technology");
    symbols["sex"] = "Male";
    Console.WriteLine("The keys are: ");
    foreach (Object key in symbols.Keys)
      Console.WriteLine(key);
    Console.WriteLine();
    Console.WriteLine("The values are: ");
    foreach (Object value in symbols.Values)
      Console.WriteLine(value);
  }
}
```

Retrieving a Value Based on the Key

Retrieving a value using its associated key can be accomplished using an indexer, which works just like an indexer for an array. A key is passed in as the index value, and the value associated with the key is returned, unless the key doesn't exist, in which a null is returned.

The following short code segment demonstrates how this technique works:

```
Object value = symbols.Item["name"];
Console.WriteLine("The variable name's value is: " +
                  value.ToString());
```

The value returned is "David Durr".

We can use an indexer along with the Keys method to retrieve all the data stored in a hash table:

```
using System;
using System.Collections;
```

```
class chapter10 {
  static void Main() {
    Hashtable symbols = new Hashtable(25);
    symbols.Add("salary", 100000);
    symbols.Add("name", "David Durr");
    symbols.Add("age", 45);
    symbols.Add("dept", "Information Technology");
    symbols["sex"] = "Male";
    Console.WriteLine();
    Console.WriteLine("Hash table dump - ");
    Console.WriteLine();
    foreach (Object key in symbols.Keys)
      Console.WriteLine(key.ToString() + ": " +
                        symbols[key].ToString());
  }
}
```

The output is:

Utility Methods of the Hashtable Class

There are several methods in the Hashtable class that help you be more pro-
ductive with Hashtable objects. In this section, we examine several of them,
including methods for determining the number of elements in a hash table,
clearing the contents of a hash table, determining if a specified key (and value)
is contained in a hash table, removing elements from a hash table, and copying
the elements of a hash table to an array.

The number of elements in a hash table is stored in the Count property, which returns an integer:

```
int numElements;
numElements = symbols.Count;
```

We can immediately remove all the elements of a hash table using the Clear method:

```
symbols.Clear();
```

To remove a single element from a hash table, you can use the Remove method. This method takes a single argument, a key, and the method removes both the specified key and its associated value. Here's an example:

```
symbols.Remove("sex");
foreach(Object key In symbols.Keys)
  Console.WriteLine(key.ToString() + ": " +
                    symbols[key].ToString());
```

Before you remove an element from a hash table, you may want to check to see if either the key or the value is in the table. We can determine this information with the ContainsKey method and the ContainsValue method. The following code fragment demonstrates how to use the ContainsKey method:

```
string aKey;
Console.Write("Enter a key to remove: ");
aKey = Console.ReadLine();
if (symbols.ContainsKey(aKey))
  symbols.Remove(aKey);
```

Using this method ensures that the key–value pair to remove exists in the hash table. The ContainsValue method works similarly with values instead of keys.

A HASHTABLE APPLICATION: COMPUTER TERMS GLOSSARY

One common use of a hash table is to build a glossary, or dictionary, of terms. In this section, we demonstrate one way to use a hash table for just such a use—a computer terms glossary.

The program works by first reading in a set of terms and definitions from a text file. This process is coded in the BuildGlossary subroutine. The structure of the text file is: *word,definition*, with the comma being the delimiter between a word and the definition. Each word in this glossary is a single word, but the glossary could easily work with phrases instead. That's why a comma is used as the delimiter, rather than a space. Also, this structure allows us to use the word as the key, which is the proper way to build this hash table.

Another subroutine, DisplayWords, displays the words in a list box so the user can pick one to get a definition. Since the words are the keys, we can use the Keys method to return just the words from the hash table. The user can then see which words have definitions.

To retrieve a definition, the user simply clicks on a word in the list box. The definition is retrieved using the Item method and is displayed in the text box.

Here's the code:

```
using System;
using System.Drawing;
using System.Collections;
using System.ComponentModel;
using System.Windows.Forms;
using System.IO;

namespace Glossary
{
  public class Form1 : System.Windows.Forms.Form
  {

    private System.Windows.Forms.ListBox lstWords;
    private System.Windows.Forms.TextBox txtDefinition;
    private Hashtable glossary = new Hashtable();
    private System.ComponentModel.Container
      components = null;
    public Form1()
```

```
    {
      InitializeComponent();
    }

  protected override void Dispose( bool disposing )
  {
    if( disposing )
    {
      if (components != null)
      {
        components.Dispose();
      }
    }
    base.Dispose( disposing );
  }

  #region Windows Form Designer generated code
    [STAThread]
    static void Main()
    {
      Application.Run(new Form1());
    }
    private void BuildGlossary(Hashtable g)
    {
      StreamReader inFile;
      string line;
      string[] words;
      inFile = File.OpenText("c:\\words.txt");
      char[] delimiter = new char[]{','};
      while (inFile.Peek() != -1)
      {
        line = inFile.ReadLine();
        words = line.Split(delimiter);
        g.Add(words[0], words[1]);
      }
      inFile.Close();
    }

    private void DisplayWords(Hashtable g)
```

```
    {
      Object[] words = new Object[100];
      g.Keys.CopyTo(words, 0);
      for(int i = 0; i <= words.GetUpperBound(0); i++)
        if (!(words[i] == null))
          lstWords.Items.Add((words[i]));
    }
    private void Form1_Load(object sender,
      System.EventArgs e)
    {
      BuildGlossary(glossary);
      DisplayWords(glossary);
    }
    private void lstWords_SelectedIndexChanged
      (object sender, System.EventArgs e)
    {
      Object word;
      word = lstWords.SelectedItem;
      txtDefinition.Text = glossary[word].ToString();

    }
  }
}
```

The text file looks like this:

adder,an electronic circuit that performs an addition operation on binary
    values
addressability,the number of bits stored in each addressable location in
    memory
bit,short for binary digit
block,a logical group of zero or more program statements
call,the point at which the computer begins following the instructions in
    a subprogram
compiler,a program that translates a high-level program into machine code
data,information in a form a computer can use
database,a structured set of data

. . .

Here's how the program looks when it runs:

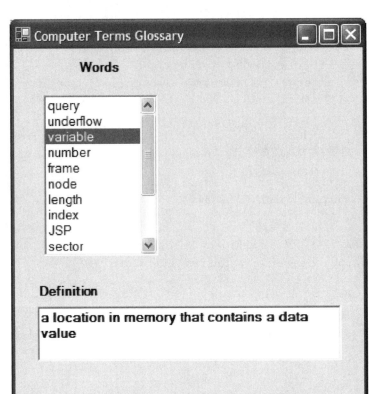

If a word is entered that is not in the glossary, the Item method returns Nothing. There is a test for Nothing in the GetDefinition subroutine so that the string "not found" is displayed if the word entered is not in the hash table.

SUMMARY

A hash table is a very efficient data structure for storing key–value pairs. The implementation of a hash table is mostly straightforward, with the tricky part having to do with choosing a strategy for collisions. This chapter discussed several techniques for handling collisions.

For most C# applications, there is no reason to build a custom hash table, when the Hashtable class of the .NET Framework library works quite well. You can specify your own hash function for the class or you can let the class calculate hash values.

EXERCISES

1. Rewrite the computer terms glossary application using the custom-designed Hash class developed in this chapter. Experiment with different hash functions and collision-resolution strategies.
2. Using the Hashtable class, write a spelling checker program that reads through a text file and checks for spelling errors. You will, of course, have to limit your dictionary to several common words.
3. Create a new Hash class that uses an arraylist instead of an array for the hash table. Test your implementation by rewriting (yet again) the computer terms glossary application.

CHAPTER 11

Linked Lists

For many applications, data are best stored as lists, and lists occur naturally in day-to-day life: to-do lists, grocery lists, and top-ten lists. In this chapter, we explore one particular type of list, the linked list. Although the .NET Framework class library contains several list-based collection classes, the linked list is not among them. The chapter starts with an explanation of why we need linked lists, then we explore two different implementations of the data structure—object-based linked lists and array-based linked lists. The chapter finishes up with several examples of how linked lists can be used for solving computer programming problems you may run across.

THE PROBLEM WITH ARRAYS

The array is the natural data structure to use when working with lists. Arrays provide fast access to stored items and are easy to loop through. And, of course, the array is already part of the language and you don't have to use extra memory and processing time using a user-defined data structure.

But as we've seen, the array is not the perfect data structure. Searching for an item in an unordered array is slow because you have to possibly visit every element in the array before finding the element you're searching for. Ordered (sorted) arrays are much more efficient for searching, but insertions

FIGURE **11.1. An Example Linked List.**

and deletions are slow because you have to shift the elements up or down to either make space for an insertion or remove space with a deletion. Not to mention that in an ordered array, you have to search for the proper space to insert an element into the array.

When you determine that the operations performed on an array are too slow for practical use, you can consider using the linked list as an alternative. The linked list can be used in almost every situation where an array is used, except if you need random access to the items in the list, when an array is probably the best choice.

LINKED LISTS DEFINED

A linked list is a collection of class objects called nodes. Each node is linked to its successor node in the list using a reference to the successor node. A node is made up of a field for storing data and the field for the node reference. The reference to another node is called a link. An example linked list is shown in Figure 11.1.

A major difference between an array and a linked list is that whereas the elements in an array are referenced by position (the index), the elements of a linked list are referenced by their relationship to the other elements of the array. In Figure 11.1, we say that "Bread" follows "Milk", not that "Bread" is in the second position. Moving through a linked list involves following the links from the beginning node to the ending node.

Another thing to notice in Figure 11.1 is that we mark the end of a linked list by pointing to the value null. Since we are working with class objects in memory, we use the null object to denote the end of the list.

Marking the beginning of a list can be a problem in some cases. It is common in many linked list implementations to include a special node, called the "header", to denote the beginning of a linked list. The linked list of Figure 11.1 is redesigned with a header node in Figure 11.2.

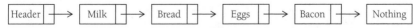

FIGURE **11.2. A Linked List with a Header Node.**

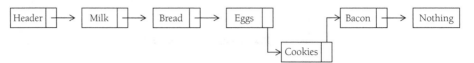

FIGURE 11.3. Inserting Cookies.

Insertion becomes a very efficient task when using a linked list. All that is involved is changing the link of the node previous to the inserted node to point to the inserted node, and setting the link of the new node to point to the node the previous node pointed to before the insertion. In Figure 11.3, the item "Cookies" is added to the linked list after "Eggs".

Removing an item from a linked list is just as easy. We simply redirect the link of the node before the deleted node to point to the node the deleted node points to and set the deleted node's link to null. The diagram of this operation is shown in Figure 11.4, where we remove "Bacon" from the linked list.

There are other methods we can, and will, implement in the LinkedList class, but insertion and deletion are the two methods that define why we use linked lists over arrays.

AN OBJECT-ORIENTED LINKED LIST DESIGN

Our design of a linked list will involve at least two classes. We'll create a Node class and instantiate a Node object each time we add a node to the list. The nodes in the list are connected via references to other nodes. These references are set using methods created in a separate LinkedList class. Let's start by looking at the design of the Node class.

The Node Class

A node is made up of two data members: Element, which stores the node's data; and Link, which stores a reference to the next node in the list. We'll use Object for the data type of Element, just so we don't have to worry about what

FIGURE 11.4. Removing Bacon.

kind of data we store in the list. The data type for Link is Node, which seems strange but actually makes perfect sense. Since we want the link to point to the next node, and we use a reference to make the link, we have to assign a Node type to the link member.

To finish up the definition of the Node class, we need at least two construc- tor methods. We definitely want a default constructor that creates an empty Node, with both the Element and Link members set to null. We also need a parameterized constructor that assigns data to the Element member and sets the Link member to null.

Here's the code for the Node class:

```
public class Node {

  public Object Element;

  public Node Link;

public Node() {
  Element = null;
  Link = null;
}
public Node(Object theElement) {
  Element = theElement;
  Link = null;
  }
}
```

The LinkedList Class

The LinkedList class is used to create the linkage for the nodes of our linked list. The class includes several methods for adding nodes to the list, removing nodes from the list, traversing the list, and finding a node in the list. We also need a constructor method that instantiates a list. The only data member in the class is the header node.

```
public class LinkedList {

  protected Node header;

  public LinkedList() {
```

```
      header = new Node("header");
  }
  .  .  .
}
```

The header node starts out with its Link field set to null. When we add the first node to the list, the header node's Link field is assigned a reference to the new node, and the new node's Link field is assigned the null value.

The first method we'll examine is the Insert method, which we use to put a node into our linked list. To insert a node into the list, you have to specify the node you want to insert before or after. This is necessary to adjust all the necessary links in the list. We'll choose to insert a new node after an existing node in the list.

To insert a new node after an existing node, we have to first find the "after" node. To do this, we create a Private method, Find, that searches through the Element field of each node until a match is found.

```
private Node Find(Object item) {
  Node current = new Node();
  current = header;
  while(current.header != item)
    current = current.Link;
  return current;
}
```

This method demonstrates how we move through a linked list. First, we instantiate a Node object, current, and assign it as the header node. Then we check to see if the value in the node's Element field equals the value we're searching for. If not, we move to the next node by assigning the node in the Link field of current as the new value of current.

Once we've found the "after" node, the next step is to set the new node's Link field to the Link field of the "after" node, and then set the "after" node's Link field to a reference to the new node. Here's how it's done:

```
public void Insert(Object newItem, Object after) {
  Node current = new Node();
  Node newNode = new Node(newItem);
  current = Find(after);
```

```
    newNode.Link = current.Link;
    current.Link = newNode;
}
```

The next linked list operation we explore is Remove. To remove a node from a linked list, we simply have to change the link of the node that points to the removed node to point to the node after the removed node.

Since we need to find the node before the node we want to remove, we'll define a method, FindPrevious, that does this. This method walks down the list, stopping at each node and looking ahead to the next node to see if that node's Element field holds the item we want to remove.

```
private Node FindPrevious(Object n) {
  Node current = header;
  while(!(current.Link == null) && (current.Link.
                                    Element != n))
    current = current.Link;
  return current;
}
```

Now we're ready to see how the code for the Remove method looks:

```
public void Remove(Object n)
  Node p = FindPrevious(n);
  if (!(p.Link == null))
    p.Link = p.Link.Link;
}
```

The Remove method removes the first occurrence of an item in a linked list only. You will also notice that if the item is not in the list, nothing happens.

The last method we'll define in this section is PrintList, which traverses the linked list and displays the Element fields of each node in the list.

```
public void PrintList() {
  Node current = new Node();
  current = header;
  while (!(current.Link == null)) {
    Console.WriteLine(current.Link.Element);
    current = current.Link;
  }
}
```

LINKED LIST DESIGN MODIFICATIONS

There are several modifications we can make to our linked list design in order to better solve certain problems. Two of the most common modifications are the doubly linked list and the circularly linked list. A doubly linked list makes it easier to move backward through a linked list and to remove a node from the list. A circularly linked list is convenient for applications that move more than once through a list. We'll look at both of these modifications in this section. Finally, we'll look at a modification to the LinkedLast class that is common only to object-oriented implementations of a linked list—an Iterator class for denoting position in the list.

The Doubly Linked List

Although traversing a linked list from the first node in the list to the last node is very straightforward, it is not as easy to traverse a linked list backward. We can make this procedure much easier if we add a field to our Node class that stores the link to the previous node. When we insert a node into the list, we'll have to perform more operations in order to assign data to the new field, but we gain efficiency when we have to remove a node from the list, since we don't have to look for the previous node. Figure 11.5 illustrates graphically how a doubly linked list works.

    We first need to modify the Node class to add an extra link to the class. To distinguish between the two links, we'll call the link to the next node the FLink, and the link to the previous node the BLink. These fields are set to Nothing when a Node is instantiated. Here's the code:

```
public class Node {

  public Object Element;
  public Node Flink;
  public Node Blink;

  public Node() {
    Element = null;
```

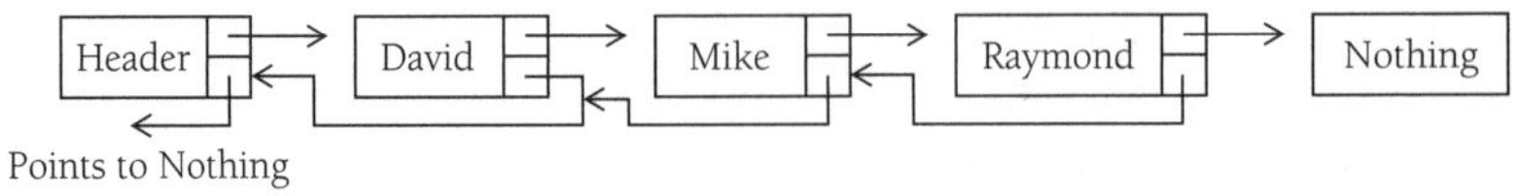

FIGURE 11.5. A Doubly Linked List.

```
      Flink = null;
      Blink = null;
  }

  public Node(Object theElement) {
    Element = theElement;
    Flink = null;
    Blink = null;
  }
}
```

The Insertion method is similar to the same method in a singularly linked list, except we have to set the new node's back link to point to the previous node.

```
public void Insert(Object newItem, Object after) {
  Node current = new Node();
  Node newNode = new Node(newItem);
  current = Find(after);
  newNode.Flink = current.Link;
  newNode.Blink = current;
  current.Flink = newNode;
}
```

The Remove method for a doubly linked list is much simpler to write than for a singularly linked list. We first need to find the node in the list; then we set the node's back link property to point to the node pointed to in the deleted node's forward link. Then we need to redirect the back link of the link the deleted node points to and point it to the node before the deleted node.

Figure 11.6 illustrates a special case of deleting a node from a doubly linked list when the node to be deleted is the last node in the list (other than the Nothing node).

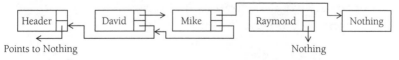

FIGURE 11.6. Removing a Node From a Doubly Linked.

The code for the Remove method of a doubly linked list is as follows.

```
public void Remove(Object n) {
  Node p = Find(n);
  if (!(p.Flink == null)) {
    p.Blink.Flink = p.Flink;
    p.Flink.Blink = p.Blink;
    p.Flink = null;
    p.Blink = null;
  }
}
```

We'll end this section on implementing doubly linked lists by writing a method that prints the elements of a linked list in reverse order. In a singularly linked list, this could be somewhat difficult, but with a doubly linked list, the method is easy to write.

First, we need a method that finds the last node in the list. This is just a matter of following each node's forward link until we reach a link that points to null. This method, called FindLast, is defined as follows:

```
private Node FindLast() {
  Node current = new Node();
  current = header;
  while(!(current.Flink == null))
    current = current.Flink;
  return current;
}
```

Once we find the last node in the list, to print the list in reverse order we just follow the backward link until we get to a link that points to null, which indicates we're at the header node. Here's the code:

```
public void PrintReverse() {
  Node current = new Node();
  current = FindLast();
  while (!(current.Blink == null)) {
    Console.WriteLine(current.Element);
    current = current.Blink;
  }
}
```

FIGURE **11.7. A Circularly Linked List.**

The Circularly Linked List

A circularly linked list is a list where the last node points back to the first node (which may be a header node). Figure 11.7 illustrates how a circularly linked list works.

This type of linked list is used in certain applications that require the last node pointing back to the first node (or the header). Many programmers choose to use circularly linked lists when a linked list is called for.

The only real change we have to make to our code is to point the Header node to itself when we instantiate a new linked list. If we do this, every time we add a new node the last node will point to the Header, since that link is propagated from node to node.

The code for a circularly linked list is shown. For clarity, we show the complete class (and not just to pad book page length):

```
public class Node {

  public Object Element;
  public Node Flink;
  public Node Blink;

  public Node() {
    Element = null;
    Flink = null;
    Blink = null;
  }

  public Node(Object theElement) {
    Element = theElement;
    Flink = null;
    Blink = null;
  }
  }

public class LinkedList {
  protected Node current;
```

```
    protected Node header;
    private int count;

    public LinkedList() {
      count = 0;
      header = new Node("header");
      header.Link = header;
}

    public bool IsEmpty() {
      return (header.Link == null);
    }

    public void MakeEmpty() {
     header.Link = null;
    }

    public void PrintList() {
      Node current = new Node();
      current = header;
      while (!(current.Link.Element = "header")) {
        Console.WriteLine(current.Link.Element);
        current = current.Link;
      }
}

    private Node FindPrevious(Object n) {
      Node current = header;
      while (!(current.Link == null) && current.Link.
             Element != n)
        current = current.Link;
      return current;
    }

     private Node Find(Object n) {
      Node current = new Node();
      current = header.Link;
      while (current.Element != n)
        current = current.Link;
      return current;
    }
```

```
public void Remove(Object n) {
  Node p = FindPrevious(n);
  if (!(p.Link == null)
     p.Link = p.Link.Link;
  count--;
}

public void Insert(Object n1, n2) {
  Node current = new Node();
  Node newnode = new Node(n1);
  current = Find(n2);
  newnode.Link = current.Link;
  current.Link = newnode;
  count++;
}

public void InsertFirst(Object n) {
  Node current = new Node(n);
  current.Link = header;
  header.Link = current;
  count++;
}

public Node Move(int n) {
  Node current = header.Link;
  Node temp;
  for(int i = 0, i <= n; i++)
     current = current.Link;
  if (current.Element = "header")
     current = current.Link;
  temp = current;
  return temp;
  }
}
```

In the .NET Framework Library, the ArrayList data structure is implemented using a circularly linked list. There are also many problems that can
be solved using a circularly linked list. We look at one typical problem in the
exercises.

USING AN ITERATOR CLASS

One problem the LinkedList class has is that you can't refer to two positions in the linked list at the same time. We can refer to any one position in the list (the current node, the previous node, etc.), but if we want to specify two or more positions, such as if we want to remove a range of nodes from the list, we'll need some other mechanism. This mechanism is an iterator class.

The iterator class consists of three data fields: a field that stores the linked list, a field that stores the current node, and a field that stores the current node. The constructor method is passed a linked list object, and the method sets the current field to the header node of the list passed into the method. Let's look at our definition of the class so far:

```
public class ListIter {

   private Node current;
   private Node previous;
   LinkedList theList;
   public ListIter(LinkedList list) {
    theList = list;
    current = theList.getFirst();
    previous = null;
}
```

The first thing we want an Iterator class to do is allow us to move from node to node through the list. The method nextLink does this:

```
public void NextLink() {
   previous = current;
   current = current.link;
}
```

Notice that in addition to establishing a new current position, the previous node is also set to the node that is current before the method has finished executing. Keeping track of the previous node in addition to the current node makes insertion and removal easier to perform.

The getCurrent method returns the node pointed to by the iterator:

```
public Node GetCurrent()
    return current;
}
```

Two insertion methods are built in the Iterator class: InsertBefore and InsertAfter. InsertBefore inserts a new node before the current node; InsertAfter inserts a new node after the current node. Let's look at the Insert-Before method first.

The first thing we have to do when inserting a new node before the current object is check to see if we are at the beginning of the list. If we are, then we can't insert a node before the header node, so we throw an exception. This exception is defined below. Otherwise, we set the new node's Link field to the Link field of the previous node, set the previous node's Link field to the new node, and reset the current position to the new node. Here's the code:

```
public void InsertBefore(Object theElement) {
    Node newNode = new Node(theElement);
    if (current == header)
        throw new InsertBeforeHeaderException();
    else {
        newNode.Link = previous.Link;
        previous.Link = newNode;
        current = newNode;
    }
}
```

The InsertBeforeHeader Exception class definition is:

```
public class InsertBeforeHeaderException {

    public InsertBeforeHeaderException() {
    base("Can't insert before the header node.");
    }
}
```

The InsertAfter method in the Iterator class is much simpler than the method we wrote in the LinkedList class. Since we already know the position of the current node, the method just needs to set the proper links and set the current node to the next node.

```
public void InsertAfter(Object theElement) {
   Node newnode = new Node(theElement);
   newNode.Link = current.Link;
   current.Link = newnode;
   NextLink();
}
```

Removing a node from a linked list is extremely easy using an Iterator class. The method simply sets the Link field of the previous node to the node pointed to by the current node's Link field:

```
public void Remove() {
   prevous.Link = current.Link;
}
```

Other methods we need in an Iterator class include methods to reset the iterator to the header node (and the previous node to null) and a method to test if we're at the end of the list. These methods are shown as follows.

```
public void Reset()
   current = theList.getFirst();
   previous = null;
}

public bool AtEnd() {
   return (current.Link == null);
}
```

The New LinkedList Class

With the Iterator class doing a lot of the work now, we can slim down the LinkedList class quite a bit. Of course, we still need a header field and a constructor method to instantiate the list.

```
public class LinkedList() {

   private Node header;

   public LinkedList() {
```

```
   header = new Node("header");
   }

   public bool IsEmpty() {
     return (header.Link == null);
   }

   public Node GetFirst() {
     return header;
   }

   public void ShowList() {
     Node current = header.Link;
     while (!(current == null)) {
        Console.WriteLine(current.Element);
       current = current.Link;
     }
   }
}
```

Demonstrating the Iterator Class

Using the Iterator class, it's easy to write an interactive program to move through a linked list. This also gives us a chance to put all the code for both the Iterator class and the LinkedList class in one place.

```
using System;

public class Node
{
    public Object Element;
    public Node Link;

    public Node()
    {
      Element = null;
      Link = null;
    }

    public Node(Object theElement)
    {
```

```
      Element = theElement;
      Link = null;
    }
}

public class InsertBeforeHeaderException : System.
  ApplicationException
{
  public InsertBeforeHeaderException(string message) :
    base(message)
  {
}
  }

public class LinkedList {

  private Node header;

  public LinkedList() {
    header = new Node("header");
  }

  public bool IsEmpty() {
    return (header.Link == null);
  }

  public Node GetFirst() {
    return header;
  }

  public void ShowList() {
    Node current = header.Link;
    while (!(current == null)) {
      Console.WriteLine(current.Element);
      current = current.Link;
    }
  }
}

public class ListIter {

  private Node current;
```

```
  private Node previous;
  LinkedList theList;

  public ListIter(LinkedList list) {
    theList = list;
    current = theList.GetFirst();
    previous = null;
  }

  public void NextLink() {
    previous = current;
    current = current.Link;
  }

  public Node GetCurrent() {
    return current;
  }

  public void InsertBefore(Object theElement) {
    Node newNode = new Node(theElement);
    if (previous.Link == null)
      throw new InsertBeforeHeaderException
        ("Can't insert here.");
    else {
      newNode.Link = previous.Link;
      previous.Link = newNode;
      current = newNode;
    }
  }
}

public void InsertAfter(Object theElement) {
  Node newNode = new Node(theElement);
  newNode.Link = current.Link;
  current.Link = newNode;
  NextLink();
}
  public void Remove() {
    previous.Link = current.Link;
  }

  public void Reset() {
```

```
      current = theList.GetFirst();
      previous = null;
  }

  public bool AtEnd() {
    return (current.Link == null);
    }
  }

  class chapter11 {
    static void Main() {
      LinkedList MyList = new LinkedList();
      ListIter iter = new ListIter(MyList);
      string choice, value;
       try
       {
         iter.InsertAfter("David");
         iter.InsertAfter("Mike");
         iter.InsertAfter("Raymond");
         iter.InsertAfter("Bernica");
         iter.InsertAfter("Jennifer");
         iter.InsertBefore("Donnie");
         iter.InsertAfter("Michael");
         iter.InsertBefore("Terrill");
         iter.InsertBefore("Mayo");
         iter.InsertBefore("Clayton");
         while (true)
         {
           Console.WriteLine("(n) Move to next node");
           Console.WriteLine("(g) Get value in current node");
           Console.WriteLine("(r) Reset iterator");
           Console.WriteLine("(s) Show complete list");
           Console.WriteLine("(a) Insert after");
           Console.WriteLine("(b) Insert before");
           Console.WriteLine("(c) Clear the screen");
           Console.WriteLine("(x) Exit");
           Console.WriteLine();
           Console.Write("Enter your choice: ");
           choice = Console.ReadLine();
           choice = choice.ToLower();
```

```csharp
char[] onechar = choice.ToCharArray();
switch(onechar[0])
{
  case 'n' :
    if (!(MyList.IsEmpty()) &&
       (!(iter.AtEnd())))
         iter.NextLink();
    else
      Console.WriteLine("Can' move to
                         next link.");
    break;
  case 'g' :
    if (!(MyList.IsEmpty()))
      Console.WriteLine("Element: " +
        iter.GetCurrent().Element);
    else
      Console.WriteLine ("List is empty.");
    break;
  case 'r' :
    iter.Reset();
    break;
  case 's' :
    if (!(MyList.IsEmpty()))
         MyList.ShowList();
    else
      Console.WriteLine("List is empty.");
    break;
  case 'a' :
    Console.WriteLine();
    Console.Write("Enter value to insert:");
    value = Console.ReadLine();
    iter.InsertAfter(value);
    break;
  case 'b' :
    Console.WriteLine();
    Console.Write("Enter value to insert:");
    value = Console.ReadLine();
      iter.InsertBefore(value);
      break;
```

```
        case 'c' :
          // clear the screen
          break;
        case 'x' :
          // end of program
          break;
    }
  }
}
catch (InsertBeforeHeaderException e)
{
  Console.WriteLine(e.Message);
}
}
}
```

Yes, this program is a Console application and doesn't use a GUI. You will get a chance to remedy this in the exercises, however.

THE GENERIC LINKED LIST CLASS AND THE GENERIC NODE CLASS

The System.Collections.Generic namespace provides two generic classes for building linked lists: the LinkedList class and the LinkedListNode class. The Node class provides two data fields for storing a value and a link, whereas the LinkedList class implements a doubly linked list with methods for inserting before a node as well as inserting after a node. The class also provides method for removing nodes, finding the first and last nodes in the linked list, as well as other useful methods.

A Generic Linked List Example

Like other generic classes, LinkedListNode and LinkedList require a data type placeholder when instantiating objects. Here are some examples:

```
LinkedListNode<string> node1 = new LinkedListNode<string>_
  ("Raymond");
```

```
LinkedList<string> names = new LinkedList<string>();
```

From here, it's just a matter of using the classes to build and use a linked list. A simple example demonstrates how easy it is to use these classes:

```
using System;
using System.Collections.Generic;
using System.Text;

class Program {

  static void Main(string[] args) {
   LinkedListNode<string> node = new
     LinkedListNode<string>("Mike");
   LinkedList<string> names = new LinkedList<string>();
   names.AddFirst(node);
   LinkedListNode<string> node1 = new
                              LinkedListNode<string>
                                        ("David");
   names.AddAfter(node, node1);
   LinkedListNode<string> node2 = new
                              LinkedListNode<string>
                                   ("Raymond");
   names.AddAfter(node1, node2);
   LinkedListNode<string> node3 = new LinkedListNode
                                   <string>(null);
   LinkedListNode<string> aNode = names.First;
   while(aNode != null) {
      Console.WriteLine(aNode.Value);
      aNode = aNode.Next;
   }
   aNode = names.Find("David");
   if (aNode != null) aNode = names.First;
   while (aNode != null) {
      Console.WriteLine(aNode.Value);
      aNode = aNode.Next;
   }
   Console.Read()
   }
}
```

The linked list in this example does not use a header node because we can easily find the first node in the linked list with the First property. Although it wasn't used in this example, there is also a Last property that could be used in the previous While loop to check for the end of the list:

```
while (aNode != names.Last) {
  Console.WriteLine(aNode.Value);
  aNode = aNode.Next;
}
```

There are two other methods, not shown here, that could prove useful in a linked list implementation: AddFirst and AddLast. These methods can help you implement a linked list without having to provide header and tail nodes in your list.

SUMMARY

In the traditional study of computer programming, linked lists are often the first data structure studied. In C#, however, it is possible to use one of the built-in data structures, such as the ArrayList, and achieve the same result as implementing a linked list. However, it is well worth every programming student's time to learn how linked lists work and how to implement them. The .NET Framework library uses a circularly linked list design to implement the ArrayList data structure.

C# 2.0 provides both a generic linked list class and a generic Node class. These classes make it easier to write linked lists that can adapt to different data type values for the nodes in the list.

There are several good books that discuss linked lists, though none of them use C# as the target language. The definitive source, as usual, is Knuth's *The Art of Computer Programming, Volume I, Fundamental Algorithms*. Other books you might consult for more information include *Data Structures with C++*, by Ford and Topp, and, if you're interested in Java implementations (and you should be because you can almost directly convert a Java implementation to C#) consult *Data Structures and Algorithm Analysis In Java*, by Mark Allen Weiss.

EXERCISES

1. Rewrite the Console application that uses an iterator-based linked list as a Windows application.
2. According to legend, the first century Jewish historian, Flavius Josephus, was captured along with a band of 40 compatriots by Roman soldiers during the Jewish–Roman war. The captured soldiers decided that they preferred suicide to being captured and devised a plan for their demise. They were to form a circle and kill every third soldier until they were all dead. Joseph and one other decided they wanted no part of this and quickly calculated where they needed to place themselves in the circle so that they would both survive. Write a program that allows you to place *n* people in a circle and specify that every *m* person will be killed. The program should determine the number of the last person left in the circle. Use a circularly linked list to solve the problem.
3. Write a program that can read an indefinite number of lines of VB.NET code and store reserved words in one linked list and identifiers and literals in another linked list. When the program has finished reading input, display the contents of each linked list.
4. Design and implement a ToArray method for the LinkedList class that takes a linked list instance and returns an array.

CHAPTER 12

Binary Trees and Binary Search Trees

Trees are a very common data structure in computer science. A tree is a nonlinear data structure that is used to store data in a hierarchical manner. We examine one primary tree structure in this chapter, the binary tree, along with one implementation of the binary tree, the binary search tree. Binary trees are often chosen over more fundamental structures, such as arrays and linked lists, because you can search a binary tree quickly (as opposed to a linked list) and you can quickly insert data and delete data from a binary tree (as opposed to an array).

THE DEFINITION OF A TREE

Before we examine the structure and behavior of the binary tree, we need to define what we mean by a tree. A *tree* is a set of *nodes* connected by *edges*. An example of a tree is a company's organization chart (see Figure 12.1).

The purpose of an organization chart is to communicate to the viewer the structure of the organization. In Figure 12.1, each box is a node and the lines connecting the boxes are the edges. The nodes, obviously, represent the entities (people) that make up an organization. The edges represent the relationship between the entities. For example, the Chief Information Officer (CIO), reports directly to the CEO, so there is an edge between these two

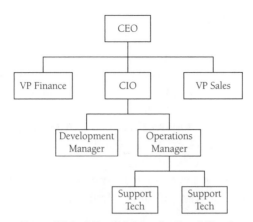

FIGURE **12.1. A Partial Organizational Chart.**

nodes. The IT manager reports to the CIO so there is an edge connecting them. The Sales VP and the Development Manager in IT do not have a direct edge connecting them, so there is not a direct relationship between these two entities.

Figure 12.2 displays another tree that defines a few terms we need when discussing trees. The top node of a tree is called the *root* node. If a node is connected to other nodes below it, the top node is called the parent, and

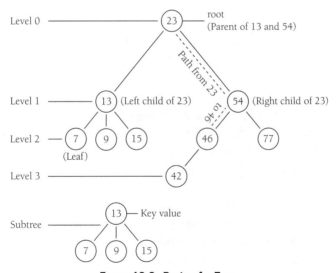

FIGURE **12.2. Parts of a Tree.**

the nodes below it are called the parent's children. A node can have zero, one, or more nodes connected to it. Special types of trees, called *binary* trees, restrict the number of children to no more than two. Binary trees have certain computational properties that make them very efficient for many operations. Binary trees are discussed extensively in the sections of this chapter. A node without any child node is called a *leaf*.

Continuing to examine Figure 12.2, you can see that by following certain edges, you can travel from one node to other nodes that are not directly connected. The series of edges you follow to get from one node to another is called a *path* (depicted in the figure with dashed lines). Visiting all the nodes in a tree in some particular order is known as a tree *transversal*.

A tree can be broken down into *levels*. The root node is at Level 0, its children at Level 1, those node's children are at Level 2, and so on. A node at any level is considered the root of a *subtree*, which consists of that root node's children, its children's children, and so on. We can define the *depth* of a tree as the number of layers in the tree.

Finally, each node in a tree has a value. This value is sometimes referred to as the *key* value.

BINARY TREES

A binary tree is defined as a tree where each node can have no more than two children. By limiting the number of children to 2, we can write efficient programs for inserting data, deleting data, and searching for data in a binary tree.

Before we discuss building a binary tree in C#, we need to add two terms to our tree lexicon. The child nodes of a parent node are referred to as the *left* node and the *right* node. For certain binary tree implementations, certain data values can only be stored in left nodes and other data values must be stored in right nodes. An example binary tree is shown in Figure 12.3.

Identifying the child nodes is important when we consider a more specific type of binary tree—the *binary search tree*. A binary search tree is a binary tree where data with lesser values are stored in left nodes and values with greater values are stored in right nodes. This property provides for very efficient searches, as we shall soon see.

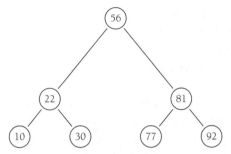

FIGURE **12.3. A Binary Tree.**

Building a Binary Search Tree

A binary search tree is made up of nodes, so we need a Node class that is similar to the Node class we used in the linked list implementation. Let's look at the code for the Node class first:

```
public class Node {

    public int Data;
    public Node left;
    public Node right;

    public void DisplayNode() {
      Console.Write(iData);
    }
}
```

We include Public data members for the data stored in the node and for each child node. The displayNode method allows us to display the data stored in a node. This particular Node class holds integers, but we could adopt the class easily to hold any type of data, or even declare iData of Object type if we need to.

Next we're ready to build a BinarySearchTree (BST) class. The class consists of just one data member—a Node object that represents the root node of the BST. The default constructor method for the class sets the root node to null, creating an empty node.

We next need an Insert method to add new nodes to our tree. This method is somewhat complex and will require some explanation. The first step in the method is to create a Node object and assign the data the Node holds to the iData variable. This value is passed in as the only argument to the method.

The second step to insertion is to see if our BST has a root node. If not, then this is a new BST and the node we are inserting is the root node. If this is the case, then the method is finished. Otherwise, the method moves on to the next step.

If the node being added is not the root node, then we have to prepare to traverse the BST in order to find the proper insertion point. This process is similar to traversing a linked list. We need a Node object that we can assign to the current node as we move from level to level. We also need to position ourselves inside the BST at the root node.

Once we're inside the BST, the next step is to determine where to put the new node. This is performed inside a while loop that we break once we've found the correct position for the new node. The algorithm for determining the proper position for a node is as follows:

1. Set the parent node to be the current node, which is the root node.
2. If the data value in the new node is less than the data value in the current node, set the current node to be the left child of the current node. If the data value in the new node is greater than the data value in the current node, skip to Step 4.
3. If the value of the left child of the current node is null, insert the new node here and exit the loop. Otherwise, skip to the next iteration of the While loop.
4. Set the current node to the right child node of the current node.
5. If the value of the right child of the current node is null, insert the new node here and exit the loop. Otherwise, skip to the next iteration of the While loop.

The code for the Insert method, along with the rest of the code for the BST class (that has been discussed) and the Node class is as follows:

```
public class Node {

    public int Data;
    public Node Left;
```

```
    public Node Right;

    public void DisplayNode() {
      Console.Write(Data + " ");
    }
}

public class BinarySearchTree {

    public Node root;

    public BinarySearchTree() {
      root = null;
    }

    public void Insert(int i) {
      Node newNode = new Node();
      newNode.Data = i;
      if (root == null)
        root = newNode;
      else {
        Node current = root;
        Node parent;
        while (true) {
            parent = current;
            if (i < current.Data) {
                current = current.Left;
                if (current == null) {
                   parent.Left = newNode;
                   break;
                }
            }
          else {
              current = current.Right;
              if (current == null) {
                 parent.Right = newNode;
                 break;
            }
        }
      }
    }
  }
}
```

Traversing a Binary Search Tree

We now have the basics to implement the BST class, but all we can do so far is insert nodes into the BST. We need to be able to traverse the BST so that we can visit the different nodes in several different orders.

There are three traversal methods used with BSTs: *inorder*, *preorder*, and *postorder*. An inorder traversal visits all the nodes in a BST in ascending order of the node key values. A preorder traversal visits the root node first, followed by the nodes in the subtrees under the left child of the root, followed by the nodes in the subtrees under the right child of the root. Although it's easy to understand why we would want to perform an inorder traversal, it is less obvious why we need preorder and postorder traversals. We'll show the code for all three traversals now and explain their uses in a later section.

An inorder traversal can best be written as a recursive procedure. Since the method visits each node in ascending order, the method must visit both the left node and the right node of each subtree, following the subtrees under the left child of the root before following the subtrees under the right side of the root. Figure 12.4 diagrams the path of an inorder traversal.

Here's the code for a inorder traversal method:

```
public void InOrder(Node theRoot) {
    if (!(theRoot == null)) {
        InOrder(theRoot.Left);
        theRoot.DisplayNode();
        InOrder(theRoot.Right);
    }
}
```

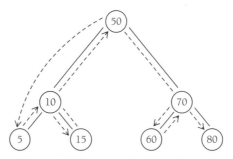

FIGURE **12.4. Inorder Traversal Order.**

To demonstrate how this method works, let's examine a program that inserts a series of numbers into a BST. Then we'll call the inOrder method to display the numbers we've placed in the BST. Here's the code:

```
static void Main() {
    BinarySearchTree nums = new BinarySearchTree();
    nums.Insert(23);
    nums.Insert(45);
    nums.Insert(16);
    nums.Insert(37);
    nums.Insert(3);
    nums.Insert(99);
    nums.Insert(22);
    Console.WriteLine("Inorder traversal: ");
    nums.inOrder(nums.root);
}
```

Here's the output:

```
Inorder traversal:
3 16 22 23 37 45 99
```

This list represents the contents of the BST in ascending numerical order, which is exactly what an inorder traversal is supposed to do.

Figure 12.5 illustrates the BST and the path the inorder traversal follows.

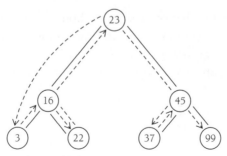

FIGURE **12.5. Inorder Traversal Path.**

Now let's examine the code for a preorder traversal:

```
public void PreOrder(Node theRoot) {
    if (!(theRoot == null)) {
        theRoot.displayNode();
        preOrder(theRoot.Left);
        preOrder(theRoot.Right);
    }
}
```

Notice that the only difference between the preOrder method and the inOrder method is where the three lines of code are placed. The call to the displayNode method was sandwiched between the two recursive calls in the inOrder method and it is the first line of the preOrder method.

If we replace the call to inOrder with a call to preOrder in the previous sample program, we get the following output:

```
Preorder traversal:

23 16 3 22 45 37 99
```

Finally, we can write a method for performing postorder traversals:

```
public void PostOrder(Node theRoot) {
    if (!(theRoot == null)) {
        PostOrder(theRoot.Left);
        PostOrder(theRoot.Right);
        theRoot.DisplayNode();
    }
}
```

Again, the difference between this method and the other two traversal methods is where the recursive calls and the call to displayNode are placed. In a postorder traversal, the method first recurses over the left subtrees and then over the right subtrees. Here's the output from the postOrder method:

```
Postorder traversal:

3 22 16 37 99 45 23
```

We'll look at some practical programming examples using BSTs that use these traversal methods later in this chapter.

Finding a Node and Minimum/Maximum Values in a Binary Search Tree

Three of the easiest things to do with BSTs are find a particular value, find the minimum value, and find the maximum value. We examine these operations in this section.

The code for finding the minimum and maximum values is almost trivial in both cases, due to the properties of a BST. The smallest value in a BST will always be found at the last left child node of a subtree beginning with the left child of the root node. On the other hand, the largest value in a BST is found at the last right child node of a subtree beginning with the right child of the root node.

We provide the code for finding the minimum value first:

```
public int FindMin() {
    Node current = root;
    while (!(current.Left == null))
        current = current.Left;
    return current.Data;
}
```

The method starts by creating a Node object and setting it to the root node of the BST. The method then tests to see if the value in the left child is null. If a non-Nothing node exists in the left child, the program sets the current node to that node. This continues until a node is found whose left child is equal to null. This means there is no smaller value below and the minimum value has been found.

Now here's the code for finding the maximum value in a BST:

```
public int FindMax() {
    Node current = root;
    while (!(current.Right == null))
        current = current.Right;
    return current.Data;
}
```

This method looks almost identical to the FindMin() method, except the method moves through the right children of the BST instead of the left children.

The last method we'll look at here is the Find method, which is used to determine if a specified value is stored in the BST. The method first creates a Node object and sets it to the root node of the BST. Next it tests to see if the key (the data we're searching for) is in that node. If it is, the method simply returns the current node and exits. If the data isn't found in the root node, the data we're searching for is compared to the data stored in the current node. If the key is less than the current data value, the current node is set to the left child. If the key is greater than the current data value, the current node is set to the right child. The last segment of the method will return null as the return value of the method if the current node is null (Nothing), indicating the end of the BST has been reached without finding the key. When the While loop ends, the value stored in current is the value being searched for.

Here's the code for the Find method:

```
public Node Find(int key) {
   Node current = root;
   while (current.iData != key) {
      if (key < current.iData)
         current = current.Left;
      Else
         current = current.Right;
      if (current == null)
         return null;
   }
   return current;
}
```

Removing a Leaf Node From a BST

The operations we've performed on a BST so far have not been that complicated, at least in comparison with the operation we explore in this section—removal. For some cases, removing a node from a BST is almost trivial; for other cases, it is quite involved and demands that we pay special care to the code we right, otherwise we run the risk of destroying the correct hierarchical order of the BST.

Let's start our examination of removing a node from a BST by discussing the simplest case—removing a leaf. Removing a leaf is the simplest case since there are no child nodes to take into consideration. All we have to do is set each child node of the target node's parent to null. Of course, the node will still be there, but there will not be any references to the node.

The code fragment for deleting a leaf node is as follows (this code also includes the beginning of the Delete method, which declares some data members and moves to the node to be deleted):

```
public Node Delete(int key) {
    Node current = root;
    Node parent = root;
    bool isLeftChild = true;
    while (current.Data != key) {
        parent = current;
        if (key < current.Data) {
            isLeftChild = true;
            current = current.Right;
        else {
            isLeftChild = false;
            current = current.Right;
        }
        if (current == null)
            return false;
    }
    if ((current.Left == null) & (current.Right == null))
        if (current == root)
            root == null;
        else if (isLeftChild)
            parent.Left = null;
        else
            parent.Right = null;
    }

    // the rest of the class goes here
}
```

The while loop takes us to the node we're deleting. The first test is to see if the left child and the right child of that node are null. Then we test to see if this node is the root node. If so, we set it to null, otherwise, we either set the left node of the parent to null (if isLeftChild is true) or we set the right node of the parent to null.

Deleting a Node With One Child

When the node to be deleted has one child, there are four conditions we have to check for: 1. the node's child can be a left child; 2. the node's child can be a right child; 3. the node to be deleted can be a left child; or 4. the node to be deleted can be a right child.

Here's the code fragment:

```
else if (current.Right == null)
   if (current == root)
      root = current.Left;
   else if (isLeftChild)
      parent.Left = current.Left;
   else
      parent.Right = current.Right;
else if (current.Left == null)
   if (current == root)
      root = current.Right;
   else if (isLeftChild)
      parent.Left = parent.Right;
   else
      parent.Right = current.Right;
```

First, we test to see if the right node is null. If so, then we test to see if we're at the root. If we are, we move the left child to the root node. Otherwise, if the node is a left child we set the new parent left node to the current left node, or if we're at a right child, we set the parent right node to the current right node.

Deleting a Node With Two Children

Deletion now gets tricky when we have to delete a node with two children. Why? Look at Figure 12.6. If we need to delete the node marked 52, what do we do to rebuild the tree. We can't replace it with the subtree starting at the node marked 54 because 54 already has a left child.

The answer to this problem is to move the inorder successor into the place of the deleted node. This works fine unless the successor itself has children,

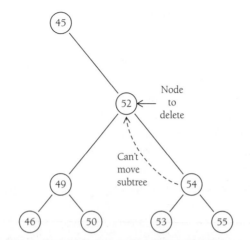

FIGURE **12.6. Deleting A Node With Two Children.**

but there is a way around that scenario also. Figure 12.7 diagrams how using the inorder successor works.

To find the successor, go to the original node's right child. This node has to be larger than the original node by definition. Then it begins following left child paths until it runs out of nodes. Since the smallest value in a subtree (like a tree) must be at the end of the path of left child nodes, following this path to the end will leave us with the smallest node that is larger than the original node.

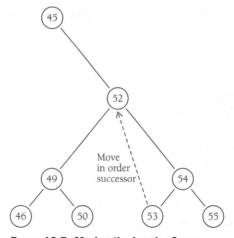

FIGURE **12.7. Moving the Inorder Successor.**

Here's the code for finding the successor to a deleted node:

```
public Node GetSuccessor(Node delNode) {
    Node successorParent = delNode;
    Node successor = delNode;
    Node current = delNode.Right;
    while (!(current == null)) {
        successorParent = current;
        successor = current;
        current = current.Left;
    }
    if (!(successor == delNode.Right)) {
        successorParent.Left = successor.Right;
        successor.Right = delNode.Right;
    }
    return successor;
}
```

Now we need to look at two special cases: the successor is the right child of the node to be deleted and the successor is the left child of the node to be deleted. Let's start with the former.

First, the node to be deleted is marked as the current node. Remove this node from the right child of its parent node and assign it to point to the successor node. Then, remove the current node's left child and assign to it the left child node of the successor node. Here's the code fragment for this operation:

```
else {
    Node successor = GetSuccessor(current);
    if (current == root)
        root = successor;
    else if (isLeftChild)
        parent.Left = successor;
    else
        parent.Right = successor;
    successor.Left = current.Left;
}
```

Now let's look at the situation when the successor is the left child of the node to be deleted. The algorithm for performing this operation is as follows:

1. Assign the right child of the successor to the successor's parent left child node.
2. Assign the right child of the node to be deleted to the right child of the successor node.
3. Remove the current node from the right child of its parent node and assign it to point to the successor node.
4. Remove the current node's left child from the current node and assign it to the left child node of the successor node.

Part of this algorithm is carried out in the GetSuccessor method and part of it is carried out in the Delete method. The code fragment from the GetSuccessor method is:

```
if (!(successor == delNode.Right)) {
    successorParent.Left = successor.Right;
    successor.Right = delNode.Right;
}
```

The code from the Delete method is:

```
if (current == root)
    root = successor;
else if (isLeftChild)
    parent.Left = successor;
else
    parent.Right = successor;
successor.Left = current.Left;
```

This completes the code for the Delete method. Because this code is somewhat complicated, some binary search tree implementations simply mark nodes for deletion and include code to check for the marks when performing searches and traversals.

Here's the complete code for Delete:

```
public bool Delete(int key) {
    Node current = root;
```

```
Node parent = root;
bool isLeftChild = true;

while (current.Data != key) {
    parent = current;
    if (key < current.Data) {
      isLeftChild = true;
      current = current.Right;
  } else {
      isLeftChild = false;
      current = current.Right;
  }
    if (current == null)
      return false;
}
 if ((current.Left == null) && (current.Right == null))
    if (current == root)
      root = null;
    else if (isLeftChild)
      parent.Left = null;
    else
      parent.Right = null;
else if (current.Right == null)
    if (current == root)
      root = current.Left;
    else if (isLeftChild)
     parent.Left = current.Left;
    else
      parent.Right = current.Right;
else if (current.Left == null)
    if (current == root)
      root = current.Right;
    else if (isLeftChild)
      parent.Left = parent.Right;
    else
      parent.Right = current.Right;
 else
      Node successor = GetSuccessor(current);
      if (current == root)
```

```
          root = successor;
      else if (isLeftChild)
          parent.Left = successor;
      else
          parent.Right = successor;
      successor.Left = current.Left;
  }
  return true;
}
```

SUMMARY

Binary search trees are a special type of data structure called a tree. A tree is a collection of nodes (objects that consist of fields for data and links to other nodes) that are connected to other nodes. A binary tree is a specialized tree structure where each node can have only two child nodes. A binary search tree is a specialization of the binary tree that follows the condition that lesser values are stored in left child nodes and greater values are stored in right nodes.

Algorithms for finding the minimum and maximum values in a binary search tree are very easy to write. We can also simply define algorithms for traversing binary search trees in different orders (inorder, preorder, postorder). These definitions make use of recursion, keeping the number of lines of code to a minimum while making their analysis a bit harder.

Binary search trees are most useful when the data stored in the structure are obtained in a random order. If the data in the tree are obtained in sorted or close-to-sorted order, the tree will be unbalanced and the search algorithms will not work as well.

EXERCISES

1. Write a program that generates 10,000 random integers in the range of 0–9 and store them in a binary search tree. Using one of the algorithms discussed in this chapter, display a list of each of the integers and the number of times they appear in the tree.
2. Add a function to the BinarySearchTree class that counts the number of edges in a tree.

3. Rewrite Exercise 1 so that it stores the words from a text file. Display all the words in the file and the number of times they occur in the file.
4. An arithmetic expression can be stored in a binary search tree. Modify the BinarySearchTree class so that an expression such as $2 + 3 * 4 / 5$ can be properly evaluated using the correct operator precedence rules.

CHAPTER 13

Sets

A set is a collection of unique elements. The elements of a set are called *members*. The two most important properties of sets are that the members of a set are unordered and no member can occur in a set more than once. Sets play a very important role in computer science but are not included as a data structure in C#.

This chapter discusses the development of a Set class. Rather than providing just one implementation, however, we provide two. For nonnumeric items, we provide a fairly simple implementation using a hash table as the underlying data store. The problem with this implementation is its efficiency. A more efficient Set class for numeric values utilizes a bit array as its data store. This forms the basis of our second implementation.

FUNDAMENTAL SET DEFINITIONS, OPERATIONS AND PROPERTIES

A set is defined as an unordered collection of related members in which no member occurs more than once. A set is written as a list of members surrounded by curly braces, such as {0,1,2,3,4,5,6,7,8,9}. We can write a set in any order, so the previous set can be written as {9,8,7,6,5,4,3,2,1,0} or any other combination of the members so that all members are written just once.

237

Set Definitions

Here are some definitions you need to know in order to work with sets.

1. A set that contains no members is called the *empty set*. The *universe* is the set of all possible members.
2. Two sets are considered *equal* if they contain exactly the same members.
3. A set is considered a *subset* of another set if all the members of the first set are contained in the second set.

Set Operations

The following describes the fundamental operations performed on sets.

1. *Union*: A new set is obtained by combining the members of one set with the members of a second set.
2. *Intersection*: A new set is obtained by adding all the members of one set that also exist in a second set.
3. *Difference*: A new set is obtained by adding all the members of one set except those that also exist in a second set.

Set Properties

The following properties are defined for sets.

1. The intersection of a set with the empty set is the empty set. The union of a set with the empty set is the original set.
2. The intersection of a set with itself is the original set. The union of a set with itself is the original set.
3. Intersection and union are *commutative*. In other words, set1 intersection set2 is equal to set2 intersect set1, and the same is true for the union of the two sets.
4. Intersection and union are *associative*. set1 intersection (set2 intersection set3) is equal to (set1 intersection set2) intersection s3. The same is true for the union of multiple sets.
5. The intersection of a set with the union of two other sets is *distributive*. In other words, set1 intersection (set2 union set3) is equal to (set1

intersection set2) union (set1 intersection set3). This also works for the union of a set with the intersection of two other sets.
6. The intersection of a set with the union of itself and another set yields the original set. This is also true for the union of a set with the intersection of itself and another set. This is called the *absorption law*.
7. The following equalities exist when the difference of the union or intersection of two sets is taken from another set. The equalities are:

set1 difference (set2 union set3) equals (set1 difference set2) intersection (set1 difference set3)
and
set1 difference (set2 intersection set3) equals (set1 difference set2) union (set1 difference set3)

These equalities are known as *DeMorgan's Laws*.

A FIRST SET CLASS IMPLEMENTATION USING A HASH TABLE

Our first Set class implementation will use a hash table to store the members of the set. The HashTable class is one of the more efficient data structures in the.NET Framework library and it should be your choice for most class implementations when speed is important. We will call our class CSet since Set is a reserved word in C#.

Class Data Members and Constructor Method

We only need one data member and one constructor method for our CSet class. The data member is a hash table and the constructor method instantiates the hash table. Here's the code:

```
public class CSet {

  private Hashtable data;

  public CSet() {

      data = new Hashtable();
    }
    // More code to follow
}
```

The Add Method

To add members to a set, the Add method needs to first check to make sure the member isn't already in the set. If it is, then nothing happens. If the member isn't in the set, it is added to the hash table.

```
public void Add(Object item) {
  if (!(data.ContainsValue(item))
     data.Add(Hash(item), item);
}
```

Since items must be added to a hash table as a key–value pair, we calculate a hash value by adding the ASCII value of the characters of the item being added to the set. Here's the Hash function:

```
private string Hash(Object item) {
  char[] chars;
  string s = item.ToString();
  chars = s.ToCharArray();
  for(int i = 0; i <= chars.GetUpperBound(0); i++)
    hashValue += (int)chars[i];
  return hashValue.ToString();
}
```

The Remove and Size Methods

We also need to be able to remove members from a set and we also need to determine the number of members (size) in a set. These are straightforward methods:

```
public void Remove(Object item) {
  data.Remove(Hash(item));
}
public int Size() {
  return data.Count;
}
```

The Union Method

The Union method combines two sets using the Union operation discussed previously to form a new set. The method first builds a new set by adding all the members of the first set. Then the method checks each member of the second set to see if it is already a member of the first set. If it is, the member is skipped over, and if not, the member is added to the new set.

Here's the code:

```
public CSet Union(CSet aSet) {
  CSet tempSet = new CSet();
  foreach (Object hashObject in data.Keys)
    tempSet.Add(this.data[hashObject]);
  foreach (Object hashObject in aSet.data.Keys)
    if (!(this.data.ContainsKey(hashObject)))
      tempSet.Add(aSet.data[hashObject]);
  return tempSet;
}
```

The Intersection Method

The Intersection method loops through the keys of one set, checking to see if that key is found in the passed-in set. If so, the member is added to the new set and skipped otherwise.

```
public CSet Intersection(CSet aSet) {
  CSet tempSet = new CSet();
  foreach (Object hashObject in data.Keys)
    if (aSet.data.Contains(hashObject))
      tempSet.Add(aSet.GetValue(hashObject))
  return tempSet;
}
```

The isSubset Method

The first requirement for a set to be a subset of another set is that the first set must be smaller in size in the second set. The Subset method checks the size of the sets first, and if the first set qualifies, then checks to see that every member of the first set is a member of the second set. The code is shown as follows:

```
public bool Subset(CSet aSet) {
  if (this.Size > aSet.Size)
    return false;
  else
    foreach(Object key in this.data.Keys)
      if (!(aSet.data.Contains(key)))
        return false;
  return true;
}
```

The Difference Method

We've already examined how to obtain the difference of two sets. To perform this computationally, the method loops over the keys of the first set, looking for any matches in the second set. A member is added to the new set if it exists in the first set and is not found in the second set. Here's the code (along with a ToString method):

```
public CSet Difference(CSet aSet) {
  CSet tempSet = new CSet();
  foreach (Object hashObject in data.Keys)
  if (!(aSet.data.Contains(hashObject)))
    tempSet.Add(data[hashObject]);
  return tempSet;
}
public override string ToString() {
  string s;
  foreach(Object key in data.Keys)
    s += data[key] + " ";
  return s;
}
```

A Program to Test the CSet Implementation

Here's a program that tests our implementation of the CSet class by creating two sets, performing a union of the two sets, an intersection of the two sets, finding the subset of the two sets, and the difference of the two sets.

Here is the program:

```
static void Main() {
CSet setA = new CSet();
CSet setB = new CSet();
setA.add("milk");
setA.add("eggs");
setA.add("bacon");
setA.add("cereal");
setB.add("bacon");
setB.add("eggs");
setB.add("bread")
CSet setC = new CSet();
setC = setA.Union(setB);
Console.WriteLine();
Console.WriteLine("A: " & setA.ToString());
Console.WriteLine("B: " & setB.ToString())
Console.WriteLine("A union B: " & setC.ToString());
setC = setA.Intersection(setB);
Console.WriteLine("A intersect B: " &
                  setC.ToString());
setC = setA.Difference(setB);
Console.WriteLine("A diff B: " & setC.ToString());
setC = setB.Difference(setA);
Console.WriteLine("B diff A: " & setC.ToString());
if (setB.isSubset(setA))
   Console.WriteLine("b is a subset of a");
else
   Console.WriteLine("b is not a subset of a");
}
```

The output from this program is:

```
C:\Documents and Settings\Administrator\My Documents\Visual Studio Projects\Set\bin\Set...  _ □ ×
A: bacon cereal eggs milk
B: bacon eggs bread
A union B: bacon cereal eggs milk bread
A intersect B: bacon eggs
A diff B: cereal milk
B diff A: bread
b is not a subset of a
```

If we comment out the line where "bread" is added to setB, we get the following output:

```
C:\Documents and Settings\Administrator\My Documents\Visual Studio Projects\Set\bin\Set...  _ □ ×
A: bacon cereal eggs milk
B: bacon eggs
A union B: bacon cereal eggs milk
A intersect B: bacon eggs
A diff B: cereal milk
B diff A:
b is a subset of a
```

In the first example, setB could not be a subset of subA because it contained bread. Removing bread as a member makes setB a subset of subA, as shown in the second screen.

A BitArray Implementation of the CSet Class

The previous implementation of the CSet class works for objects that are not numbers, but is still somewhat inefficient, especially for large sets. When we have to work with sets of numbers, a more efficient implementation uses the BitArray class as the data structure to store set members. The BitArray class was discussed in depth in Chapter 7.

Overview of Using a BitArray Implementation

There are several advantages to using a BitArray to store integer set members. First, because we are really only storing Boolean values, the storage space requirement is small. The second advantage is that the four main operations we want to perform on sets (union, intersection, difference, and subset) can be performed using simple Boolean operators (And, Or, and Not). The implementations of these methods are much faster than the implementations using a hash table.

The storage strategy for creating a set of integers using a BitArray is as follows: Consider adding the member 1 to the set. We simply set the array element in index position 1 to True. If we add 4 to the set, the element at position 4 is set to True, and so on.

We can determine which members are in the set by simply checking to see if the value at that array position is set to True. We can easily remove a member from the set by setting that array position to False.

Computing the union of two sets using Boolean values is simple and efficient. Since the union of two sets is a combination of the members of both sets, we can build a new union set by Oring the corresponding elements of the two BitArrays. In other words, a member is added to the new set if the value in the corresponding position of either BitArray is True.

Computing the intersection of two sets is similar to computing the union; only for this operation we use the And operator instead of the Or operator. Similarly, the difference of two sets is found by executing the And operator with a member from the first set and the negation of the corresponding member of the second set. We can determine if one set is a subset of another set by using the same formula we used for finding the difference. For example, if:

```
setA(index) && !(setB(index))
```

evaluates to False then setA is not a subset of setB.

The BitArray Set Implementation

The code for a CSet class based on a BitArray is shown as follows:

```
public class CSet {
  private BitArray data;
  public BitArray() {
    data = new BitArray(5);
}
  public void Add(int item) {
    data[item] = true;
```

```
  }
  public bool IsMember(int item) {
    return data[item];
  }
  public void Remove(int item) {
    data[item] = false;
  }
  public CSet Union(CSet aSet) {
    CSet tempSet = new CSet();
    for(int i = 0; i <= data.Count-1; i++)
      tempSet.data[index] = (this.data[index ||
                             aSet.data[index]);
    return tempSet;
  }

    public CSet Intersection(CSet aSet) {
      CSet tempSet = new CSet();
      for(int i = 0; i <= data.Count-1; i++)
        tempSet.data[index] = (this.data[index] &&
                               aSet.data[index]);
      return tempSet;
  }
  public CSet Difference(CSet aSet) {
    CSet tempSet = new CSet();
    for(int i = 0; i <= data.Count-1; i++)
      tempSet.data[index] = (this.data[index] &&
                             (!(aSet.data[index])));
    return tempSet;
  }
  public bool IsSubset(CSet aSet) {
    CSet tempSet = new CSet();
    for(int i = 0; i <= data.Count-1; i++)
      if (this.data[index] && (!(aSet.data[index])))
        return false;
    return true;
  }
  public override string ToString() {
    string s = "";
    for(int i = 0; i <= data.Count-1; i++)
       if (data[index])
      str += index;
```

```
        return st;
    }
}
```

Here's a program to test our implementation:

```
static void Main()
    CSet setA = new CSet();
    CSet setB = new CSet();
    setA.Add(1);
    setA.Add(2);
    setA.Add(3);
    setB.Add(2);
    setB.Add(3);
    CSet setC = new CSet();
    setC = setA.Union(setB);
    Console.WriteLine();
    Console.WriteLine(setA.ToString());
    Console.WriteLine(setC.ToString());
    setC = setA.Intersection(setB);
    Console.WriteLine(setC.ToString());
    setC = setA.Difference(setB);
    Console.WriteLine(setC.ToString());
    Dim flag As Boolean = setB.isSubset(setA);
    if (flag)
        Console.WriteLine("b is a subset of a");
    else
        Console.WriteLine("b is not a subset of a");
}
```

The output from this program is:

SUMMARY

Sets and set theory provide much of the foundation of computer science theory. Although some languages provide a built-in set data type (Pascal), and other languages provide a set data structure via a library (Java), C# does not provide a set data type or data structure.

The chapter discussed two different implementations of a set class, one using a hash table as the underlying data store and the other implementation using a bit array as the data store. The bit array implementation is only applicable for storing integer set members, whereas the hash table implementation will store members of any data type. The bit array implementation is inherently more efficient than the hash table implementation and should be used any time you are storing integer values in a set.

EXERCISES

1. Create two pairs of sets using both the hash table implementation and the bit array implementation. Both implementations should use the same sets. Using the Timing class, compare the major operations (union, intersection, difference, isSubset) of each implementation and report the actual difference in times.
2. Modify the hash table implementation so that it uses an ArrayList to store the set members rather than a hash table. Compare the running times of the major operations of this implementation with the hash table implementation. What is the difference in times?

CHAPTER 14

Advanced Sorting Algorithms

In this chapter, we examine algorithms for sorting data that are more complex than the algorithms examined in Chapter 4. These algorithms are also more efficient, and one of them, the QuickSort algorithm, is generally considered to be the most efficient sort to use in most situations. The other sorting algorithms we'll examine are the ShellSort, the MergeSort, and the HeapSort.

To compare these advanced sorting algorithms, we'll first discuss how each of them is implemented, and in the exercises you will use the Timing class to determine the efficiency of these algorithms.

THE SHELLSORT ALGORITHM

The ShellSort algorithm is named after its inventor Donald Shell. This algorithm is fundamentally an improvement of the insertion sort. The key concept in this algorithm is that it compares items that are distant rather than adjacent items, as is done in the insertion sort. As the algorithm loops through the data set, the distance between each item decreases until at the end the algorithm is comparing items that are adjacent.

ShellSort sorts distant elements by using an increment sequence. The sequence must start with 1, but can then be incremented by any amount.

A good increment to use is based on this code fragment:

```
while (h <= numElements / 3)
   h = h * 3 + 1;
```

where numElements is the number of elements in the data set being sorted, such as an array.

For example, if the sequence number generated by the code is 4, every fourth element of the data set is sorted. Then a new sequence number is chosen, using this code:

```
h = (h - 1) / 3;
```

Then the next *h* elements are sorted, and so on.

Let's look at the code for the ShellSort algorithm (we are using the Array-Class code from Chapter 4):

```
public void ShellSort() {
   int inner, temp;
   int h = 1;
   while (h <= numElements / 3)
      h = h * 3 + 1;
   while (h > 0) {
      for(int outer = h; h <= numElements-1;h++) {
         temp = arr[outer];
      inner = outer;
      while ((inner > h-1) && arr[inner-h] >= temp) {
         arr[inner] = arr[inner-h];
         inner -= h;
      }
      arr[inner] = temp;
   }
   h = (h-1) / 3;
   }
}
```

Here's some code to test the algorithm:

```
static void Main() {
  const int SIZE = 19;
  CArray theArray = new CArray(SIZE);
  For(int index = 0; index <= SIZE; index++)
    theArray.Insert(Int(100 * Rnd() + 1));
  Console.WriteLine();
  theArray.showArray();
  Console.WriteLine();
  theArray.ShellSort();
  theArray.showArray();
}
```

The output from this code is:

The ShellSort is often considered a good advanced sorting algorithm to use because it is fairly easy to implement but its performance is acceptable even for data sets in the tens of thousands of elements.

THE MERGESORT ALGORITHM

The MergeSort algorithm is a very good example of a recursive algorithm. This algorithm works by breaking the data set up into two halves and recursively sorting each half. When the two halves are sorted, they are brought together using a merge routine.

The easy work comes when sorting the data set. Let's say we have the following data in the set: 71 54 58 29 31 78 2 77. First, the data set is broken up into two separate sets: 71 54 58 29 and 31 78 2 77. Then each half is sorted: 29 54 58 71 and 2 31 77 78. Then the two sets are merged, 2 29 31 54 58 71 77 78. The merge process compares the first two elements of each data set (stored in temporary arrays), copying the smaller value to yet another array. The element not added to the third array is then compared to the next element in the other array. The smaller element is added to the third array, and this process continues until both arrays are out of data.

But what if one array runs out of data before the other? This is likely to happen and the algorithm makes provisions for this situation. Two extra loops are used that are called only if one or the other of the two arrays still has data in it after the main loop finishes.

Now we can see the code for performing a MergeSort. The first two methods are the MergeSort and the recMergeSort methods. The first method simply launches the recursive subroutine recMergeSort, which performs the sorting of the array:

```
public void MergeSort() {
  int[] tempArray = new int[numElements];
  RecMergeSort(tempArray, 0, numElements-1);
}
public void RecMergeSort(int[] tempArray, int lbount,
                         int ubound) {
  if (lbound == ubound)
    return
  else {
    int mid = (int)(lbound + ubound) / 2;
    RecMergeSort(tempArray, lbound, mid);
    RecMergeSort(tempArray, mid+1, ubound);
    RecMergeSort(tempArray, lbound, mid+1, ubound);
  }
}
```

In RecMergeSort, the first if statement is the base case of the recursion, returning to the calling program when the condition becomes true. Otherwise, the middle point of the array is found and the routine is called recursively on the bottom half of the array (the first call to RecMergeSort) and then on the top half of the array (the second call to RecMergeSort). Finally, the entire array is merged by calling the merge method.

Here is the code for the merge method:

```
public void Merge(int[] tempArray, int lowp, int highp,
                  int ubound) {
  int lbound = lowp;
  int mid = highp - 1;
  int n = (ubound-lbound) + 1;
  while ((lowp <= mid) && (highp <= ubound))
    if (arr[lowp] < arr[highp]) {
      tempArray[j] = arr[lowp];
      j++;
      lowp++;
    } else {
      tempArray[j] = arr[highp];
      j++;
      highp++;
    }
  }
  while (lowp <= mid) {
    tempArray[j] = arr[lowp];
    j++;
    lowp++;
  }
  while (highp <= ubound) {
    tempArray[j] = arr[highp];
    j++;
    highp++;
  }
  for(int j = 0; j <= n-1; j++)
    arr[lbound+j] = tempArray[j];
}
```

This method is called each time the recMergeSort subroutines perform a preliminary sort. To demonstrate better how this method works along with recMergeSort, let's add one line of code to the end of the merge method:

```
this.showArray();
```

With this one line, we can view the array in its different temporary states before it is completely sorted. Here's the output:

```
■ C:\Documents and Settings\Administrator\My Documents\Visual Studio Projects\ArrayClass\...  _ □ ×
71 54 58 29 31 78 2 77 82 71

54 71 58 29 31 78 2 77 82 71
54 58 71 29 31 78 2 77 82 71
54 58 71 29 31 78 2 77 82 71
29 31 54 58 71 78 2 77 82 71
29 31 54 58 71 2 78 77 82 71
29 31 54 58 71 2 77 78 82 71
29 31 54 58 71 2 77 78 71 82
29 31 54 58 71 2 71 77 78 82
2 29 31 54 58 71 71 77 78 82
2 29 31 54 58 71 71 77 78 82
```

The first line shows the array in the original state. The second line shows the beginning of the lower half being sorted. By the fifth line, the lower half is completely sorted. The sixth line shows that the upper half of the array is beginning to be sorted and the ninth line shows that both halves are completely sorted. The tenth line is the output from the final merge and the eleventh line is just another call to the showArray method.

THE HEAPSORT ALGORITHM

The HeapSort algorithm makes use of a data structure called a *heap*. A heap is similar to a binary tree, but with some important differences. The Heap-Sort algorithm, although not the fastest algorithm in this chapter, has some attractive features that encourage its use in certain situations.

Building a Heap

The heap data structure, as we discussed earlier, is similar to a binary tree, but not quite the same. First, heaps are usually built using arrays rather than using node references. Also, there are two very important conditions for a heap: 1. a heap must be complete, meaning that each row must be filled in; and 2. each node contains data that is greater than or equal to the data in the child nodes below it. An example of a heap is shown in Figure 14.1. The array that stores the heap is shown in Figure 14.2.

The data we store in a heap is built from a Node class, similar to the nodes we've used in other chapters. This particular Node class, however, will hold just one piece of data, its primary, or key, value. We don't need any references

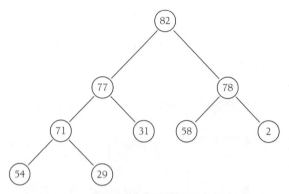

FIGURE **14.1. A Heap.**

to other nodes but we like using a class for the data so we can easily change the data type of the data being stored in the heap if we need to. Here's the code for the Node class:

```
public class Node {
   Public int data;
   public void Node(ByVal key As Integer) {
     data = key;
   }
}
```

Heaps are built by inserting nodes into the heap array, whose elements are nodes of the heap. A new node is always placed at the end of the array in an empty array element. The problem is that doing this will probably break the heap condition because the new node's data value may be greater than some of the nodes above it. To restore the array to the proper heap condition, we must shift the new node up until it reaches its proper place in the array. We do this with a method called ShiftUp. Here's the code:

```
public void ShiftUp(int index) {
   int parent = (index - 1) / 2;
```

82	77	78	71	31	58	2	54	29
0	1	2	3	4	5	6	7	8

FIGURE **14.2. An Array For Storing the Heap in Figure 14.1.**

```
Node bottom = heapArray[index];
while ((index > 0) && (heapArray[parent].data <
                       bottom.data)) {
  heapArray[index] = heapArray[parent];
  index = parent;
  parent = (parent - 1) / 2;
}
heapArray[index] = bottom;
}
```

And here's the code for the Insert method:

```
public bool Insert(int key) {
  if (currSize == maxSize)
      return False;
  Node newNode = new Node(key);
  heapArray[currSize] = newNode;
  ShiftUp[currSize];
  currSize++;
  return true;
}
```

The new node is added at the end of the array. This immediately breaks the heap condition, so the new node's correct position in the array is found by the ShiftUp method. The argument to this method is the index of the new node. The parent of this node is computed in the first line of the method. The new node is then saved in a Node variable, bottom. The while loop then finds the correct spot for the new node. The last line then copies the new node from its temporary location in bottom to its correct position in the array.

Removing a node from a heap always means removing the node with highest value. This is easy to do because the maximum value is always in the root node. The problem is that once the root node is removed, the heap is incomplete and must be reorganized. There is an algorithm for making the heap complete again:

1. Remove the node at the root.
2. Move the node in the last position to the root.
3. Trickle the last node down until it is below.

When this algorithm is applied continually, the data is removed from the heap in sorted order. Here is the code for the Remove and TrickleDown methods:

```
public Node Remove() {
  Node root = heapArray[0];
  currSize--;
  heapArray[0] = heapArray[currSize];
  ShiftDown(0);
  return root;
}
public void ShiftDown(int index) {
  int largerChild;
  Node top = heapArray[index];
  while (index < (int)(currSize / 2)) {
    int leftChild = 2 * index + 1;
    int rightChild = leftChild + 1;
    if ((rightChild < currSize) &&
          heapArray[leftChild].data
        < heapArray[righChild].data)
      largerChild = rightChild;
    else
      largerChild = leftChild;
    if (top.data >= heapArray[largerChild].data)
      break;
    heapArray[index] = heapArray[largerChild];
    index = largerChild;
  }
  heapArray[index] = top;
}
```

This is all we need to perform a heap sort, so let's look at a program that builds a heap and then sorts it:

```
static void Main() {
  const int SIZE = 9;
  Heap aHeap = new Heap(SIZE);
  Node sortedHeap = new Node[SIZE];
  for(int i = 0; i < SIZE; i++) {
```

```
      Random RandomClass = new Random();
      int rn = RandomClass.Next(1,100);
      Node aNode = new Node(rn);
      aHeap.InsertAt(i, aNode);
      aHeap.IncSize();
   }
   Console.Write("Random: ");
   aHeap.ShowArray();
   Console.WriteLine();
   Console.Write("Heap: ");
   for(int i = (int)SIZE/2-1; i >= 0; i--)
      aHeap.ShiftDown(i);
   aHeap.ShowArray();
   for(int i = SIZE-1; i >= 0; i--) {
      Node bigNode = aHeap.Remove();
      aHeap.InsertAt(i, bigNode);
   }
   Console.WriteLine();
   Console.Write("Sorted: ");
   aHeap.ShowArray();
}
```

The first for loop begins the process of building the heap by inserting random numbers into the heap. The second loop heapifies the heap and the third for loop then uses the Remove method and the TrickleDown method to rebuild the heap in sorted order. Here's the output from the program:

HeapSort is the second fastest of the advanced sorting algorithms we examine in this chapter. Only the QuickSort algorithm, which we discuss in the next section, is faster.

THE QUICKSORT ALGORITHM

QuickSort has a reputation, deservedly earned, as the fastest algorithm of the advanced algorithms we're discussing in this chapter. This is true only for large, mostly unsorted data sets. If the data set is small (100 elements or less), or if the data is relatively sorted, you should use one of the fundamental algorithms discussed in Chapter 4.

The QuickSort Algorithm Described

To understand how the QuickSort algorithm works, imagine you are a teacher and you have to alphabetize a stack of student papers. You will pick a letter that is in the middle of the alphabet, such as M, putting student papers whose name starts with A through M in one stack and names starting with N through Z in another stack. Then you split the A–M stack into two stacks and the N–Z stack into two stacks using the same technique. Then you do the same thing again until you have a set of small stacks (A–C, D–F, ..., X–Z) of two or three elements that sort easily. Once the small stacks are sorted, you simply put all the stacks together and you have a set of sorted papers.

As you should have noticed, this process is recursive, since each stack is broken up into smaller and smaller stacks. Once a stack is broken down into one element, that stack cannot be further broken up and the recursion stops.

How do we decide where to split the array into two halves? There are many choices, but we'll start by just picking the first array element:

```
mv = arr[first];
```

Once that choice is made, we next have to understand how to get the array elements into the proper "half" of the array. (The reason the word half is in quotes in the previous sentence is because it is entirely possible that the two halves will not be equal, depending on the splitting point.) We accomplish this by creating two variables, first and last, storing the second element in first and the last element in last. We also create another variable, theFirst, which stores the first element in the array. The array name is arr for the sake of this example.

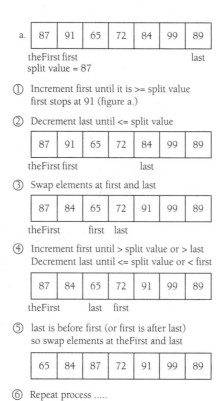

FIGURE 14.3. The Splitting an Array.

Figure 14.3 describes how the QuickSort algorithm works.

Code for the QuickSort Algorithm

Now that we've reviewed how the algorithm works, let's see how it's coded in C#:

```
public void QSort() {
  RecQSort(0, numElements-1);
}
public void RecQSort(int first, int last) {
  if ((last-first) <= 0)
    return;
```

```
    else {
     int pivot = arr[last];
     int part = this.Partition(first, last);
     RecQSort(first, part-1);
     RecQSort(part+1, last);
    }
}
public int Partition(int first, int last) {
   int pivotVal = arr[first];
   int theFirst = first;
   bool okSide;
   first++;
   do {
     okSide = true;
     while (okSide)
       if (arr[first] > pivotVal)
         okSide = false;
       else {
         first++;
         okSide = (first <= last);
     }
   okSide = (first <= last);
   while (okSide)
     if (arr[last] <= pivotVal)
       okSide = false;
    else {
      last--;
        okSide = (first <= last);
    if (first < last) {
      Swap(first, last);
      this.ShowArray();
      first++;
      last--;
    }
  } loop while (first <= last);
  Swap(theFirst, last);
  this.ShowArray();
  return last;
}
```

```
public void Swap(int item1, int item2) {
  int temp = arr[item1];
  arr[item1] = arr[item2];
  arr[item2] = temp;
}
```

An Improvement to the QuickSort Algorithm

If the data in the array is random, then picking the first value as the "pivot" or "partition" value is perfectly acceptable. Otherwise, however, making this choice will inhibit the performance of the algorithm.

A popular choice for picking this value is to determine the median value in the array. You can do this by taking the upper bound of the array and dividing it by 2. For example:

```
theFirst = arr[(int)arr.GetUpperBound(0) / 2]
```

Studies have shown that using this strategy can reduce the running time of the algorithm by about 5 percent (see Weiss 1999, p. 243).

SUMMARY

The algorithms discussed in this chapter are all quite a bit faster than the fundamental sorting algorithms discussed in Chapter 4, but it is universally accepted that the QuickSort algorithm is the fastest sorting algorithm and should be used for most sorting scenarios. The Sort method that is built into several of the .NET Framework library classes is implemented using QuickSort, which explains how dominant QuickSort is over other sorting algorithms.

EXERCISES

1. Write a program that compares all four advanced sorting algorithms discussed in this chapter. To perform the tests, create a randomly generated array of 1,000 elements. What is the ranking of the algorithms? What happens when you increase the array size to 10,000 elements and then 100,000 elements?
2. Using a small array (less than 20), compare the sorting times between the insertion sort and QuickSort. What is the difference in time? Can you explain why?

CHAPTER 15

Advanced Data Structures and Algorithms for Searching

In this chapter, we present a set of advanced data structures and algorithms for performing searching. The data structures we cover include the red–black tree, the splay tree, and the skip list. AVL trees and red–black trees are two solutions to the problem of handling unbalanced binary search trees. The skip list is an alternative to using a tree-like data structure that foregoes the complexity of the red–black and splay trees.

AVL TREES

Another solution to maintaining balanced binary trees is the AVL tree. The name AVL comes from the two computer scientists who discovered this data structure, G. M. Adelson-Velskii and E. M. Landis, in 1962. The defining characteristic of an AVL tree is that the difference between the height of the right and left subtrees can never be more than one.

AVL Tree Fundamentals

By continually comparing the heights of the left and right subtrees of a tree, the AVL tree is guaranteed to always stay "in balance." AVL trees utilize a technique, called a rotation, to keep them in balance.

FIGURE 15.1.

To understand how a rotation works, let's look at a simple example that builds a binary tree of integers. Starting with the tree shown in Figure 15.1, if we insert the value 10 into the tree, the tree becomes unbalanced, as shown in Figure 15.2. The left subtree now has a height of 2, but the right subtree has a height of 0, violating the rule for AVL trees. The tree is balanced by performing a *single right rotation*, moving the value 40 down to the right, as shown in Figure 15.3.

Now look at the tree in Figure 15.4. If we insert the value 30, we get the tree in Figure 15.5. This tree is unbalanced. We fix it by performing what is called a *double rotation*, moving 40 down to the right and 30 up to the right, resulting in the tree shown in Figure 15.6.

The AVL Tree Implementation

Our AVL tree implementation consists of two classes: a Node class used to hold data for each node in the tree, and the AVLTree class, which contains the methods for inserting nodes and rotating nodes.

The Node class for an AVL tree implementation is built similarly to nodes for a binary tree implementation, but with some important differences. Each node in an AVL tree must contain data about its height, so a data member for height is included in the class. We also have the class implement the IComparable interface in order to compare the values stored in the nodes. Also, because the height of a node is so important, we include a ReadOnly Property method to return a node's height.

Here is the code for the Node class:

```
public class Node : IComparable {

    public Object element;
    public Node left;
    public Node right;
```

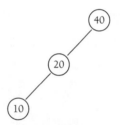

FIGURE **15.2.**

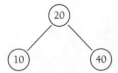

FIGURE **15.3.**

FIGURE **15.4.**

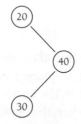

FIGURE **15.5.**

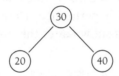

FIGURE **15.6.**

```
public int height;

public Node(Object data, Node lt, Node rt) {
  element = data;
  left = lt;
  right = rt;
  height = 0;
}

public Node(Object data) {
  element = data;
  left = null;
  right = null;
}

public int CompareTo(Object obj) {
  return (this.element.CompareTo((Node)obj.element));
}

public int GetHeight() {
  if (this == null)
    return -1;
  else
    return this.height;
}
}
```

The first method in the AVLTree class we examine is the Insert method. This method determines where to place a node in the tree. The method is recursive, either moving left when the current node is greater than the node to be inserted or moving right when the current node is less than the node to be inserted.

Once the node is in its place, the difference in heights of the two subtrees is calculated. If it is determined the tree is unbalanced, a left or right, or double left or double right rotation is performed. Here's the code (the code for the different rotation methods is shown after the Insert method):

```
private Node Insert(Object item, Node n) {
  if (n == null)
    n = new Node(item, null, null);
  else if (item.CompareTo(n.element) < 0) {
```

```
      n.left = Insert(item, n.left);
      if (height(n.left) - height(n.right) == 2)
         n = RotateWithLeftchild(n);
      else
         n = DoubleWithLeftChild(n);
   }
   else if (item.CompareTo(n.element) > 0) {
      n.right = Insert(item, n.right);
      if ((height(n.right) - height(n.left)) == 2)
         if (item.CompareTo(n.right.element) > 0)
            n = RotateWithRightChild(n);
         else
            n = DoubleWithRightChild(n);
   else
      ;// do nothing, duplicate value
   n.height = Math.Max(height(n.left), height(n.right)) + 1;
   return n
}
```

The different rotation methods are shown as follows:

```
private Node RotateWithLeftChild(Node n2) {
  Node n1 = n2.left;
  n2.left = n1.right;
  n1.right = n2;
  n2.height = Math.Max(height(n2.left), height
                            (n2.right)) + 1
  n1.height = Math.Max(height(n1.left), n2.height) + 1
  return n1
}
private Node RotateWithRightChild(Node n1) {
  Node n2 = n1.right;
  n1.right = n2.left;
  n2.left = n1;
  n1.height = Math.Max(height(n1.left),
                          height(n1.right)) + 1);
  n2.height = Math.Max(height(n2.right), n1.height) + 1;
  return n2;
}
```

```
private Node DoubleWithLeftChild(Node n3) {
  n3.left = RotateWithRightChild(n3.left);
  return RotateWithLeftChild(n3);
}

private Node DoubleWithRightChild(Node n1) {
  n1.right = RotateWithLeftChild(n1.right);
  return RotateWithRightChild(n1);
}
```

There are many other methods we can implement for this class, that is, the methods from the BinarySearchTree class. We leave the implementation of those methods to the exercises. Also, we have purposely not implemented a deletion method for the AVLTree class. Many AVL tree implementations use *lazy deletion*. This system of deletion marks a node for deletion but doesn't actually delete the node from the tree. The performance cost of deleting nodes and then rebalancing the tree is often prohibitive. You will get a chance to experiment with lazy deletion in the exercises.

RED–BLACK TREES

AVL trees are not the only solution to unbalanced binary search tree. Another data structure you can use is the *red–black tree*. A red-black tree is the one in which the nodes of the tree are designated as either red or black, depending on a set of rules. By properly coloring the nodes in the tree, the tree stays nearly perfectly balanced. An example of a red–black tree is shown in Figure 15.7 (black nodes are shaded):

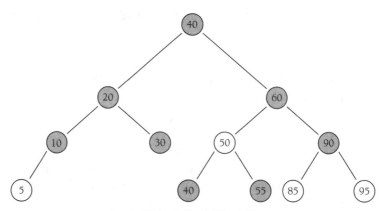

FIGURE 15.7. A Red–Black Tree.

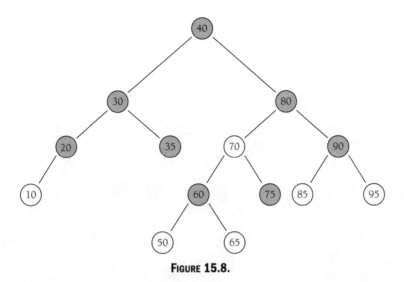

FIGURE 15.8.

Red–Black Tree Rules

The following rules are used when working with red–black trees:

1. Every node in the tree is colored either red or black.
2. The root node is colored black.
3. If a node is red, the children of that node must be black.
4. Each path from a node to a null reference must contain the same number of black nodes.

The consequence of these rules is that a red–black tree stays in very good balance, which means searching a red–black tree is quite efficient. As with AVL trees, though, these rules also make insertion and deletion more difficult.

Red–Black Tree Insertion

Inserting a new item into a red–black tree is complicated because it can lead to a violation of one of the rules shown in the earlier section. For example, look at the red-black tree in Figure 15.8.

We can insert a new item into the tree as a black node. If we do so, we are violating rule 4. So the node must be colored red. If the parent node is black,

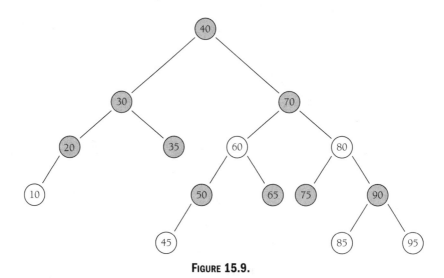

FIGURE 15.9.

everything is fine. If the parent node is red, however, then rule 3 is violated. We have to adjust the tree either by having nodes change color or by rotating nodes as we did with AVL trees.

We can make this process more concrete by looking at a specific example. Let's say we want to insert the value 55 into the tree shown in Figure 15.8. As we work our way down the tree, we notice that the value 60 is black and has two red children. We can change the color of each of these nodes (60 to red, 50 and 65 to black), then rotate 60 to 80's position, and then perform other rotations to put the subtree back in order. We are left with the red–black tree shown in Figure 15.9. This tree now follows all the red–black tree rules and is well balanced.

Red–Black Tree Implementation Code

Rather than break up the code with explanations, we show the complete code for a red–black tree implementation in one piece, with a description of the code to follow. We start with the Node class and continue with the RedBlack class.

```
public class Node {

    public string element;
    public Node left;
```

```
      public Node right;
      public int color;
      const int RED = 0;
      const int BLACK = 1;

      public Node(string element, Node left, Node right) {
        this.element = element;
        this.left = left;
        this.right = right;
        this.color = BLACK;
      }

      public Node(string element) {
        this.element = element;
        this.left = left;
        this.right = right;
        this.color = BLACK;
      }
    }
  public class RBTree {
    const int RED = 0;
    const int BLACK = 1;
    private Node current;
    private Node parent;
    private Node grandParent;
    private Node greatParent;
    private Node header;
    private Node nullNode;

    public RBTree(string element) {
      current = new Node("");
      parent = new Node("");
      grandParent = new Node("");
      greatParent = new Node("");
      nullNode = new Node("");
      nullNode.left = nullNode;
      nullNode.right = nullNode;
      header = new Node(element);
      header.left = nullNode;
```

```
    header.right = nullNode;
  }

  public void Insert(string item) {
    grandParent = header;
    parent = grandParent;
      current = parent;
    nullNode.element = item;
    while (current.element.CompareTo(item) ! = 0) {
      Node greatParent = grandParent;
      grandParent = parent;
      parent = current;
      if (item.CompareTo(current.element) < 0)
        current = current.left;
      else
        current = current.right;
    if ((current.left.color) = RED &&
        (current.right.color) = RED)
      HandleReorient(item);
  }
   if (!(current == nullNode)
      return
    current = new Node(item, nullNode, nullNode);
    if (item.CompareTo(parent.element) < 0)
      parent.left = current;
    else
      parent.right = current;
    HandleReorient(item);
  }

  public string FindMin() {
    if (this.IsEmpty())
      return null;
    Node itrNode = header.right;
    while(!(itrNode.left == nullNode))
      itrNode = itrNode.left;
    return itrNode.element;
  }

  public string FindMax() {
```

```
    if (this.IsEmpty())
       return null;
  Node itrNode = header.right;
  while (!(itrNode.right == nullNode))
    itrNode = itrNode.right;
  return itrNode.element;
}

public string Find(string e) {
  nullNode.element = e;
  Node current = header.right;
  while (true)
    if (e.CompareTo(current.element) < 0)
       current = current.left;
   else if (e.CompareTo(current.element) > 0)
       current = current.right;
   else if (! (current == nullNode))
       return current.element;
   else
       return null
}

public void MakeEmpty() {
  header.right = nullNode;
}

public bool IsEmpty() {
  return (header.right == nullNode);
}

public void PrintRBTree() {
  if (this.IsEmpty())
     Console.WriteLine("Empty");
  else
     PrintRB(header.right);
}
public void PrintRB(Node n) {
  if (!(n == nullNode)) {
     PrintRB(n.left);
     Console.WriteLine(n.element);
     PrintRB(n.right);
```

```
  }

  public void HandleReorient(string item) {
    current.Color = RED;
    current.left.color = BLACK;
    current.right.color = BLACK;
    if (parent.color == RED) {
      grandParent.color = RED;
      if ((item.CompareTo(grandParent.element) < 0) ! =
          (item.CompareTo(parent.element))) {
        current = Rotate(item, grandParent);
        current.color = BLACK;
    }

      header.right.color = BLACK;
    }
  }

  public Node Rotate(string item, Node parent) {
    if (item.CompareTo(parent.element) < 0)
      if (item.CompareTo(parent.left.element) < 0)
        parent.left = RotateWithLeftChild(parent.left);
      else
        parent.elft = RotateWithRightChild(parent.left);
      return parent.left;
    else
        if (item.CompareTo(parent.right.element) < 0)
        parent.right = RotateWithLeftChild(parent.
                                                right);
      else
        parent.right = RotateWithRightChild(parent.
                                                right);
      return parent.right;
  }

  public Node RotateWithLeftChild(Node k2) {
    Node k1 = k2.left;
    k2.left = k1.right;
    k1.right = k2;
    return k1;
  }
```

```
public Node RotateWithRightChild(Node k1) {
  Node k2 = k1.right;
  k1.right = k2.left;
  k2.left = k1;
  return k2;
  }
}
```

Then HandleReorient method is called whenever a node has two red children. The rotate methods are similar to those used with AVL trees. Also, because dealing with the root node is a special case, the RedBlack class includes a root sentinel node as well as the nullNode node, which indicates the node is a reference to null.

SKIP LISTS

Although AVL trees and red–black trees are efficient data structures for searching and sorting data, the rebalancing operations necessary with both data structures to keep the tree balanced causes a lot of overhead and complexity. There is another data structure we can use, especially for searching, that provides the efficiency of trees without the worries of rebalancing. This data structure is called a skip list.

Skip List Fundamentals

Skip lists are built from one of the fundamental data structures for searching— the linked list. As we know, linked lists are great for insertion and deletion, but not so good at searching, since we have to travel to each node sequentially. But there is no reason why we have to travel each link successively. When we want to go from the bottom of a set of stairs to the top and we want to get there quickly, what do we do? We take the stairs two or three at a time (or more if we're blessed with long legs).

We can implement the same strategy in a linked list by creating different levels of links. We start with level 0 links which point to the next node in the list. Then we have a level 1 link, which points to the second node in the list, skipping one node; a level 2 link, which points to the third node

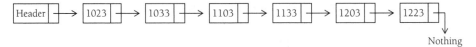

Nothing

FIGURE 15.10. Basic Linked List.

in the list, skipping two nodes; and so on. When we search for an item, we can start at a high link level and traverse the list until we get to a value that is greater than the value we're looking for. We can then back up to the previous visited node, and move down to the lowest level, searching node by node until we encounter the searched-for value. To illustrate the difference between a skip list and a linked list, study the diagrams in Figure 15.10 and 15.11.

Let's look at how a search is performed on the level 1 skip list shown in Figure 15.11. The first value we'll search for is 1133. Looking at the basic linked list first, we have to travel to four nodes to find 1133. Using a skip list, though, we only have to travel to two nodes. Clearly, using the skip list is more efficient for such a search.

Now let's look at how a search for 1203 is performed with the skip list. The level 1 links are traversed until the value 1223 is found. This is greater than 1203, so we back up to the node storing the value 1133 and drop down one level and start using level 0 links. The next node is 1203, so the search ends. This example makes the skip list search strategy clear. Start at the highest link level and traverse the list using those links until you reach a value greater than the value you're searching for. At that point, back up to the last node visited and move down to the next link level and repeat the same steps. Eventually, you will reach the link level that leads you to the searched-for value.

It turns out that we can make the skip list even more efficient by adding more links. For example, every fourth node can have a link that points four nodes ahead, every sixth node can have a link that points six nodes ahead,

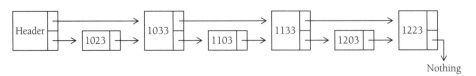

Nothing

FIGURE 15.11. Skip List With Links 2 Nodes Ahead (Level 1).

and so on. The problem with this scheme is that when we insert or delete a node, we have to rearrange a tremendous number of node pointers, making our skip list much less efficient.

The solution to this problem is to allocate nodes to the link levels randomly. The first node (after the header) might be a level 2 node, whereas the second node might be a level 4 node, the third node a level 1 node again, and so on. Distributing link levels randomly makes the other operations (other than search) more efficient, and it doesn't really affect search times. The probability distribution used to determine how to distribute nodes randomly is based on the fact that about half the nodes in a skip list will be level 0 nodes, whereas a quarter of the nodes will be level 1 nodes, 12.5% will be level 2 nodes, 5.75% will be level 3 nodes, and so on.

All that's left to explain is how we determine how many levels will be used in the skip list. The inventor of the skip list, William Pugh, a professor of Computer Science currently at the University of Maryland, worked out a formula in his paper that first described skip lists (ftp://ftp.cs.umd.edu/pub/skipLists/). Here it is, expressed in C# code:

```
(int)(Math.Ceiling(Math.Log(maxNodes) / Math.Log(1 /
PROB)) - 1);
```

where maxNodes is an approximation of the number of nodes that will be required and PROB is a probability constant, usually 0.25.

Skip List Implementation

We need two classes for a skip list implementation: a class for nodes and a class for the skip list itself. Let's start with the class for nodes.

The nodes we'll use for this implementation will store a key and a value, as well as an array for storing pointers to other nodes. Here's the code:

```
public class SkipNode {

   int key;
   Object value;
   SkipNode[] link;
   public SkipNode(int level, int key, Object value) {
```

```
      this.key = key;
      this.value = value;
      link = new SkipValue[level];
   }
}
```

Now we're ready to build the skip list class. The first thing we need to do is determine which data members we need for the class. Here's what we'll need:

- maxLevel: stores the maximum number of levels allowed in the skip list
- level: stores the current level
- header: the beginning node that provides entry into the skip list
- probability: stores the current probability distribution for the link levels
- NIL: a special value that indicates the end of the skip list
- PROB: the probability distribution for the link levels

```
public class SkipList {

   private int maxLevel;
   private int level;
   private SkipNode header;
   private float probability;
   private const int NIL = Int32.MaxValue;
   private const int PROB = 0.5;
```

The constructor for the SkipList class is written in two parts: a Public constructor with a single argument passing in the total number of nodes in the skip list, and a Private constructor that does most of the work. Let's view the methods first before explaining how they work:

```
private SkipList(float probable, int maxLevel) {
   this.probability = probable;
   this.maxLevel = maxLevel;
   level = 0;
   header = new SkipNode(maxLevel, 0, null);
   SkipNode nilElement = new SkipNode(maxLevel, NIL, null);
   for(int i = 0; i <= maxLevel-1; i++)
      header.link(i) = nilElement;
```

```
}
public SkipList(long maxNodes) {
  this.New(PROB, (int)(Math.Ceiling(Math.Log(maxNodes) /
                            Math.Log(1/PROB)-1)));
}
```

The Public constructor performs two tasks. First, the node total is passed into the constructor method as the only parameter in the method. Second, the Private constructor, where the real work of initializing a skip list object is performed, is called with two arguments. The first argument is the probability constant, which we've already discussed. The second argument is the formula for determining the maximum number of link levels for the skip list, which we've also already discussed.

The body of the Private constructor sets the values of the data members, creates a header node for the skip list, creates a "dummy" node for each of the header's links, and then initializes the links to that element.

The first thing we do with a skip list is insert nodes into the list. Here's the code for the Insert method of the SkipList class:

```
public void Insert(int key, Object value) {
  SkipNode[] update = new SkipNode[maxLevel];
  SkipNode cursor = header;
  for(int i = level; i > = level; i--) {
    while(cursor.link[i].key < key)
      cursor = cursor.link[i];
    update[i] = cursor;
  }
  cursor = cursor.link[0];
  if (cursor.key = key)
    cursor.value = value;
  else {
    int newLevel = GenRandomLevel();
    if (newlevel > level) {
      for(int i = level+1; i <= newLevel-1; i++)
        update[i] = header;
      level = newLevel;
    }
    cursor = new SkipNode(newLevel, key, value);
```

```
    for(int i = 0; i <= newLevel-1; i++) {
        cursor.link[i] = update[i].link[i];
        update[i].link[i] = cursor;
    }
    }
}
```

The first thing the method does is determine where in the list to insert the new SkipNode (the first for loop). Next, the list is checked to see if the value to insert is already there. If not, then the new SkipNode is assigned a random link level using the Private method genRandomLevel (we'll discuss this method next) and the item is inserted into the list (the line before the last for loop).

Link levels are determined using the probabilistic method genRandom-Level. Here's the code:

```
private int GenRandomLevel() {
    int newLevel = 0;
    int ran = Random.Next(0);
    while ((newLevel < maxLevel) && (ran < probability))
        newLevel++;
    return newLevel;
}
```

Before we cover the Search method, which is the focus of this section, let's look at how to perform deletion in a skip list. First, let's view the code for the Delete method:

```
public void Delete(int key) {
    SkipNode[] update = new SkipNode[maxLevel+1];
    SkipNode cursor = header;
    for(int i = level; i > = level; i--) {
        while (cursor.link[i].key < key)
        cursor = cursor.link[i];
        update[i] = cursor;
    }
    cursor = cursor.link[0];
    if (cursor.key == key) {
```

```
    for(int i = 0; i < level-1; i++)
      if (update[i].link[i] == cursor)
        update[i].link[i] == cursor.link[i];
    while((level > 0) && (header.link[level].key == NIL))
      level--;
  }
}
```

This method, like the Insert method, is split into two parts. The first part, highlighted by the first for loop, finds the item to be deleted in the list. The second part, highlighted by the if statement, adjusts the links around the deleted SkipNode and readjusts the levels.

Now we're ready to discuss the Search method. The method starts at the highest level, following those links until a key with a higher value than the key being searched for is found. The method then drops down to the next lowest level and continues the search until a higher key is found. It drops down again and continues searching. The method will eventually stop at level 0, exactly one node away from the item in question. Here's the code:

```
public Object Search(int key) {
  SkipNode cursor = header;
  for(int i = level; i <= level-1; i--) {
   SkipNode nextElement = cursor.link[i];
   while (nextElement.key < key) {
     cursor = nextElement;
     nextElement = cursor.link[i];
   }
  cursor = cursor.link[0];
  if (cursor.key == key)
    return cursor.value;
  else
    return "Object not found";
}
```

We've now provided enough functionality to implement a SkipList class. In the exercises at the end of the chapter, you will get a chance to write code that uses the class.

Skip lists offer an alternative to tree-based structures. Most programmers find them easier to implement and their efficiency is comparable to tree-like structures. If you are working with a completely or nearly sorted data set, skip lists are probably a better choice than trees.

SUMMARY

The advanced data structures discussed in this chapter are based on the discussions in Chapter 12 of Weiss (1999). AVL trees and red–black trees offer good solutions to the balancing problems experienced when using fairly sorted data with binary search trees. The major drawback to AVL and red–black trees is that the rebalancing operations come with quite a bit of overhead and can slow down performance on large data sets.

For extremely large data sets, skip lists offer an alternative even to AVL and red–black trees. Because skip lists use a linked-list structure versus a tree structure, rebalancing is unnecessary, making them more efficient in many situations.

EXERCISES

1. Write FindMin and FindMax methods for the AVLTree class.
2. Using the Timing class, compare the times for the methods implemented in Exercise 1 to the same methods in the BinarySearchTree class. Your test program should insert a sorted list of approximately 100 randomly generated integers into the two trees.
3. Write a deletion method for the AVLTree class that utilizes lazy deletion. There are several techniques you can use, but a simple one is to simply add a Boolean field to the Node class that signifies whether or not the node is marked for deletion. Your other methods must then take this field into account.
4. Write a deletion method for the RedBlack class that adheres to the red-black rules.
5. Design and implement a program that compares AVL trees and red–black trees to skip lists. Which data structure performs the best?

CHAPTER 16

Graphs and Graph Algorithms

The study of networks has become one of the great scientific hotbeds of this new century, though mathematicians and others have been studying networks for many hundreds of years. Recent developments in computer technology (i.e., the Internet), and in social theory (the social network, popularly conceived in the concept of "six degrees of separation"), have put a spotlight on the study of networks.

In this chapter, we look at how networks are modeled with graphs. We're not talking about the graphs such as pie graphs or bar graphs. We define what a graph is, how they're represented in VB.NET, and how to implement important graph algorithms. We also discuss the importance of picking the correct data representation when working with graphs, since the efficiency of graph algorithms is dependent on the data structure used.

GRAPH DEFINITIONS

A *graph* consists of a set of *vertices* and a set of *edges*. Think of a map of your state. Each town is connected with other towns via some type of road. A map is a type of graph. Each town is a vertex and a road that connects two towns is an edge. Edges are specified as a *pair*, (v1, v2), where v1 and v2 are two vertices in the graph. A vertex can also have a *weight*, sometimes also called a cost.

283

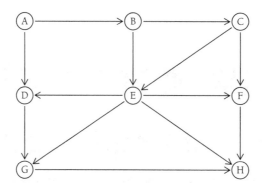

FIGURE 16.1. A Digraph (Directed Graph).

A graph whose pairs are ordered is called a *directed graph*, or just a *digraph*. An ordered graph is shown in Figure 16.1. If a graph is not ordered, it is called an *unordered graph*, or just a *graph*. An example of an unordered graph is shown in Figure 16.2.

A *path* is a sequence of vertices in a graph such that all vertices are connected by edges. The length of a path is the number of edges from the first vertex in the path to the last vertex. A path can also consist of a vertex to itself, which is called a *loop*. Loops have a length of 0.

A *cycle* is a path of at least 1 in a directed graph so that the beginning vertex is also the ending vertex. In a directed graph, the edges can be the same edge, but in an undirected graph, the edges must be distinct.

An undirected graph is considered *connected* if there is a path from every vertex to every other vertex. In a directed graph, this condition is called *strongly connected*. A directed graph that is not strongly connected, but is considered connected, is called *weakly connected*. If a graph has a edge between every set of vertices, it is said to be a *complete graph*.

REAL WORLD SYSTEMS MODELED BY GRAPHS

Graphs are used to model many different types of real world systems. One example is traffic flow. The vertices represent street intersections and the

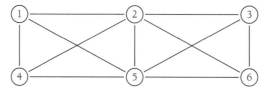

FIGURE 16.2. An Unordered Graph.

edges represent the streets themselves. Weighted edges can be used to represent speed limits or the number of lanes. Modelers can use the system to determine best routes and streets that are likely to suffer from traffic jams.

Any type of transportation system can be modeled using a graph. For example, an airline can model their flight system using a graph. Each airport is a vertex and each flight from one vertex to another is an edge. A weighted edge can represent the cost of a flight from one airport to another, or perhaps the distance from one airport to another, depending on what is being modeled.

THE GRAPH CLASS

At first glance, a graph looks much like a tree and you might be tempted to try to build a graph class like a tree. There are problems with using a reference-based implementation, however, so we will look at a different scheme for representing both vertices and edges.

Representing Vertices

The first step we have to take to build a Graph class is to build a Vertex class to store the vertices of a graph. This class has the same duties the Node class had in the LinkedList and BinarySearchTree classes.

The Vertex class needs two data members: one for the data that identifies the vertex, and the other a Boolean member we use to keep track of "visits" to the vertex. We call these data members label and wasVisited, respectively.

The only method we need for the class is a constructor method that allows us to set the label and wasVisited data members. We won't use a default constructor in this implementation because every time we make a first reference to a vertex object, we will be performing instantiation.

Here's the code for the Vertex class:

```
public class Vertex {
    public bool wasVisited;
    public string label;
```

```
public Vertex(string label) {
  this.label = label;
  wasVisited = false;
}
}
```

We will store the list of vertices in an array and will reference them in the Graph class by their position in the array.

Representing Edges

The real information about a graph is stored in the edges, since the edges detail the structure of the graph. As we mentioned earlier, it is tempting to represent a graph like a binary tree, but doing so would be a mistake. A binary tree has a fairly fixed representation, since a parent node can only have two child nodes, whereas the structure of a graph is much more flexible. There can be many edges linked to a single vertex or just one edge, for example.

The method we'll choose for representing the edges of a graph is called an adjacency matrix. This is a two-dimensional array where the elements indicate whether an edge exists between two vertices. Figure 16.3 illustrates how an adjacency matrix works for the graph in the figure.

The vertices are listed as the headings for the rows and columns. If an edge exists between two vertices, a 1 is placed in that position. If an edge doesn't exist, a 0 is used. Obviously, you can also use Boolean values here.

	V_0	V_1	V_2	V_3	V_4
V_0	0	0	1	0	0
V_1	0	0	1	0	0
V_2	1	1	0	1	1
V_3	0	0	1	0	0
V_4	0	0	1	0	0

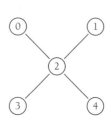

FIGURE 16.3. An Adjacency Matrix.

Building a Graph

Now that we have a way to represent vertices and edges, we're ready to build a graph. First, we need to build a list of the vertices in the graph. Here is some code for a small graph that consists of four vertices:

```
int nVertices = 0;
vertices[nVertices] = new Vertex("A");
nVertices++;
vertices[nVertices] = new Vertex("B");
nVertices++;
vertices[nVertices] = new Vertex("C");
nVertices++;
vertices[nVertices] = new Vertex("D");
```

Then we need to add the edges that connect the vertices. Here is the code for adding two edges:

```
adjMatrix[0,1] = 1;
adjMatrix[1,0] = 1;
adjMatrix[1,3] = 1;
adjMatrix[3,1] = 1;
```

This code states that an edge exists between vertices A and B and that an edge exists between vertices B and D.

With these pieces in place, we're ready to look at a preliminary definition of the Graph class (along with the definition of the Vertex class):

```
public class Vertex {

  public bool wasVisited;
  public string label;

  public Vertex(string label) {
    this.label = label;
    wasVisited = false;
  }
}
```

```
public class Graph {

  private const int NUM_VERTICES = 20;
  private Vertex[] vertices;
  private int[,] adjMatrix;
  int numVerts;

  public Graph() {
    vertices = new Vertex[NUM_VERTICES];
    adjMatrix = new int[NUM_VERTICES, NUM_VERTICES];
    numVerts = 0;
    for(int j = 0; j <= NUM_VERTICES; j++)
      for(int k = 0; k <= NUMVERTICES-1; k++)
        adjMatrix[j,k] = 0;

  }

  public void AddVertex(string label) {
    vertices[numVerts] = new Vertex(label);
    numVerts++;
  }

  public void AddEdge(int start, int eend) {
    adjMatrix[start, eend] = 1;
    adjMatrix[eend, start] = 1;
  }

  public void ShowVertex(int v) {
    Console.Write(vertices[v].label + " ");
  }
}
```

The constructor method redimensions the vertices array and the adjacency matrix to the number specified in the constant NUM_VERTICES. The data member numVerts stores the current number in the vertex list so that it is initially set to zero, since arrays are zero-based. Finally, the adjacency matrix is initialized by setting all elements to zero.

The AddVertex method takes a string argument for a vertex label, instantiates a new Vertex object, and adds it to the vertices array. The AddEdge method takes two integer values as arguments. These integers represent to vertices and indicate that an edge exists between them. Finally, the showVertex method displays the label of a specified vertex.

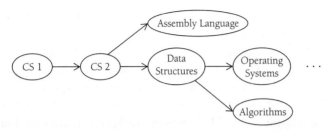

FIGURE 16.4. A Directed Graph Model of Computer Science Curriculum Sequence.

A FIRST GRAPH APPLICATION: TOPOLOGICAL SORTING

Topological sorting involves displaying the specific order in which a sequence of vertices must be followed in a directed graph. The sequence of courses a college student must take on their way to a degree can be modeled with a directed graph. A student can't take the Data Structures course until they've had the first two introductory Computer Science courses, as an example. Figure 16.4 depicts a directed graph modeling part of the typical Computer Science curriculum.

A topological sort of this graph would result in the following sequence:

1. CS1
2. CS2
3. Assembly Language
4. Data Structures
5. Operating Systems
6. Algorithms

Courses 3 and 4 can be taken at the same time, as can 5 and 6.

An Algorithm for Topological Sorting

The basic algorithm for topological sorting is very simple:

1. Find a vertex that has no successors.
2. Add the vertex to a list of vertices.
3. Remove the vertex from the graph.
4. Repeat Step 1 until all vertices are removed.

Of course, the challenge lies in the details of the implementation but this is the crux of topological sorting.

The algorithm will actually work from the end of the directed graph to the beginning. Look again at Figure 16.4. Assuming that Operating Systems and Algorithms are the last vertices in the graph (ignoring the ellipsis), neither of them have successors and so they are added to the list and removed from the graph. Next come Assembly Language and Data Structures. These vertices now have no successors and so they are removed from the list. Next will be CS2. Its successors have been removed so it is added to the list. Finally, we're left with CS1.

Implementing the Algorithm

We need two methods for topological sorting—a method to determine if a vertex has no successors and a method for removing a vertex from a graph. Let's look at the method for determining no successors first.

A vertex with no successors will be found in the adjacency matrix on a row where all the columns are zeroes. Our method will use nested for loops to check each set of columns row by row. If a 1 is found in a column, then the inner loop is exited and the next row is tried. If a row is found with all zeroes in the columns, then that row number is returned. If both loops complete and no row number is returned, then a −1 is returned, indicating there is no vertex with no successors. Here's the code:

```
public int NoSuccessors() {
  bool isEdge;
  for(int row = 0; row <= numVertices-1; row++) {
    isEdge = false;
    for(int col = 0 col <= numVertices-1; col++)
      if (adjMatrix[row, col] > 0) {
        isEdge = true;
        break;
      }
  }
    if (!(isEdge))
      return row;
  }
  return -1;
}
```

Next we need to see how to remove a vertex from the graph. The first thing we have to do is remove the vertex from the vertex list. This is easy. Then we need to remove the row and column from the adjacency matrix, followed by moving the rows and columns above and to the right of the vertex are moved down and to the left to fill the void left by the removed vertex.

To perform this operation, we write a method named delVertex, which includes two helper methods, moveRow and moveCol. Here is the code:

```
public void DelVertex(int vert)
   if (vert ! = numVertices-1) {
     for(int j = vert; j <= numVertices-1; j++)
       vertices[j] = vertices[j+1];
     for(int row = vert; row <= numVertices-1; row++)
       moveRow[row, numVertices];
     for(int col = vert; col <= numVertices-1; col++)
       moveCol[row, numVertices-1];
   }
}

private void MoveRow(int row, int length) {
   for(int col = 0; col <= length-1; col++)
     adjMatrix[row, col] = adjMatrix[row+1, col];
}

private void MoveCol(int col, int length) {
   for(int row = 0; row <= length-1; row++)
     adjMatrix[row, col] = adjMatrix[row, col+1];
}
```

Now we need a method to control the sorting process. We'll show the code first and then explain what it does:

```
public void TopSort() {
   int origVerts = numVertices;
   while(numVertices > 0) {
     int currVertex = noSuccessors();
     if (currVertex == -1) {
       Console.WriteLine("Error: graph has cycles.");
       return;
```

```
    }
    gStack.Push(vertices[currVertex].label);
    DelVertex(currVertex);
  }
  Console.Write("Topological sorting order: ");
  while (gStack.Count > 0)
    Console.Write(gStack.Pop() + " ");
}
```

The TopSort method loops through the vertices of the graph, finding a vertex with no successors, deleting it, and then moving on to the next vertex. Each time a vertex is deleted, its label is pushed onto a stack. A stack is a convenient data structure to use because the first vertex found is actually the last (or one of the last) vertices in the graph. When the TopSort method is complete, the contents of the stack will have the last vertex pushed down to the bottom of the stack and the first vertex of the graph at the top of the stack. We merely have to loop through the stack popping each element to display the correct topological order of the graph.

These are all the methods we need to perform topological sorting on a directed graph. Here's a program that tests our implementation:

```
static void Main() {
  Graph theGraph = new Graph();
  theGraph.AddVertex("A");
  theGraph.AddVertex("B");
  theGraph.AddVertex("C");
  theGraph.AddVertex("D");
  theGraph.AddEdge(0, 1);
  theGraph.AddEdge(1, 2);
  theGraph.AddEdge(2, 3);
  theGraph.AddEdge(3, 4);
  theGraph.TopSort();
  Console.WriteLine();
  Console.WriteLine("Finished.");
}
```

The output from this program shows that the order of the graph is A B C D.

Now let's look at how we would write the program to sort the graph shown in Figure 16.4:

```
static void Main() {
  Graph theGraph = new Graph();
  theGraph.AddVertex("CS1");
  theGraph.AddVertex("CS2");
  theGraph.AddVertex("DS");
  theGraph.AddVertex("OS");
  theGraph.AddVertex("ALG");
  theGraph.AddVertex("AL");
  theGraph.AddEdge(0, 1);
  theGraph.AddEdge(1, 2);
  theGraph.AddEdge(1, 5);
  theGraph.AddEdge(2, 3);
  theGraph.AddEdge(2, 4);
  theGraph.TopSort();
  Console.WriteLine();
  Console.WriteLine("Finished.");
}
```

The output from this program is:

```
 C:\Documents and Settings\Administrator\My Documents\Visual Studio Projects\Graph\bin\...  _ □ ×
Topological sorting order: CS1 CS2 DS AL ALG OS
Finished.
```

SEARCHING A GRAPH

Determining which vertices can be reached from a specified vertex is a common activity performed on graphs. We might want to know which roads lead from one town to other towns on the map, or which flights can take us from one airport to other airports.

These operations are performed on a graph using a search algorithm. There are two fundamental searches we can perform on a graph: a *depth-first* search and a *breadth-first* search. In this section, we examine each of these search algorithms.

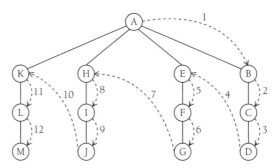

FIGURE 16.5. Depth-First Search.

Depth-First Search

Depth-first search involves following a path from the beginning vertex until it reaches the last vertex, then backtracking and following the next path until it reaches the last vertex, and so on until there are no more paths left. A diagram of a depth-first search is shown in Figure 16.5.

At a high level, the depth-first search algorithm works like this: First, pick a starting point, which can be any vertex. Visit the vertex, push it onto a stack, and mark it as visited. Then you go to the next vertex that is unvisited, push it on the stack, and mark it. This continues until you reach the last vertex. Then you check to see if the top vertex has any unvisited adjacent vertices. If it doesn't, then you pop it off the stack and check the next vertex. If you find one, you start visiting adjacent vertices until there are no more, check for more unvisited adjacent vertices, and continue the process. When you finally reach the last vertex on the stack and there are no more adjacent, unvisited vertices, you've performed a depth-first search.

The first piece of code we have to develop is a method for getting an unvisited, adjacent matrix. Our code must first go to the row for the specified vertex and determine if the value 1 is stored in one of the columns. If so, then an adjacent vertex exists. We can then easily check to see if the vertex has been visited or not. Here's the code for this method:

```
private int GetAdjUnvisitedVertex(int v) {
    for(int j = 0; j <= numVertices-1; j++)
        if ((adjMatrix(v,j) = 1) && (vertices[j].WasVisited_
                                == false))
            return j;
    return -1;
}
```

Now we're ready to look at the method that performs the depth-first search:

```
public void DepthFirstSearch() {
  vertices[0].WasVisited = true;
  ShowVertex(0);
  gStack.Push(0);
  int v;
  while (gStack.Count > 0) {
    v = GetAdjUnvisitedVertex(gStack.Peek());
    if (v == -1)
      gStack.Pop();
    else {
      vertices[v].WasVisited = true;
      ShowVertex(v);
      gStack.Push(v);
    }
  }
  for(int j = 0; j <= numVertices-1; j++)
    vertices[j].WasVisited = false;
}
```

Here is a program that performs a depth-first search on the graph shown in Figure 16.5:

```
static void Main() {
  Graph aGraph = new Graph();
  aGraph.AddVertex("A");
  aGraph.AddVertex("B");
  aGraph.AddVertex("C");
  aGraph.AddVertex("D");
  aGraph.AddVertex("E");
  aGraph.AddVertex("F");
  aGraph.AddVertex("G");
  aGraph.AddVertex("H");
  aGraph.AddVertex("I");
  aGraph.AddVertex("J");
  aGraph.AddVertex("K");
  aGraph.AddVertex("L");
  aGraph.AddVertex("M");
```

```
aGraph.AddEdge(0, 1);
aGraph.AddEdge(1, 2);
aGraph.AddEdge(2, 3);
aGraph.AddEdge(0, 4);
aGraph.AddEdge(4, 5);
aGraph.AddEdge(5, 6);
aGraph.AddEdge(0, 7);
aGraph.AddEdge(7, 8);
aGraph.AddEdge(8, 9);
aGraph.AddEdge(0, 10);
aGraph.AddEdge(10, 11);
aGraph.AddEdge(11, 12);
aGraph.DepthFirstSearch();
Console.WriteLine();
}
```

The output from this program is:

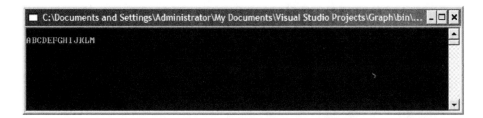

Breadth-First Search

A breadth-first search starts at a first vertex and tries to visit vertices as close to the first vertex as possible. In essence, this search moves through a graph layer by layer, examining the layers closer to the first vertex first and moving down to the layers farthest away from the starting vertex. Figure 16.6 demonstrates how breadth-first search works.

The algorithm for breadth-first search uses a queue instead of a stack, though a stack could be used. The algorithm is as follows:

1. Find an unvisited vertex that is adjacent to the current vertex, mark it as visited, and add to a queue.

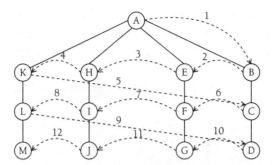

FIGURE 16.6. Breath-First Search.

2. If an unvisited, adjacent vertex can't be found, remove a vertex from the queue (as long as there is a vertex to remove), make it the current vertex, and start over.
3. If the second step can't be performed because the queue is empty, the algorithm is finished.

Now let's look at the code for the algorithm:

```
public void BreadthFirstSearch() {
  Queue gQueue = new Queue();
  vertices[0].WasVisited = true;
  ShowVertex(0);
  gQueue.EnQueue(0);
  int vert1, vert2;
  while (gQueue.Count > 0) {
    vert1 = gQueue.Dequeue();
    vert2 = GetAdjUnvisitedVertex(vert1);
    while (vert2 != -1) {
      vertices[vert2].WasVisited = true;
      ShowVertex(vert2);
      gQueue.Enqueue(vert2);
      vert2 = GetAdjUnvisitedVertex(vert1);
    }
  }
  for(int i = 0; i <= numVertices-1; i++)
    vertices[index].WasVisited = false;
}
```

Notice that there are two loops in this method. The outer loop runs while the queue has data in it, and the inner loop checks adjacent vertices to see if they've been visited. The for loop simply cleans up the vertices array for other methods.

A program that tests this code, using the graph from Figure 16.6, is shown as follows:

```
static void Main() {
  Graph aGraph = new Graph();
  aGraph.AddVertex("A");
  aGraph.AddVertex("B");
  aGraph.AddVertex("C");
  aGraph.AddVertex("D");
  aGraph.AddVertex("E");
  aGraph.AddVertex("F");
  aGraph.AddVertex("G");
  aGraph.AddVertex("H");
  aGraph.AddVertex("I");
  aGraph.AddVertex("J");
  aGraph.AddVertex("K");
  aGraph.AddVertex("L");
  aGraph.AddVertex("M");
  aGraph.AddEdge(0, 1);
  aGraph.AddEdge(1, 2);
  aGraph.AddEdge(2, 3);
  aGraph.AddEdge(0, 4);
  aGraph.AddEdge(4, 5);
  aGraph.AddEdge(5, 6);
  aGraph.AddEdge(0, 7);
  aGraph.AddEdge(7, 8);
  aGraph.AddEdge(8, 9);
  aGraph.AddEdge(0, 10);
  aGraph.AddEdge(10, 11);
  aGraph.AddEdge(11, 12);
  Console.WriteLine();
  aGraph.BreadthFirstSearch();
}
```

The output from this program is:

MINIMUM SPANNING TREES

When a network is first designed, it is possible that there can be more than the minimum number of connections between the nodes of the network. The extra connections are a wasted resource and should be eliminated, if possible. The extra connections also just make the network unnecessarily complex for others to study and understand. What we want is a network that contains just the minimum number of connections necessary to connect the nodes. Such a network, when applied to a graph, is called a *minimum spanning tree*.

A minimum spanning tree is called such because it is constructed from the minimum of number of edges necessary to cover every vertex (spanning), and it is in tree form because the resulting graph is acyclic. There is one important point you need to keep in mind: One graph can contain multiple minimum spanning trees; the minimum spanning tree you create depends entirely on the starting vertex.

A Minimum Spanning Tree Algorithm

Figure 16.7 depicts a graph for which we want to construct a minimum spanning tree.

The algorithm for a minimum spanning tree is really just a graph search algorithm (either depth-first or breadth-first) with the additional component of recording each edge that is traveled. The code also looks similar. Here's the method:

```
public void Mst() {
  vertices[0].WasVisited = true;
  gStack.Push(0);
```

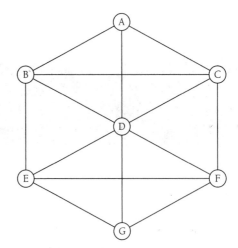

Figure 16.7. Graph For Minimum Spanning Tree.

```
int currVertex, ver;
while (gStack.Count > 0) {
  currVertex = gStack.Peek();
  ver = GetAdjUnvisitedVertex(currVertex);
  if (ver == -1)
    gStack.Pop();
  else {
    vertices[ver].WasVisited = true;
    gStack.Push(ver);
    ShowVertex(currVertex);
    ShowVertex(ver);
    Console.Write(" ");
  }
}
for (int j = 0; j <= numVertices-1; j++)
  vertices[j].WasVisited = false;
}
```

If you compare this method to the method for depth-first search, you'll see that the current vertex is recorded by calling the showVertex method with the current vertex as the argument. Calling this method twice, as shown in the code, creates the display of edges that define the minimum spanning tree.

Here is a program that creates the minimum spanning tree for the graph in Figure 16.7:

```
static void Main() {
  Graph aGraph = new Graph();
  aGraph.AddVertex("A");
  aGraph.AddVertex("B");
  aGraph.AddVertex("C");
  aGraph.AddVertex("D");
  aGraph.AddVertex("E");
  aGraph.AddVertex("F");
  aGraph.AddVertex("G");
  aGraph.AddEdge(0, 1);
  aGraph.AddEdge(0, 2);
  aGraph.AddEdge(0, 3);
  aGraph.AddEdge(1, 2);
  aGraph.AddEdge(1, 3);
  aGraph.AddEdge(1, 4);
  aGraph.AddEdge(2, 3);
  aGraph.AddEdge(2, 5);
  aGraph.AddEdge(3, 5);
  aGraph.AddEdge(3, 4);
  aGraph.AddEdge(3, 6);
  aGraph.AddEdge(4, 5);
  aGraph.AddEdge(4, 6);
  aGraph.AddEdge(5, 6);
  Console.WriteLine();
  aGraph.Mst();
}
```

The output from this program is:

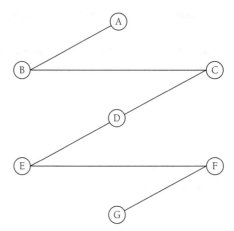

FIGURE **16.8. The Minimum Spanning Tree for Figure 16.7.**

A diagram of the minimum spanning tree is shown in Figure 16.8.

FINDING THE SHORTEST PATH

One of the most common operations performed on graphs is finding the shortest path from one vertex to another. For vacation, you are going to travel to 10 major league baseball cities to watch games over a two-week period. You want to minimize the number of miles you have to drive to visit all ten cities using a shortest-path algorithm. Another shortest-path problem is creating a network of computers, where the cost could be the time to transmit between two computers or the cost of establishing and maintaining the connection. A shortest-path algorithm can determine the most effective way you can build the network.

Weighted Graphs

We mentioned weighted graphs at the beginning of the chapter. Each edge in the graph has an associated weight, or cost. A weighted graph is shown in Figure 16.9. Weighted graphs can have negative weights, but we will limit our discussion here to positive weights. We also focus here only on directed graphs.

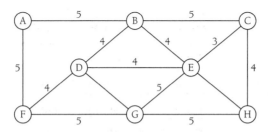

FIGURE 16.9. A Weighted Graph.

Dijkstra's Algorithm for Determining the Shortest Path

One of the most famous algorithms in computer science is *Dijkstra's algorithm* for determining the shortest path of a weighted graph, named for the late computer science Edsger Dijkstra, who discovered the algorithm in the late 1950s.

Dijkstra's algorithm finds the shortest path from any specified vertex to any other vertex, and it turns out, to all the other vertices in the graph. It does this by using what is commonly termed a *greedy* strategy or algorithm. A greedy algorithm (about which we'll have more to say in Chapter 17) breaks a problem into pieces, or stages, determining the best solution at each stage, with each subsolution contributing to the final solution. A classic example of a greedy algorithm is making change with coins. For example, if you buy something at the store for 74 cents using a dollar bill, the cashier, if he or she is using a greedy algorithm and wants to minimize the number of coins returned, will return to you a quarter and a penny. Of course, there are other solutions to making change for 26 cents, but a quarter and a penny is the optimal solution.

We use Dijkstra's algorithm by creating a table to store known distances from the starting vertex to the other vertices in the graph. Each adjacent vertex from the original vertex is visited, and the table is updated with information about the weight of the adjacent edge. If a distance between two vertices is known, but a shorter distance is discovered by visiting a new vertex, that information is changed in the table. The table is also updated by indicating which vertex leads to the shortest path.

The following tables show us the progress the algorithm makes as it works through the graph. The first table shows us the table values before vertex A is visited (the value Infinity indicates we don't know the distance, and in code we use a large value that cannot represent a weight):

Vertex	Visited	Weight	Via Path
A	False	0	0
B	False	Infinity	n/a
C	False	Infinity	n/a
D	False	Infinity	n/a
E	False	Infinity	n/a
F	False	Infinity	n/a
G	False	Infinity	n/a

After A is visited, the table looks like this:

Vertex	Visited	Weight	Via Path
A	True	0	0
B	False	2	A
C	False	Infinity	n/a
D	False	1	A
E	False	Infinity	n/a
F	False	Infinity	n/a
G	False	Infinity	n/a

Next we visit vertex D:

Vertex	Visited	Weight	Via Path
A	True	0	0
B	False	2	A
C	False	3	D
D	True	1	A
E	False	3	D
F	False	9	D
G	False	5	D

The vertex B is next visited:

Vertex	Visited	Weight	Via Path
A	True	0	0
B	True	2	A
C	False	3	D
D	True	1	A
E	False	3	D
F	False	9	D
G	False	5	D

And so on until we visit the last vertex G:

Vertex	Visited	Weight	Via Path
A	True	0	0
B	True	2	A
C	True	3	D
D	True	1	A
E	True	3	D
F	True	6	D
G	False	5	D

Code for Dijkstra's Algorithm

The first piece of code for the algorithm is the Vertex class, which we've seen before:

```
public class Vertex {
    public string label;
    public bool isInTree;
```

```
public Vertex(string lab) {
  label = lab;
  isInTree = false;
}
}
```

We also need a class that helps keep track of the relationship between a distant vertex and the original vertex used to compute shortest paths. This is called the DistOriginal class:

```
public class DistOriginal {

  public int distance;
  public int parentVert;

  public DistOriginal(int pv, int d) {
    distance = d;
    parentVert = pv;
  }
}
```

The Graph class that we've used before now has a new set of methods for computing shortest paths. The first of these is the Path() method, which drives the shortest path computations:

```
public void Path() {
  int startTree = 0;
  vertexList[startTree].isInTree = true;
  nTree = 1;
  for(int j = 0; j <= nVerts-1; j++) {
    int tempDist = adjMat(startTree, j);
    sPath[j] = new DistOriginal(startTree, tempDist);
  }
  while (nTree < nVerts) {
    int indexMin = GetMin();
    int minDist = sPath[indexMin].distance;
    currentVert = indexMin;
    startToCurrent = sPath[indexMin].distance;
    vertexList[currentVert].isInTree = true;
```

```
        nTree++;
        AdjustShortPath();
    }
    DisplayPaths();
    nTree = 0;
    for(int j = 0; j <= nVerts-1; j++)
        vertexList[j].isInTree = false;
}
```

This method uses two other helper methods, getMin and adjustShortPath. Those methods are explained shortly. The for loop at the beginning of the method looks at the vertices reachable from the beginning vertex and places them in the sPath array. This array holds the minimum distances from the different vertices and will eventually hold the final shortest paths.

The main loop (the while loop) performs three operations:

1. Find the entry in sPath with the shortest distance.
2. Make this vertex the current vertex.
3. Update the sPath array to show distances from the current vertex.

Much of this work is performed by the getMin and adjustShortPath methods:

```
public int GetMin() {
    double minDist = Double.PositiveInfinity;
    int indexMin = 0;
    for(int j = 1; j <= nVerts-1; j++)
        if (!(vertexList[j].isInTree) &&
            (sPath[j].distance < minDist)) {
            minDist = sPath[j].distance;
            indexMin = j;
        }
    return indexMin;
}

public void AdjustShortPath() {
    int column = 1;
    while (column < nVerts)
        if (vertexList[column].isInTree)
            column++;
```

```
      else {
        int currentToFringe = adjMat[currentVert, column];
        int startToFringe = startToCurrent +
                            currentToFringe;
        int sPathDist = sPath[column].distance;
        if (startToFringe < sPathDist) {
          sPath[column].parentVert = currentVert;
          sPath[column].distance = startToFringe;
        }
      }
    }
  }
}
```

The getMin method steps through the sPath array until the minimum distance
is determined, which is then returned by the method. The adjustShortPath
method takes a new vertex, finds the next set of vertices connected to this
vertex, calculates shortest paths, and updates the sPath array until a shorter
distance is found.

Finally, the displayPaths method shows the final contents of the sPath array.
To make the graph available for other algorithms, the nTree variable is set to
0 and the isInTree flags are all set to false.

To put all this into context, here is a complete application that includes all
the code for computing the shortest paths using Dijkstra's algorithm, along
with a program to test the implementation:

```
public class DistOriginal {

  int distance;
  int parentVert;

  public DistOriginal(int pv, int d) {
    distance = d;
    parentVert = pv;
  }
}
public class Vertex {
  public string label;
  public bool isInTree;

  public Vertex(string lab) {
    label = lab;
```

```
        isInTree = false;
    }
}
public class Graph {
    private const int max_verts = 20;
    int infinity = 1000000;
    Vertex[] vertexList;
    int[,] adjMat;
    int nVerts;
    int nTree;
    DistOriginal[] sPath;
    int currentVert;
    int startToCurrent;

    public Graph() {
        vertexList = new Vertex(max_verts);
        adjMat = new int(max_verts, max_verts);
        nVerts = 0;
        nTree = 0;
        for(int j = 0; j <= max_verts-1; j++)
            for(int k = 0;, <= max_verts-1; k++)
                adjMat[j,k] = infinity;
        sPath = new DistOriginal[max_verts];
    }

    public void AddVertex(string lab) {
        vertexList[nVerts] = new Vertex[lab];
        nVerts++;
    }

    public void AddEdge(int start, int theEnd, int weight){
        adjMat[start, theEnd] = weight;
    }

    public void Path() {
        int startTree = 0;
        vertexList[startTree].isInTree = true;
        nTree = 1;
        for(int j = 0; j <= nVerts; j++) {
            int tempDist = adjMat[startTree, j];
            sPath[j] = new DistOriginal[startTree, tempDist];
        }
```

```
  while (nTree < nVerts) {
    int indexMin = GetMin();
    int minDist = sPath[indexMin].distance;
    currentVert = indexMin;
    startToCurrent = sPath[indexMin].distance;
    vertexList[currentVert].isInTree = true;
    nTree++;
    AdjustShortPath();
  }
  DisplayPaths();
  nTree = 0;
  for(int j = 0; j <= nVerts-1; j++)
    vertexList[j].isInTree = false;
}

public int GetMin() {
  int minDist = infinity;
  int indexMin = 0;
  for(int j = 1; j <= nVerts-1; j++)
    if (!(vertexList[j].isInTree) &&
          sPath[j].distance < minDist)) {
      minDist = sPath[j].distance;
      indexMin = j;
    }
  return indexMin;
}

public void AdjustShortPath() {
  int column = 1;
  while (column < nVerts)
    if (vertexList[column].isInTree)
        column++;
    else {
      int currentToFring = adjMat[currentVert, column];
      int startToFringe = startToCurrent +
                          currentToFringe;
      int sPathDist = sPath[column].distance;
      if (startToFringe < sPathDist) {
        sPath[column].parentVert = currentVert;
        sPath[column].distance = startToFringe;
      }
```

```
            column++;
        }
      }
    }

    public void DisplayPaths() {
      for(int j = 0; j <= nVerts-1; j++) {
        Console.Write(vertexList[j].label + "=");
        if (sPath[j].distance = infinity)
          Console.Write("inf");
        else
          Console.Write(sPath[j].distance);
        string parent = vertexList[sPath[j].parentVert].
                                  label;
        Console.Write("(" + parent + ") ");
      }
    }
  }

  class chapter16 {
    static void Main() {
      Graph theGraph = new Graph();
      theGraph.AddVertex("A");
      theGraph.AddVertex("B");
      theGraph.AddVertex("C");
      theGraph.AddVertex("D");
      theGraph.AddVertex("E");
      theGraph.AddVertex("F");
      theGraph.AddVertex("G");
      theGraph.AddEdge(0, 1, 2);
      theGraph.AddEdge(0, 3, 1);
      theGraph.AddEdge(1, 3, 3);
      theGraph.AddEdge(1, 4, 10);
      theGraph.AddEdge(2, 5, 5);
      theGraph.AddEdge(2, 0, 4);
      theGraph.AddEdge(3, 2, 2);
      theGraph.AddEdge(3, 5, 8);
      theGraph.AddEdge(3, 4, 2);
      theGraph.AddEdge(3, 6, 4);
      theGraph.AddEdge(4, 6, 6);
      theGraph.AddEdge(6, 5, 1);
      Console.WriteLine();
```

```
        Console.WriteLine("Shortest paths:");
        Console.WriteLine();
        theGraph.Path();
        Console.WriteLine();
    }
}
```

The output from this program is:

```
■ C:\Documents and Settings\Administrator\My Documents\Visual Studio Projects\GraphW\bi...  _ □ ×
Shortest paths:
A=inf(A)  B=2(A)  C=3(D)  D=1(A)  E=3(D)  F=6(G)  G=5(D)
■
```

SUMMARY

Graphs are one of the most important data structures used in computer science. Graphs are used regularly to model everything from electrical circuits to university course schedules to truck and airline routes.

Graphs are made up of vertices that are connected by edges. Graphs can be searched in several ways; the two most common are depth-first search and breadth-first search. Another important algorithm performed on graph is determining the minimum spanning tree, which is the minimum number of edges necessary to connect all the vertices in a graph.

The edges of a graph can have weights, or costs. When working with weighted graphs, an important operation is determining the shortest path from a starting vertex to the other vertices in the graph. This chapter looked at one algorithm for computing shortest paths, Dijkstra's algorithm.

Weiss (1999) contains a more technical discussion of the graph algorithms covered in this chapter, whereas LaFore (1998) contains very good practical explanations of all the algorithms we covered here.

EXERCISES

1. Build a weighted graph that models a section of your home state. Use Dijkstra's algorithm to determine the shortest path from a starting vertex to the last vertex.

2. Take the weights off the graph in Exercise 1 and build a minimum spanning tree.
3. Still using the graph from Exercise 1, write a Windows application that allows the user to search for a vertex in the graph using either a depth-first search or a breadth-first search.
4. Using the Timing class, determine which of the searches implemented in Exercise 3 is more efficient.

CHAPTER 17

Advanced Algorithms

In this chapter, we look at two advanced topics: dynamic programming and greedy algorithms. *Dynamic programming* is a technique that is often considered to be the reverse of recursion—a recursive solution starts at the top and breaks the problem down solving all small problems until the complete problem is solved; a dynamic programming solution starts at the bottom, solving small problems and combining them to form an overall solution to the big problem.

A *greedy algorithm* is an algorithm that looks for "good solutions" as it works toward the complete solution. These good solutions, called *local optima*, will hopefully lead to the correct final solution, called the *global optimum*. The term "greedy" comes from the fact these algorithms take whatever solution looks best at the time. Often, greedy algorithms are used when it is almost impossible to find a complete solution, due to time and/or space considerations, yet a suboptimal solution is acceptable.

Dynamic Programming

Recursive solutions to problems are often elegant but inefficient. The C# compiler, along with other language compilers, will not efficiently translate the recursive code to machine code, resulting in an inefficient, though elegant computer program.

Many programming problems that have recursive solutions can be rewritten using the techniques of dynamic programming. A dynamic programming solution builds a table, usually using an array, which holds the results of the different subsolutions. Finally, when the algorithm is complete, the solution is found in a distinct spot in the table.

A Dynamic Programming Example: Computing Fibonacci Numbers

The Fibonacci numbers can be described by the following sequence

0, 1, 1, 2, 3, 5, 8, 13, 21, 34, 55, . . .

There is a simple recursive program you can use to generate any specific number in this sequence. Here is the code for the function:

```
static long recurFib(int n) {
  if (n < 2)
    return n
  else
    return recurFib(n - 1) + recurFib(n - 2);
}
```

And here is a program that uses the function:

```
static void Main() {
  int num = 5;
  long fibNumber = recurFib(num);
  Console.Write(fibNumber);
}
```

The problem with this function is that it is extremely inefficient. We can see exactly how inefficient this recursion is by examining the tree in Figure 17.1.

The problem with the recursive solution is that too many values are recomputed during a recursive call. If the compiler could keep track of the values that are already computed, the function would not be nearly so inefficient. We can design an algorithm using dynamic programming techniques that is much more efficient than the recursive algorithm.

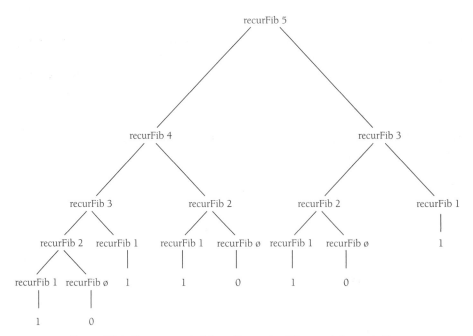

FIGURE **17.1. Tree generated from Recursive Fibonacci Computation.**

An algorithm designed using dynamic programming techniques starts by solving the simplest subproblem it can solve, using that solution to solve more complex subproblems until the problem is solved. The solutions to each subproblem are typically stored in an array for easy access.

We can easily comprehend the essence of dynamic programming by examining the dynamic programming algorithm for computing a Fibonacci number. Here's the code followed by an explanation of how it works:

```
static long iterFib(int n) {
  int[] val = new int[n];
  if ((n == 1) || (n == 2))
     return 1;
  else {
     val[1] = 1;
     val[2] = 2;
     for(int i = 3; i <= n-1; i++)
        val[i] = val[i-1] + val[i-2];
  }
  return val[n-1];
}
```

The array val is where we store our intermediate results. The first part of the If statement returns the value 1 if the argument is 1 or 2. Otherwise, the values 1 and 2 are stored in the indices 1 and 2 of the array. The for loop runs from 3 to the input argument, assigning each array element the sum of the previous two array elements, and when the loop is complete, the last value in the array is returned.

Let's compare the times it takes to compute a Fibonacci number using both the recursive version and the iterative version. First, here's the program we use for the comparison:

```
static void Main() {
  Timing tObj = new Timing();
  Timing tObj1 = new Timing();
  int num = 10;
  int fibNumber;
  tObj.StartTime();
  fibNumber = recurFib(num);
  tObj.StopTime();
  Console.WriteLine("Calculating Fibonacci number: " +
                    num);
  Console.WriteLine(fibNumber + " in: " +
                    tObj.Result.TotalMilliseconds);
  tObj1.StartTime();
  fibNumber = iterFib(num);
  tObj1.StopTime();
  Console.WriteLine(fibNumber + " in: " +
                    tObj.Result.TotalMilliseconds);

}
```

If we run this program to test the two functions for small Fibonacci numbers, we'll see little difference, or even see that the recursive function is a little faster:

If we try a larger number, say 20, we get the following results:

```
■ C:\Documents and Settings\Administrator\My Documents\Visual Studio Projects\DynProg\bi...  _ □ ×
Calculating Fibonacci number: 20
6765 in: 10.0144
6765 in: 0
```

For a really large number, such as 35, the disparity is even greater:

```
■ C:\Documents and Settings\Administrator\My Documents\Visual Studio Projects\DynProg\bi...  _ □ ×
Calculating Fibonacci number: 35
9227465 in: 540.7776
9227465 in: 10.0144
```

This is a typical example of how dynamic programming can help improve the performance of an algorithm. As we mentioned earlier, a program using dynamic programming techniques usually utilizes an array to store intermediate computations, but we should point out that in some situations, such as the Fibonacci function, an array is not necessary. Here is the iterFib function written without the use of an array:

```
static long iterFib1(int n) {
  long last, nextLast, result;
  last = 1;
  nextLast = 1;
  result = 1;
  for(int i = 2; i <= n-1; i++) {
    result = last + nextLast;
    nextLast = last;
    last = result;
  }
  return result;
}
```

Both iterFib and iterFib1 calculate Fibonacci numbers in about the same time.

Finding the Longest Common Substring

Another problem that lends itself to a dynamic programming solution is finding the longest common substring in two strings. For example, in the words "raven" and "havoc", the longest common substring is "av".

Let's look first at the brute force solution to this problem. Given two strings, A and B, we can find the longest common substring by starting at the first character of A and comparing each character to the characters in B. When a nonmatch is found, move to the next character of A and start over with the first character of B, and so on.

There is a better solution using a dynamic programming algorithm. The algorithm uses a two-dimensional array to store the results of comparisons of the characters in the same position in the two strings. Initially, each element of the array is set to 0. Each time a match is found in the same position of the two arrays, the element at the corresponding row and column of the array is incremented by 1, otherwise the element is set to 0.

To reproduce the longest common substring, the second through the next to last rows of the array are examined and a column entry with a value greater than 0 corresponds to one character in the substring. If no common substring was found, all the elements of the array are 0.

Here is a complete program for finding a longest common substring:

```
using System;

class chapter17 {

  static void LCSubstring(string word1, string word2,
                          string[] warr1; string[]
                          warr2, int[,] arr) {
    int len1, len2;
    len1 = word1.Length;
    len2 = word2.Length;
    for(int k = 0; k <= word1.Length-1; k++) {
      warr1[k] = word1.Chars(k);
      warr2[k] = word2.Chars(k);
  }
    for(int i = len1-1; i >= 0; i--)
      for(int j = len2-1; j >= 0; j--)
        if (warr1[i] = warr2[j])
            arr[i,j] = 1 + arr[i+1, j+1];
```

```
    else
      arr[i,j] = 0;
}

static string ShowString(int[,] arr, string[] wordArr) {
  string substr = "";
  for(int i = 0; i <= arr.GetUpperBound(0))
    for(int j = 0; j <= arr.GetUpperBound(1))
      if (arr[i,j]>0)
        substr + = wordArr[j];
  return substr;
}

static void DispArray(int arr[,]) {
  for(int row = 0; row <= arr.GetUpperBound(0))
    for(int col = 0; col <= arr.GetUpperBound(1))
      Console.Write(arr[row, col]);
  Console.WriteLine();
}

static void Main() {
  string word1 = "maven";
  string word2 = "havoc";
  string[] warray1 = new string[word1.Length];
  string[] warray2 = new string[word2.Length];
  string substr;
  int[,] larray = new int[word1.Length, word2.Length];
  LCSubstring(word1, word2, warray1, warray2, larray);
  Console.WriteLine();
  DispArray(larray);
  substr = ShowString(larray, warray1);
  Console.WriteLine();
  Console.WriteLine("The strings are: " + word1 + " "
                    + word2);
  if (substr>"")
    Console.WriteLine("The longest common substring
                       is: " + substr);
  else
    Console.WriteLine("There is no common substring");
}
}
```

The function LCSubstring does the work of building the two-dimensional array that stores the values that determine the longest common substring. The first for loop simply turns the two strings into arrays. The second for loop performs the comparisons and builds the array.

The function ShowString examines the array built in LCSubstring, checking to see if any elements have a value greater than 0, and returning the corresponding letter from one of the strings if such a value is found.

The subroutine DispArray displays the contents of an array, which we use to examine the array built by LCSubstring when we run the preceding program:

The encoding stored in larray shows us that the second and third characters of the two strings make up the longest common substring of "maven" and "havoc". Here's another example:

Clearly, these two strings have no common substring, so the array is filled with zeroes.

The Knapsack Problem

A classic problem in the study of algorithms is the knapsack problem. Imagine you are a safecracker and you break open a safe filled with all sorts of treasures but all you have to carry the loot is a small backpack. The items in the safe differ in both size and value. You want to maximize your take by filling your backpack with those items that are worth the most.

There is, of course, a brute force solution to this problem but the dynamic programming solution is more efficient. The key idea to solving the knapsack problem with a dynamic programming solution is to calculate the maximum value for every value up to the total capacity of the knapsack. See Sedgewick (1990, pp. 596–598) for a very clear and succinct explanation of the knapsack problem. The example problem in this section is based on the material from that book.

If the safe in the example discussed earlier has five items, the items have a size of 3, 4, 7, 8, and 9, respectively, and values of 4, 5, 10, 11, 13, respectively, and the knapsack has a capacity of 16, then the proper solution is to pick items 3 and 5 with a total size of 16 and a total value of 23.

The code for solving this problem is quite short, but it won't make much sense without the context of the whole program, so let's look at a program to solve the knapsack problem:

```
using System;

class chapter17 {
    static void Main() {
        int capacity = 16;
        int[] size = new int[] {3, 4, 7, 8, 9};
        int[] values = new int[] {4, 5, 10, 11, 13};
        int[] totval = new int[capacity];
        int[] best = new int[capacity];
        int n = values.Length;
        for (int j = 0; j <= n-1; j++)
            for (int i = 0; i <= capacity; i++)
                if (i >= size[j])
                    if (totval[i] < (totval[i-size[j]] + values[j]) {
                        totval[i] = totval[i-size[j]] + values[j];
                        best[i] = j;
                    }
```

```
  Console.WriteLine("The maximum value is: " +
                     totval[capacity]);
  }
}
```

The items in the safe are modeled using both the size array and the values array. The totval array is used to store the highest total value as the algorithm works through the different items. The best array stores the item that has the highest value. When the algorithm is finished, the highest total value will be in the last position of the totval array, with the next highest value in the next-to-last position, and so on. The same situation holds for the best array. The item with the highest value will be stored in the last element of the best array, the item with the second highest value in the next-to-last position, and so on.

The heart of the algorithm is the second if statement in the nested for loop. The current best total value is compared to the total value of adding the next item to the knapsack. If the current best total value is greater, nothing happens. Otherwise, this new total value is added to the totval array as the best current total value and the index of that item is added to the best array. Here is the code again:

```
if (totval[i] < totval[i - size[j]] + values[j]) {
  totval[i] = totval[i - size[j]] + values[j];
  best[i] = j;
}
```

If we want to see the items that generated the total value, we can examine them in the best array:

```
Console.WriteLine("The items that generate this value
                   are: ");
int totcap = 0;
i = capacity;
while (totcap <= capacity) {
  Console.WriteLine("Item with best value: " + best[i]);
  totcap + = values[best[i]];
  i--;
}
```

Remember, all the items that generate a previous best value are stored in the array, so we move down through the best array, returning items until their sizes equal the total capacity of the knapsack.

GREEDY ALGORITHMS

In the previous section, we examined dynamic programming algorithms that can be used to optimize solutions that are found using some less-efficient algorithm, often based on recursion. For many problems, though, resorting to dynamic programming is overkill and a simpler algorithm will suffice.

One type of simpler algorithm is the *greedy* algorithm. A greedy algorithm is the one that always chooses the best solution at the time, with no regard for how that choice will affect future choices. Using a greedy algorithm generally indicates that the implementer hopes that the series of "best" local choices made will lead to a final "best" choice. If so, then the algorithm has produced an optimal solution; if not, a suboptimal solution has been found. However, for many problems, it is not worth the trouble to find an optimal solution, so using a greedy algorithm works just fine.

A First Greedy Algorithm Example: The Coin-Changing Problem

The classic example of following a greedy algorithm is making change. Let's say you buy some items at the store and the change from your purchase is 63 cents. How does the clerk determine the change to give you? If the clerk follows a greedy algorithm, he or she gives you two quarters, a dime, and three pennies. That is the smallest number of coins that will equal 63 cents (given that we don't allow fifty-cent pieces).

It has been proven that an optimal solution for coin changing can always be found using the current American denominations of coins. However, if we introduce some other denomination to the mix, the greedy algorithm doesn't produce an optimal solution.

Here's a program that uses a greedy algorithm to make change (this code assumes change of less than one dollar):

```
using System;

class chapter17 {
```

```
    static void MakeChange(double origAmount, double
                        remainAmount, int[] coins) {
      if ((origAmount % 0.25) < origAmount) {
        coins[3] = (int)(origAmount / 0.25);
        remainAmount = origAmount % 0.25;
        origAmount = remainAmount;
      }
      if ((origAmount % 0.1) < origAmount) {
        coins[2] = (int)(origAmount / 0.1);
        remainAmount = origAmount % 0.1;
        origAmount = remainAmount;
      }
      if ((origAmount % 0.05) < origAmount) {
        coins[1] = (int)(origAmount / 0.05);
        remainAmount = origAmount % 0.05;
        origAmount = remainAmount;
      }
      if ((origAmount % 0.01) < origAmount) {
        coins[0] = (int)(origAmount / 0.01);
        remainAmount = origAmount % 0.01;
      }
    }
    static void ShowChange(int[] arr) {
      if (arr[3] > 0)
        Console.WriteLine("Number of quarters: " +
arr[3]);
      if (arr[2] > 0)
        Console.WriteLine("Number of dimes: " + arr[2]);
      if (arr[1] > 0)
        Console.WriteLine("Number of nickels: " + arr[1]);
      if (arr[0] > 0)
        Console.WriteLine("Number of pennies: " + arr[0]);
    }
    static void Main() {
      double origAmount = 0.63;
      double toChange = origAmount;
      double remainAmount = 0.0;
      int[] coins = new int[4];
      MakeChange(origAmount, remainAmount, coins);
```

```
Console.WriteLine("The best way to change " +
                  toChange + " cents is: ");
    ShowChange(coins);
  }
}
```

The MakeChange subroutine starts with the highest denomination, quarters, and tries to make as much change with them as possible. The total number of quarters is stored in the coins array. Once the original amount is less than a quarter, the algorithm moves to dimes, again trying to make as much change with dimes as possible. The algorithm proceeds to nickels and then to pennies, storing the total number of each coin type in the coins array. Here's some output from the program:

As we mentioned earlier, this greedy algorithm always finds the optimal solution using the standard American coin denominations. What would happen, though, if a new coin, say a 22-cent piece, is put into circulation? In the exercises, you'll get a chance to explore this question.

Data Compression Using Huffman Coding

Compressing data is an important technique for the practice of computing. Data sent over the Internet needs to be sent as compactly as possible. There are many different schemes for compressing data, but one particular scheme makes use of a greedy algorithm—*Huffman coding*. Data compressed using a Huffman code can achieve savings of 20% to 90%. This algorithm is named for the late David Huffman, an information theorist and computer scientist who invented the technique in the 1950s.

When data is compressed, the characters that make up the data are usually translated into some other representation in order to save space. A typical compression scheme is to translate each character to a binary character code, or bit string. For example, we can encode the character "a" as 000, the character "b" as 001, the character "c" as 010, and so on. This is called a *fixed-length code*.

A better idea, though, is to use a *variable-length code*, where the characters with the highest frequency of occurrence in the string have shorter codes and the lower frequency characters have longer codes, since these characters are used as much. The encoding process then is just a matter of assigning a bit string to a character based on the character's frequency. The Huffman code algorithm takes a string of characters, translates them to a variable-length binary string, and creates a binary tree for the purpose of decoding the binary strings. The path to each left child is assigned the binary character 0 and each right child is assigned the binary character 1.

The algorithm works as follows: Start with a string of characters you want to compress. For each character in the string, calculate its frequency of occurrence in the string. Then sort the characters into order from the lowest frequency to the highest frequency. Take the two characters with the smallest frequencies and create a node with each character (and its frequency) as children of the node. The parent node's data element consists of the sum of the frequencies of the two child nodes. Insert the node back into the list. Continue this process until every character is placed into the tree.

When this process is complete, you have a complete binary tree that can be used to decode the Huffman code. Decoding involves following a path of 0s and 1s until you get to a leaf node, which will contain a character.

To see how all this works, examine Figure 17.2.

Now we're ready to examine the C# code for constructing a Huffman code. Let's start with the code for creating a Node class. This class is quite a bit different from the Node class for binary search trees, since all we want to do here is store some data and a link:

```
public class Node {

    HuffmanTree data;
    Node link;
    public Node(HuffmanTree newData) {
      data = newData;
    }
}
```

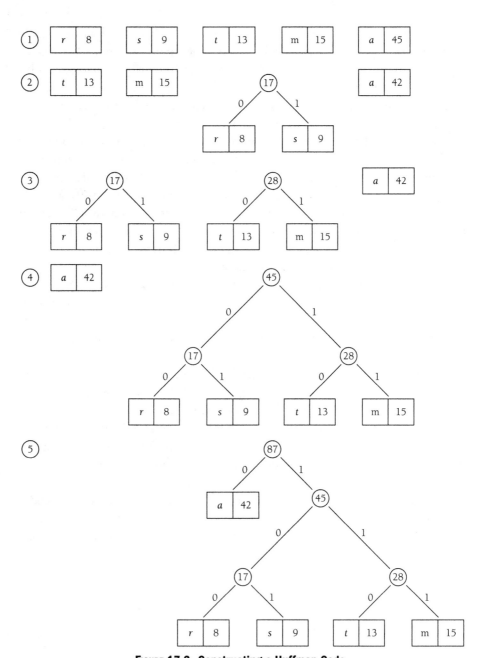

FIGURE **17.2. Constructing a Huffman Code.**

The next class to examine is the TreeList class. This class is used to store the list of nodes that are placed into the binary tree, using a linked list as the storage technique. Here's the code:

```
public class TreeList {

  private int count = 0;
  Node first;

  public void AddLetter(string letter) {
    HuffmanTree hTemp = new HuffmanTree(letter);
    Node eTemp = new Node(hTemp);
    if (first == null)
      first = eTemp;
    else {
      eTemp.link = first;
      first = eTemp;
    }
    count++;
  }

  public void SortTree() {
    TreeList otherList = new TreeList();
    HuffmanTree aTemp;
    while (!(this.first == null) {
      aTemp = this.RemoveTree();
      otherList.InsertTree(aTemp);
    }
    this.first = otherList.first;
  }

  public void MergeTree() {
    if (!(first == null))
      if (!(first.link == null)) {
        HuffmanTree aTemp = RemoveTree();
        HuffmanTree bTemp = RemoveTree();
        HuffmanTree sumTemp = new HuffmanTree();
        sumTemp.SetLeftChild(aTemp);
        sumTemp.SetRightChild(bTemp);
```

```java
            sumTemp.SetFreq(aTemp.GetFreq() +
                            bTemp.GetFreq());
            InsertTree(sumTemp);
        }
    }

    public HuffmanTree RemoveTree() {
        if (!(first == null)) {
            HuffmanTree hTemp;
            hTemp = first.data;
            first = first.link;
            count--;
            return hTemp;
        }
        return null;
    }

    public void InsertTree(HuffmanTree hTemp) {
        Node eTemp = new Node(hTemp);
        if (first == null)
            first = eTemp;
        else {
            Node p = first;
            while (!(p.link == null)) {
                if ((p.data.GetFreq()<= hTemp.GetFreq()) &&
                    (p.link.data.GetFreq() >= hTemp.GetFreq()))
                  break;
                p = p.link;
          }
            eTemp.link = p.link;
            p.link = eTemp;
        }
        count++;
    }

    public int Length() {
     return count;
    }
}
```

This class makes use of the HuffmanTree class, so let's view that code now:

```
public class HuffmanTree {

  private HuffmanTree leftChild;
  private HuffmanTree rightChild;
  private string letter;
  private int freq;

  public HuffmanTree() {
    this.letter = letter;
  }

  public void SetLeftChild(HuffmanTree newChild) {
    leftChild = newChild;
  }

  public void SetRightChild(HuffmanTree newChild) {
    rightChild = newChild;
  }

  public void SetLetter(string newLetter) {
    letter = newChild;
  }

  public void IncFreq() {
    freq++;
  }

  public void SetFreq(int newFreq) {
    freq = newFreq;
  }

  public HuffmanTree GetLeftChild() {
    return leftChild;
  }

  public HuffmanTree GetRightChild() {
    return rightChild;
  }

  public int GetFreq() {
    return freq;
  }
}
```

Finally, we need a program to test the implementation:

```
static void Main() {
  string input;
  Console.Write("Enter a string to encode: ");
  input = Console.ReadLine();
  TreeList treeList = new TreeList();
  for(int i = 0; i < input.Length; i++)
    treeList.AddSign(input.Chars(i));
  treeList.SortTree();
  int[] signTable = new int[input.Length];
  int[] keyTable = new int[input.Length];
  while(treeList.length > 1)
    treeList.MergeTree();
  MakeKey(treeList.RemoveTree(), "");
  string newStr = translate(input);
  for(int i = 0; i <= signTable.Length - 1; i++)
    Console.WriteLine(signTable[i] + ": " +
                        keyTable[i]);
  Console.WriteLine("The original string is " + input.
                      Length * 16 + " bits long.");
  Console.WriteLine("The new string is " + newStr.Length
                      + " bits long.");
  Console.WriteLine("The coded string looks like this:
                      " + newStr);
}

static string translate(string original) {
  string newStr = "";
  for(int i = 0; i <= original.Length-1; i++
    for(int j = 0; j <= signTable.Length-1; j++)
      if (original.Chars(i) == signTable[j])
        newStr + = keyTable[j];
  return newStr;
}

static void MakeKey(HuffmanTree tree, string code) {
  int pos = 0;
  if (tree.GetLeftChild == null) {
    signTable[pos] = tree.GetSign();
```

```
      keyTable[pos] = code;
      pos++;
   } else {
      MakeKey(tree.GetLeftChild, code + "0");
      MakeKey(tree.GetRightChild, code + "1");
   }
}
```

A Greedy Solution to the Knapsack Problem

Earlier in this chapter, we examined the knapsack problem and wrote a program to solve the problem using dynamic programming techniques. In this section, we look at the problem again, this time looking for a greedy algorithm to solve the problem.

To use a greedy algorithm to solve the knapsack problem, the items we are placing in the knapsack need to be "continuous" in nature. In other words, they must be items like cloth or gold dust that cannot be counted discretely. If we are using these types of items, then we can simply divide the unit price by the unit volume to determine the value of the item. An optimal solution is to place as much of the item with the highest value in the knapsack as possible until the item is depleted or the knapsack is full, followed by as much of the second highest item as possible, and so on. The reason we can't find an optimal greedy solution using discrete items is that we can't put "half a television" into a knapsack.

Let's look at an example. You are a carpet thief and you have a knapsack that will store only 25 "units" of carpeting. Therefore, you want to get as much of the "good stuff" as you can in order to maximize your take. You know that the carpet store you're going to hit has the following carpet styles and quantities on hand (with unit prices):

- Saxony: 12 units, $1.82
- Loop: 10 units, $1.77
- Frieze: 12 units, $1.75
- Shag: 13 units, $1.50

The greedy strategy dictates that you take as many units of Saxony as possible, followed by as many units of Loop, then Frieze, and finally Shag.

Being the computational type, you first write a program to model your heist. Here is the code you come up with:

```
public class Carpet : IComparable {
  private string item;
  private float val;
  private int unit;

  public Carpet(string i, float v, int u) {
    item = i;
    val = v;
    unit = u;
  }

  public int CompareTo(Carpet c) {
    return (this.val.CompareTo(c.val));
  }

  public int GetUnit() {
    return unit;
  }

  public string GetItem() {
    return item;
  }

  public float GetVal() {
    return val * unit;
  }

  public float ItemVal() {
    return val;
  }
}

public class Knapsack {
 private float quantity;
 SortedList items = new SortedList();
 string itemList;

  public Knapsack(float max) {
   quantity = max;
  }
```

```
public void FillSack(ArrayList objects) {
  int pos = objects.Count-1;
  int totalUnits = 0;
  float totalVal = 0.0;
  int tempTot = 0;
  while (totalUnits < quantity) {
    tempTot + = (Carpet)objects[pos].GetUnit();
    if (tempTot <= quantity) {
      totalUnits + = (Carpet)objects[pos].GetUnit();
      totalVal + = (Carpet)objects[pos].GetVal();
      items.Add((Carpet)objects[pos].GetItem(),
                (Carpet)objects[pos].GetUnit());
    } else {
      float tempUnit = quantity - totalUnits;
      float tempVal = (Carpet)objects[pos].ItemVal()*
                      tempUnit;
      totalVal + = tempVal;
      totalUnits + = (int)tempUnit;
      items.Add((Carpet)objects[pos].GetItem(), tempUnit);
    }
    pos--;
  }
}

public string GetItems() {
  foreach (Object k in items.GetKeyList())
    itemList + = k.ToString() + ": " + items[k].
                ToString() + " ";
  return itemList;
}
}

static void Main() {
  Carpet c1 = new Carpet("Frieze", 1.75, 12);
  Carpet c2 = new Carpet("Saxony", 1.82, 9);
  Carpet c3 = new Carpet("Shag", 1.5, 13);
  Carpet c4 = new Carpet("Loop", 1.77, 10);
  ArrayList rugs = new ArrayList();
  rugs.Add(c1);
  rugs.Add(c2);
```

```
    rugs.Add(c3);
    rugs.Add(c4);
    rugs.Sort();
    Knapsack k = new Knapsack(25);
    k.FillSack(rugs)
    Console.WriteLine(k.getItems);
}
```

The Carpet class is used for two reasons: to encapsulate the data about each type of carpeting and to implement the IComparable interface, so we can sort the carpet types by their unit cost.

The Knapsack class does most of the work in this implementation. It provides a list to store the carpet types and it provides a method, FillSack, to determine how the knapsack gets filled. Also, the constructor method allows the user to pass in a quantity that sets the maximum number of units the knapsack can hold.

The FillSack method loops through the carpet types, adding as much of the most valuable carpeting as possible into the knapsack, then moving on to the next type. At the point where the knapsack becomes full, the code in the Else clause of the If statement puts the proper amount of carpeting into the knapsack.

This code works because we can cut the carpeting wherever we want. If we were trying to fill the knapsack with some other item that does not come in continuous quantities, we would have to move to a dynamic programming solution.

SUMMARY

This chapter examined two advanced techniques for algorithm design: dynamic programs and greedy algorithms. Dynamic programming is a technique where a bottom-up approach is taken to solving a problem. Rather than working its way down to the bottom of a calculation, such as done with recursive algorithm, a dynamic programming algorithm starts at the bottom and builds on those results until the final solution is reached.

Greedy algorithms look for solutions as quickly as possible and then stop before looking for all possible solutions. A problem solved with a greedy algorithm will not necessarily be the optimal solution because the greedy algorithm will have stopped with a "sufficient" solution before finding the optimal solution.

EXERCISES

1. Rewrite the longest common substring code as a class.
2. Write a program that uses a brute force technique to find the longest common substring. Use the Timing class to compare the brute force method with the dynamic programming method. Use the program from Exercise 1 for your dynamic programming solution.
3. Write a Windows application that allows the user to explore the knapsack problem. The user should be able to change the capacity of the knapsack, the sizes of the items, and the values of the items. The user should also create a list of item names that is associated with the items used in the program.
4. Find at least two new coin denominations that make the greedy algorithm for coin changing shown in the chapter produce suboptimal results.
5. Using a "commercial" compression program, such as WinZip, compress a small text file. Then compress the same text file using a Huffman code program. Compare the results of the two compression techniques.
6. Using the code from the "carpet thief" example, change the items being stolen to televisions. Can you fill up the knapsack completely? Make changes to the example program to answer the question.

References

Cormen, Thomas H., Leiserson, Charles E., Rivest, Ronald L., and Clifford-Stein. *Introduction to Algorithms*. Cambridge, MA: The MIT Press, 2001.

Ford, William and William Topp. *Data Structures with C++*. Upper Saddle River, NJ: Prentice Hall, 1996.

Friedel, Jeffrey E. F. *Mastering Regular Expressions*, Sebastopol, CA: O'Reilly and Associates, 1997.

LaFore, Robert. *Data Structures and Algorithms in Java*, Corte Madera, CA: Waite Group Press, 1998.

McMillan, Michael. *Object-Oriented Programming With Visual Basic.NET*, New York: Cambridge University Press, 2004.

Sedgewick, Robert. *Algorithms in C*, Reading, MA: Addison-Wesley, 1998.

Weiss, Mark Allen. *Data Structures and Algorithm Analysis in Java*, Reading, MA: Addison-Wesley, 1999.

Index